M. + J. Wa____
May 1989
Princeton

Political Equality

CHARLES R. BEITZ

Political Equality

An Essay in Democratic Theory

PRINCETON UNIVERSITY PRESS

PRINCETON, NEW JERSEY

Published by Princeton University Press, 41 William Street,
Princeton, New Jersey 08540
In the United Kingdom: Princeton University Press, Guildford,
Surrey

Library of Congress Cataloging-in-Publication Data

Beitz, Charles R.
Political equality : an essay in democratic theory / Charles R. Beitz.
p. cm.   Bibliography: p.   Includes index.
ISBN 0-691-07791-6 (alk. paper)
1. Equality. 2. Democracy. I. Title.
JC575.B45 1989   321.8—dc19   88-29276

This book has been composed in Linotron Trump

Clothbound editions of Princeton University Press books
are printed on acid-free paper, and binding materials are
chosen for strength and durability. Paperbacks, although satisfactory
for personal collections, are not usually suitable for library rebinding

Printed in the United States of America by Princeton University Press,
Princeton, New Jersey

Designed by Laury A. Egan

FOR
Jean H. Beitz
AND IN MEMORY OF
Richard C. Beitz

Contents

Preface

Political theories can be "democratic" in two different, although related, senses. Democratic theories in the narrower (and more traditional) sense speak to the question, what is the best form of government? Those in the broader sense ask, instead, what is the best society?

In recent years, philosophers and political theorists have concentrated their attention on democratic theory in the broader sense, with particular emphasis on the subject of social justice. This departure from tradition has been enormously fruitful: philosophical thought about the basis and character of a democratic society has attained a richness and texture it has not known for decades.

So it is not a criticism of recent writing in democratic theory to observe that, with a few significant exceptions, it has given more narrowly political and institutional problems less than their due. Nevertheless, these problems need attention. Without a clear grasp of the foundations of democracy as a political form, we have no basis in political morality for resolving important issues concerning the structure and processes of the institutions of self-government. Moreover, there is a risk that the public character of democratic political life will be misunderstood.

For the subject of political equality, the need for closer theoretical attention is especially acute. In the last twenty-five years, a set of ostensibly egalitarian institutional reforms has taken place in the United States whose historic dimensions have perhaps not yet been fully appreciated.[1] The reform era dates from the Supreme Court's early reapportionment decisions,[2] but subsequent efforts have gone far beyond implementation of "one person, one vote." They also included reapportionment of the lower house of the Congress and of

---

[1] For a discussion that places the recent reforms in historical perspective, see J. R. Pole, *The Pursuit of Equality in American History* (Berkeley: University of California Press, 1978).

[2] Particularly the landmark "one person, one vote" decisions of *Wesberry v. Sanders*, 376 U.S. 1 (1964), and *Reynolds v. Sims*, 377 U.S. 533 (1964).

state and local legislatures to eliminate or restrict partisan and racial gerrymandering; legislation requiring affirmative action in the
reapportionment process to correct racial and other forms of "vote
dilution";[3] revision of the processes of candidate selection within
the major political parties to provide for greater participation by the
rank and file; alleviation of long-standing limitations on the access
of independent and minor-party candidates to the general election
ballot; and enactment of a system of public subsidies for presidential election campaigns and of restrictions on private financial contributions and expenditures in campaigns for all federal offices.[4]

All of these reforms were defended by their proponents as requirements of political equality. Yet, as continuing controversy in the
courts, the legislatures, and the political parties attests, there is no
consensus about the meaning of this principle. Even the most ar-
dent supporter of the reforms is bound to be troubled by this ques-
tioning: while we feel confident that political equality means something, it is surprisingly difficult to give it a clear explanation and
defense. The legislators and judges who designed and carried out the
reforms are not much help, since they themselves were seldom articulate about their principles. Nor can much guidance be found in
the recent work of political theorists. Owing to the concentration
on issues of democratic theory in its larger sense, there is little in
the way of coherent political doctrine to fall back on when, as now,
procedural reforms come under political challenge; we are forced to
rely on unexamined intuitions and a crude balancing of interests in
assessing the merits of contending positions.

This book is a contribution to democratic theory in the narrower
sense. It has two main aims. The first and more philosophical is to
arrive at a systematic theory of political equality that will clarify
the meaning of the egalitarian ideal in light of the reasons we have
for accepting it. This would be an important task for democratic
theorists even if the subject were not the focus of political controversy. For although nothing is to be gained by claiming that equality

[3] Most importantly, the Voting Rights Act of 1965 with subsequent amendments;
42 U.S. Code, secs. 1971–1973cc.

[4] The main legislation is the Federal Election Campaign Act (1971) as amended in
1974; 2 U.S. Code, secs. 431–55; 26 U.S. Code, secs. 9001–42. Several important elements of the 1974 amendments were held to be unconstitutional in *Buckley v. Valeo*, 424 U.S. 1 (1976).

is part of the definition of democracy, any philosophical theory of
democracy that failed to take up the grounds and content of political equality would be seriously deficient. To be sure, no account of
political equality, no matter how comprehensive, can hope to en-
compass all of the reasons why democratic institutions might be
valued or all of the desiderata that their procedures should satisfy.
But no theory of democracy that failed to give the egalitarian idea a
central place could possibly yield a faithful representation of the
extraordinary grip of democracy on the modern political imagina-
tion.

Contemporary controversy about how political equality bears on
institutional reform points toward a second and more practical aim.
Just as an adequate democratic theory should give a central place to
the ideal of equality, so too it should be framed in a way that illuminates matters about which people actually argue, revealing the
extent to which disagreement turns on philosophical dispute about
first principles and that to which it involves conflict about historical or casuistical questions instead. Although it would be naive to
expect a philosophical theory, by itself, to resolve controverted
questions of institutional design, an adequate theory should at least
identify the central values at issue and provide a structure that informs their application. Accordingly, I shall try to show how dispute about the meaning and grounds of political equality is reflected
in contemporary disagreement about how the institutions of democratic politics should be arranged and to illustrate how the theory
of political equality that I shall set forth would influence our judgments about these questions.

SYNOPSIS

Political equality refers to a set of requirements that apply to the
institutions that enable citizens to participate in political decision
making in a constitutional democracy. The basic idea of this book
is that these requirements are best understood in the perspective of
a substantive ideal of democratic citizenship that explains how we
should construe them and why they should matter to us.

The presentation is divided into two parts, the first concerned primarily with theoretical considerations and the second with their

application to institutions. I begin in chapter 1 with the question of the subject of political equality, or what a theory of political equality can be *about*. According to what I shall call "the simple view," the main problem is merely to say in what respects the terms of participation in democratic institutions should apply equally to all citizens—that is, how equality of political right should be conceived. In contrast, I shall argue that considerations of equality operate at a greater remove from institutional judgments, which are more accurately seen as judgments about *fair* participation than about *equal* participation. Fair institutions should treat people as equals, but whether this implies that any particular political rights should be distributed equally to all citizens is part of the problem a theory should resolve rather than a premise to be taken for granted.

Once the subject of political equality is understood in this way, it is possible to identify several prominent theories. The leading alternatives I shall consider are *best result*, *popular will*, and *procedural* theories. The examination of these alternatives in chapters 2–4 is not comprehensive; in each case I concentrate on instances of the view in question that seem particularly interesting or problematic and simply speculate about the extent to which my criticisms can be generalized. For example, the discussion of best result theories, in chapter 2, takes up what is perhaps the most striking example of inegalitarianism in modern democratic theory—the defense of plural voting set forth by John Stuart Mill. I try to show that an accurate understanding of Mill's error casts doubt as well on any theory of political equality that holds that the conditions of fair participation derive from a conception of the overall results that the political system should promote.

The discussion of popular will theories, in chapter 3, is devoted to certain aspects of the theory of social choice, where scholarly thought about political equality has found its most technically sophisticated analytical expression. I believe that technical sophistication has exacted too high a price: modern popular will theories bring a spurious unity to the subject of political equality by adopting an artificially narrow conception of the democratic process and by attributing a primacy to the popular will that cannot be sustained. Once this is recognized, the most important result of social choice theory—the impossibility theorem due to Arrow—comes to seem much less troubling. In this connection I consider, if only briefly, the foundations of majority rule, mainly to argue that this principle is wrongly conceived as expressing a foundational requirement of political equality. Its significance is far more modest.

In chapter 4, I examine simple versions of proceduralism that conceive of fairness as an intrinsic property of political procedures. These views are unexpectedly problematic. For one thing, it is surprisingly difficult to give an account of procedural fairness that avoids the twin dangers of misrepresenting its requirements as the outcomes of self-interested strategic bargaining or of collapsing it into a result-oriented conception in which the characteristics of procedures have instrumental rather than intrinsic significance. Moreover, the common forms of proceduralism lack sufficient theoretical richness to illuminate problems of institutional structure that are not best understood as involving the distribution of abstract procedural opportunities to influence outcomes.

These criticisms of received views prepare the way for the alternative conception of political fairness presented in chapter 5. It is based on the idea of a social contract: fair terms of participation are those that no citizen has a sufficient reason to refuse to accept, given that everyone shares a desire to come to agreement on some mechanism for participation. The main difficulty in working out this idea is to explain what should count as a sufficient reason for refusal. To answer this question, I provide an account of certain higher-order political interests (the *regulative interests of citizenship*) that we may presume to be among the chief normative concerns of democratic citizens. These include interests in public acknowledgment of one's status as an equal member of the polity (*recognition*), protection against political outcomes that would place one's prospects in serious jeopardy (*equitable treatment*), and conditions of public deliberation conducive to responsible judgment about public affairs (*deliberative responsibility*).

I call this theory *complex proceduralism*. The term is awkward but, I think, accurate: the view is a hybrid form of proceduralism, its complexity deriving from the irreducible plurality of substantive interests associated with the idea of political fairness. The two parts of the view—the contractualist framework and the account of the regulative interests—are an attempt to represent a familiar ideal of democratic citizenship in a theoretically fruitful way. Although I shall not provide a systematic defense of the theory, I shall make three kinds of claims on its behalf: the ideal it articulates is an attractive one that is present in the modern democratic tradition and implicit in many of our intuitive judgments about the fairness of democratic institutions, it is philosophically preferable to various more conventional alternatives, and it illuminates and helps resolve several practical problems of contemporary dispute.

In part 2 we examine how complex proceduralism applies to some of these problems, including proportional representation, the representation of groups in systems employing territorial constituencies, the structuring of the political agenda (primarily through rules governing access to the ballot and the candidate selection procedures of political parties), and regulation of the system of political finance. I shall not try to summarize the substantive conclusions reached about these issues, which seem straightforward enough. The main reasons to examine them here are to shed light on the theory and to illustrate how considerations of principle and of historical and political experience should be brought together in resolving practical dispute. I believe that theorists have tended to underestimate the importance of historical considerations and to misunderstand their place in practical reasoning about political fairness. Although a doctrine of political equality imposes constraints on the design of democratic institutions, one must take care not to conceive these theoretical constraints too concretely or to assume that they operate in a similar fashion in social contexts with varying historical and social characteristics.

Both the content of the theory and the claims I shall advance on its behalf will raise methodological questions in the minds of many readers. I have resisted the temptation to pursue these matters in the central parts of the book, where they would distract attention from more pressing normative concerns. However, some of these questions cannot be ignored altogether, and I consider them very briefly in the Conclusion.

Paths Not Taken

This is a large agenda for a book of this length, but even so it hardly exhausts the range of problems that arise under the heading of political equality. I note here three topics of particular importance that I must leave for another occasion. First, there is no systematic discussion of some basic questions in the theory of value. For example, foundational issues regarding the structure and plausibility of rival moral conceptions are left aside, as, for the most part, are disputes about the standards of value that such conceptions should employ. These questions are obviously important, but I can do no more than acknowledge the need for more systematic analysis elsewhere and rely in what follows on less systematic, intuitive judgments.

Second, the consideration of institutional issues is highly selective. For example, I discuss only in passing what many will regard as the central institutional question of political equality—the issue of voting weights, or the foundations of "one person, one vote." This is not an unimportant matter, but it is hard to discern much contemporary disagreement about it. Another institutional issue left aside involves the choice of voting systems, a problem that has engaged theoretical attention at least since the pioneering efforts of Borda and Condorcet.[5] Although some of my remarks bear on this subject, I cannot pretend to have given it the attention it would require in a more comprehensive study. I have tried to confine the discussion to issues that have arisen in the wake of recent reform efforts in the United States and that have gained attention beyond the fairly narrow confines of specialized circles of scholarly interest. (The discussion of proportional representation may seem to be an exception; but, as I hope will be clear, a grasp of the theoretical problems associated with it is required to frame the examination of issues considered later.)

Finally, I do not take up what might be called the structural prerequisites of fair political choice. By this I mean how institutions should regulate the distribution of wealth and the bases of social status that influence both the salience of the formal democratic process within the overall system of social decision making and the relative capacities of different persons and groups to advance their

---

[5] The seminal discussion is due to Duncan Black, *The Theory of Committees and Elections* (Cambridge: Cambridge University Press, 1958); there is a convenient historical survey in chap. 18, pp. 156–84. Recently there has been renewed interest in these matters; see, for example, Steven J. Brams and Peter C. Fishburn, *Approval Voting* (Boston: Birkhauser, 1983), and Michael Dummett, *Voting Procedures* (Oxford: Clarendon Press, 1984).

interests within the formal process. Some related concerns are taken up in connection with ballot access (in chapter 8) and political finance (in chapter 9), but it is unrealistic to maintain that procedural arrangements in these areas, by themselves, can effectively regulate the political influence of background inequalities. I stop short of the larger subject mainly because broader issues involving distributive justice are more familiar in recent political theory than the more narrowly procedural issues discussed here; there is less need to address them and probably less to say about them that has not already been said.[6] In addition, there is the temptation, once the larger subject has been broached, to believe that no more needs to be said about narrower issues of procedural design. This would be a mistake: not only because these issues are pressing today, but also because they (or close analogs) would be likely to arise even in a society in which the background distribution was fully just.

Beyond this, we must keep in mind that historically a main goal of democratic movements has been to seek redress in the political sphere for the effects of inequalities in the economy and society. Political equality, in particular, has more often functioned as a "protest ideal" than as a constructive one: it does not describe a goal to be realized so much as it expresses grounds for criticism of the status quo.[7] It is natural to expect to find some reflection of this fact in a philosophical theory of political equality. For this to be so, the possibility of these background inequalities must be taken for granted. Moreover, we must resist as far as possible philosophical pressure toward idealization that would obscure issues that distinctively arise in the presence of background injustice. In setting aside larger issues involving the justice of the social and economic structure, therefore, I do not suggest that they are unimportant. My aim, instead, is to set forth the outline of a normative theory of political equality that will shed light on the main issues of practical controversy that confront us today.

[6] Among recent works that explore the influence of the social and economic background on the functioning of democratic political devices, see particularly Charles E. Lindblom, *Politics and Markets* (New York: Basic Books, 1977); and Joshua Cohen and Joel Rogers, *On Democracy* (Harmondsworth, Middlesex: Penguin Books, 1983).

[7] Giovanni Sartori, *The Theory of Democracy Revisited* (Chatham, N.J.: Chatham House, 1987), vol. 2, pp. 337–38.

Acknowledgments

This book has been a long time in the making and would have been even longer were it not for the generous advice and encouragement of many friends and colleagues. Thomas Scanlon stimulated my interest in the subject of political fairness in a series of conversations beginning several years ago; the influence of his ideas, particularly in the first part, has been fundamental. Amy Gutmann, William Nelson, and Dennis Thompson read earlier versions of the entire manuscript and supplied criticisms and suggestions that affected virtually every part of it. Brian Barry, Douglas Bennett, Owen Fiss, Charles Gilbert, Russell Hardin, David Hoekema, the late Richard Krouse, Diana Meyers, J. Roland Pennock, Nancy Rosenblum, Ian Shapiro, Kenneth Sharpe, Judith Shklar, Henry Shue, and Huntington Terrell contributed valuable comments at various stages. Sanford Thatcher went well beyond the call of duty in helping me to distinguish the forest from the trees.

I am grateful for the financial support of the American Council of Learned Societies and of Swarthmore College's unusually generous program of faculty research assistance. Final revisions were completed during the tenure of a MacArthur Foundation Fellowship when I was associated with the Center for Science and International Affairs of the Kennedy School of Government at Harvard. I must thank both the MacArthur Foundation and the Center for allowing me to take time away from other pursuits so that I could finish the work on this book.

Passages from articles that appeared elsewhere are included here by arrangement with the original publishers: New York University Press, for "Procedural Equality in Democratic Theory: A Preliminary Examination," from *Nomos XXV: Liberal Democracy*, ed. J. Roland Pennock and John W. Chapman (1983); the University of Chicago Press, for "Political Finance in the United States: A Survey of Research," from *Ethics* 95 (1984); and Westview Press, for "Equal

Opportunity in Political Representation," from *Equal Opportunity*, ed. Norman Bowie (1988).

I owe a different order of thanks to Ann and Caroline Cyl-kowski—to Ann, for encouraging my work even when it dragged on considerably longer than either of us expected; and to Caroline, for reminding me with such wonderful exuberance that there are more important things than writing books.

Introduction

CHAPTER ONE

The Subject of

Political Equality

"[R]eally I think that the poorest he that is in England hath a life to live as the greatest he." Thomas Rainsborough, member of Parliament and colonel in Cromwell's New Model Army, spoke these words in the course of arguing that parliamentary constituencies "ought to be more indifferently proportioned."[1] But they also express—most famously, perhaps, if not for the first time[2]—an enduring and powerful ideal. We call it political equality, and, like Rainsborough, we appeal to it in defense of proposals for political reform. Yet, though we are sure the ideal means something, it is difficult to say what; and though we are sure we accept it, it is difficult to say why. These abstract difficulties have practical consequences. Being uncertain what political equality means, we are unable to explain

[1] The Rainsborough passage is from the Putney debates of the General Council of the Army, the session of 29 October 1647. The subject of debate was a radical proposal for political reform—the first "Agreement of the People," advanced by a dissident movement of officers but probably drafted by civilian Leveller leaders—that included the provision for reapportionment of parliamentary constituencies in its first clause. G. E. Aylmer, ed., *The Levellers in the English Revolution* (Ithaca: Cornell University Press, 1975), pp. 90 (clause 1 of the "Agreement"), 100 (Rainsborough). The best account of the debates is Austin Woolrych, *Soldiers and Statesmen: The General Council of the Army and Its Debates, 1647–1648* (Oxford: Clarendon Press, 1987), chap. 9.

[2] When was the first time? It is impossible to say; but surely it was at least as early as the speech of Otanes, reported in Herodotus's account of the Persian dialog ("the rule of the many . . . has . . . the fairest of names, to wit, equality"). *The History of Herodotus*, trans. George Rawlinson (New York: Tudor Publishing, 1928), bk. 3, p. 177. See Gregory Vlastos, "Isonomia," *American Journal of Philology* 74 (1953), pp. 337–66; and Martin Ostwald, *Nomos and the Beginnings of the Athenian Democracy* (Oxford: Clarendon Press, 1969), pp. 111–13.

what it requires of our institutions; and being uncertain why we should accept it, we are unable to explain why our institutions should conform to these procedural requirements rather than to others, or to none at all.

This book is meant to help resolve both kinds of uncertainty. The theory of political equality set forth in part 1 is a philosophical interpretation of the egalitarian ideal, which aims to explain its content and to show why, so understood, it is worthy of our support. The examination of practical problems in part 2 illustrates how the theory might be applied in the criticism and reform of the institutions of democratic participation. But as we shall see, the theory and practice of political equality are more closely intertwined than this division of the topic might suggest: the institutional problems that a theory must address help shape our conception of its subject matter, and the content of the theory informs our understanding of the issues of principle that the practical problems pose.[3]

THE SIMPLE VIEW

Not everybody will agree that there is any need for a theory of political equality. In fact, the most widely held view of the subject seems to deny it. According to this view, political equality is the requirement that democratic institutions should provide citizens with equal procedural opportunities to influence political decisions (or, more briefly, with *equal power over outcomes*).[4] Alternatively, it might be said that the political preferences expressed by each cit-

[3] Indeed, as Douglas Rae and others have observed, the complexity of the idea of equality is only revealed when we try to bring it to bear on concrete problems of political practice. *Equalities* (Cambridge: Harvard University Press, 1981), p. 4.

[4] Formulations of this idea, differing mainly in details, can be found, for example, in Carole Pateman, *Participation and Democratic Theory* (Cambridge: Cambridge University Press, 1970), p. 43; John Rawls, *A Theory of Justice* (Cambridge: Harvard University Press, 1971), p. 221; Jack Lively, *Democracy* (Oxford: Basil Blackwell, 1975), pp. 8, 16, 49–50; David Miller, "Democracy and Social Justice," *British Journal of Political Science* 8 (1978), p. 3; Amy Gutmann, *Liberal Equality* (Cambridge: Cambridge University Press, 1980), pp. 180–81; Jane Mansbridge, *Beyond Adversary Democracy* (New York: Basic Books, 1980), pp. 17–18, 30–31; and Ronald Dworkin, *Law's Empire* (Cambridge: Harvard University Press, 1986), p. 178.

izen should receive equal weight in the decision-making process.[5] Something like this conception of political equality represents a persistent conviction among contemporary democratic theorists; indeed, it has become a kind of philosophical orthodoxy, perhaps because it has seemed to express so obvious a truth as not to require systematic defense. Crude forms of the same notion occur as well in many contexts of popular political debate.

The view is simple in two related ways. First, it does not distinguish among the different levels of abstraction at which the idea of equality could arise in thinking about political procedures. Thus, for example, no complex reasoning is needed to connect the abstract idea that citizens have equal political status with concretely egalitarian requirements for political procedures; political equality just *is* procedural equality.[6] Second, in identifying political equality with the institutional requirement of equal power, the simple view treats political equality as concerned exclusively with the distribution of a single unambiguous value. The distribution of power is taken to be the only concern of political equality, and the fairness of society's decision-making institutions is assessed solely with respect to their effects on this distribution.

[5] In fact, these two conceptions of political equality may not be equivalent, though the differences frequently go unnoticed. A good example of the latter view can be found in the work of Robert Dahl, who regards it as axiomatic—at least in "populistic democracy," of which he defends a variant—that democratic institutions should be arranged so that "the preference of each member is assigned an equal value." *A Preface to Democratic Theory* (Chicago: University of Chicago Press, 1956), p. 37. The main tasks for democratic theory on this view are to specify a social choice mechanism that incorporates the equality requirement and to explain how institutional equality should be compromised with the other values with which it may possibly conflict. See also Dahl, "Procedural Democracy," in *Philosophy, Politics and Society*, 5th series, ed. Peter Laslett and James Fishkin (New Haven: Yale University Press, 1979), esp. pp. 101–2.

[6] Indeed, some theorists go even farther, holding that procedural equality is part of the *meaning* of "democracy." See, for example, Lively, *Democracy*, pp. 49–50; Miller, "Democracy and Social Justice," p. 3; Brian Barry, "Is Democracy Special?" in *Philosophy, Politics, and Society*, 5th series, ed. Peter Laslett and James Fishkin (New Haven: Yale University Press, 1979), pp. 156–58. Though they agree that political equality is part of the conventional definition of democracy, these writers adopt conceptions of equality that are apparently different ("apparently," because their accounts of equality are not uniformly precise). In view of these differences, one might wonder where there *is* a conventional definition of democracy.

Taking these points together, it is plain why someone who accepted the simple view might deny the need for a philosophical theory of political equality. For the view treats the grounds and meaning of equality as unproblematic; although the interpretation of equal power for practical purposes might raise technical or analytical problems, there is no reason to suppose that we need a *theory* to resolve them.

But the simplicity of the view is deceptive. The first point, and surely the most important, is that whether political equality should be identified with *procedural* equality is itself a question that requires an answer. This is only partly because, without an answer, various issues of institutional design will remain undecided, since it will be uncertain how the requirement of equal power should be construed. It is also, and for our purposes more significantly, because the reasons for accepting procedural equality as a constraint on the structure of democratic institutions are (perhaps surprisingly) very obscure.

The most natural thought is that a requirement of procedural equality is compelled by some version of the more basic principle that persons have a right to be treated as equals. But, as we shall see, there are very deep difficulties in this relationship, and its plausibility fades on analysis. To anticipate, equal treatment might be seen either as an abstract moral requirement or as a concrete rule with determinate institutional content. If the idea is regarded abstractly enough to be noncontroversial, then its application to institutional questions will be uncertain without controversial intervening premises.[7] It does not follow directly from such abstract principles as that persons should be treated as equally autonomous, or equally responsible for the conduct of their own lives, or equally deserving of concern and respect that they should have equal procedural opportunities to influence the conduct of public life. In each case, more needs to be said, and that is where dispute will arise. If, on the other hand, the principle is taken to specify a determinate

---

[7] For an example of a view in which egalitarian procedural opportunities are said to derive from a more abstract principle of equal worth, see Peter Jones, "Political Equality and Majority Rule," in *The Nature of Political Theory*, ed. David Miller and Larry Siedentop (Oxford: Clarendon Press, 1983), esp. pp. 167ff. Jones's discussion is particularly helpful about the nature of the intervening empirical premises required for the derivation.

institutional right—for example, a right to have one's expressed interests given equal weight in the determination of policy—then it
will fail to settle the issue that provoked it. For it can always be
asked why *that* sort of right exists. Replies that bring forward still
further institutional rights supposed to be possessed equally by all
citizens will be open to the same question. Thus, it seems unlikely
that the explanation of why institutions should provide equal opportunities to participate (if indeed they should) will terminate in
an assertion of equal political right. Nor will it terminate convinc-
ingly in a definition of democracy; for any definition robust enough
to yield precise institutional requirements would be subject to similar questions. Instead, it will be necessary to provide an explanation in other terms: for example, in terms of the kinds and importance of the values that would be affected by institutions satisfying
normative conditions of the sort being defended. Of course, this is
not to say very much; indeed, each of the theories of political equality taken up later represents an alternative means by which requirements on political procedures might be derived from a deeper analysis of the interests affected. The difficult questions involve the
range of interests it is appropriate to take into account and the theoretical structure within which they should be combined to yield
definite institutional consequences. All I have suggested thus far is
that whether the content of political equality is exhausted by (or
even includes) an institutional requirement of equal power is one of
the principal problems to be resolved *within* a theory of political
equality. To suppose otherwise would be question begging.

It would also be unilluminating. It would result in a theory that
failed to clarify some of the most important institutional issues to
which considerations of political equality are commonly (and properly) thought to apply. The reason is that the concept of power is
equivocal; indeed, it is equivocal in several dimensions. As a result,
comparisons of power, and thus the principle of equal power itself,
can be interpreted in several, potentially inconsistent, ways.

To illustrate, we will consider some problems about institutional
reform that have arisen in the recent past and ask in each case how
a principle of equal power might apply. What is equality of power
equality *of*? We will see that the values in question in each context
are distinct. There is no unequivocal conception of power—and so,

no unambiguous principle of equal power—that can plausibly be taken as a basis for resolving dispute in all of these areas.

REPRESENTATION.   Consider, for example, the array of problems sometimes said to involve the "qualitative" dimension of representation,[8] such as the propriety of the gerrymander (and of the "racial gerrymander"), vote "dilution," and vote "submersion." All of these involve manipulation of the boundaries of legislative constituencies so as to alter the legislative representation, and thus the legislative strength, of various population groups. Some sorts of manipulation—for example, that associated with racial gerrymandering— seem plainly unfair and might even be described as treating those whom they disadvantage unequally. Yet, as experience illustrates, ensuring equality in the sense of "one person, one vote" does not eliminate the possibility of gerrymandering or vote dilution. It appears that a system of representation can simultaneously treat voters both equally and unequally. How can this be?

Considered abstractly, power is the capacity to realize a possible desire, or to get what one wants, despite resistance.[9] Imagine a committee of three members in which each member has one vote and the majority rules. Suppose that members A and B agree with each other, and disagree with member C, 80 percent of the time; the rest of the time, each one is as likely to agree as to disagree with C. There is one sense in which each member has equal power. Yet member C loses far more often than either A or B. So there is also a sense in which C has less power than the others. What is the difference?

Each member of the committee has equal power in the sense that, under the decision rule, each is in a position to overcome the same

[8] See *Reynolds v. Sims*, 377 U.S. 533 (1964), at 565–66; Laurence H. Tribe, *American Constitutional Law* (Mineola, N.Y.: Foundation Press, 1978), p. 749.

[9] Influential sources of this conception of power include Max Weber, *The Theory of Economic and Social Organization*, trans. A. M. Henderson and Talcott Parsons (New York: Free Press, 1947), pp. 152f, and Robert Dahl, "The Concept of Power," *Behavioral Science* 2 (1957), pp. 201–15. See also Alvin Goldman, "Toward a Theory of Social Power," *Philosophical Studies* 23 (1972), pp. 221–68; Brian Barry, "Power: An Economic Analysis," in *Power and Political Theory: Some European Perspectives*, ed. Brian Barry (London: John Wiley, 1976), pp. 67–101; and Brian Barry, "Is it Better to be Powerful or Lucky?" parts 1 and 2, *Political Studies* 28 (1980), pp. 183–94, 338–52.

amount of resistance—namely, that of (at most) one other member. According to an analysis familiar in the literature of voting theory, this means that if each member is assumed to be equally likely to vote either way on any issue, then on any issue each has an equal probability of being decisive (that is, of casting the deciding vote).[10] But such complex analytical machinery is not really necessary; that each member has equal power in the present sense follows directly from the fact that the decision rule treats each one symmetrically.[11]

What, then, of the sense in which member C might be said to have less power than the others? Without claiming anything about conventional usage, I believe that things will be clearer if we say that what C has less of is not *power* considered abstractly but *prospects of electoral success*. Regarded as an abstract capacity to overcome resistance, power is equally distributed on the committee. However, once the likely distribution of preferences—which is to say, the amount of resistance from others that each member is actually likely to face—is taken into account, we can see that not every member will do equally well; some will succeed (that is, get the outcomes they want) more often than others.[12] One reason for resisting the temptation to say that *power* is distributed unequally is that what makes the difference among the members, once preferences are taken into account, is not the abstract capacity of each member to overcome resistance (which would be the same under any distribution of preferences) but the amount of resistance that

[10] The main source is L. S. Shapley and Martin Shubik, "A Method for Evaluating the Distribution of Power in a Committee System," *American Political Science Review* 48 (1954), pp. 787–92. The Shapley/Shubik approach to the measurement of power in a committee is generalized in Alvin Goldman, "On the Measurement of Power," *Journal of Philosophy* 71 (1974), pp. 231–52.

[11] Barry, "Is it Better to be Powerful or Lucky?" part 1, p. 186. The same point could be made by saying that the voting rule satisfies the condition of *anonymity*: the outcome does not change when any two voters' preferences are interchanged. For further comments, see Jonathan Still, "Political Equality and Election Systems," *Ethics* 91 (1981), pp. 378–82.

[12] It is plain that C will succeed—that is, will get the outcome he favors—whenever at least one other member of the committee supports him. Otherwise he will fail. Given our assumptions, C will certainly fail the 80 percent of the time that he is jointly opposed by A and B, and will succeed on three-quarters of the remaining votes (since on each of them, A and B each has an equal [and independent] probability of agreeing or disagreeing with C). Thus, overall, C's probability of success on a randomly chosen issue is $(80\% \times 0) + (20\% \times 75\%) = 15\%$.

each is likely to face given some assumption about the actual distribution of preferences. But the distinction needs only to be seen
as stipulative; there is no need to insist on the terms *power* and
prospects. One could just as well distinguish between *a priori* and
actual power, or power *ex ante* and power *ex post*.[13]

One way to explain the import of the distinction between power
and prospects of success is this. Power is a counterfactual notion. In
attributing power to someone, we imply that there is some possible
world in which her action (or omission) will change the future
course of events by converting an outcome she does not want, but
that would have occurred if she had not acted (or had acted otherwise), into an outcome she wants. Having power, she has the potential to make a difference. However, the world in which one's power
makes a difference need not be the actual world—one can have (and
exercise) power without getting what one wants, and one can get
what one wants without exercising power (or by exercising it super-
fluously: when the desired outcome would have occurred anyway).
When we say that someone has power, we are saying that if, perhaps
counterfactually, the world were a certain way, her actions (or
omissions) would bring about an outcome that would not otherwise
take place.

Now there are many features of the world that could affect the
success of a person's efforts to change the future course of events;
in any assessment of that person's power, we would normally counterfactualize some of these factors but hold others fixed. For example, in deciding whether the opportunity to vote gives someone
power, we might consider whether casting a vote would affect the
outcome of an election under any possible permutation of other
people's preferences but not under contrary-to-fact hypotheses
about the person's political competence or capacity to engage in
various kinds of strategic voting. How much power we attribute to
a person (indeed, whether we attribute power to her at all) will de-

[13] Thus, for example, Rogowski refers to what I call "equal prospects of success"
as "equally powerful representation." Ronald Rogowski, "Representation in Political
Theory and in Law," *Ethics* 91 (1981), p. 399. Rae and others distinguish more generally between "means-regarding equal opportunity" and "prospect-regarding equal
opportunity." *Equalities*, pp. 65–66. Compare N. R. Miller, "Power in Game Forms,"
in *Power, Voting, and Voting Power*, ed. M. J. Holler (Würzburg, Germany: Physica-
Verlag, 1981), pp. 33–34.

pend on which factors we are prepared to counterfactualize and which we hold constant. How should this distinction be drawn? Considerations of ordinary usage suggest no general answer. Nor should they be expected to. Assessments of power are context-dependent in the sense that what counts as an appropriate assessment of someone's power (or lack of it) depends on the reasons for taking an interest in the assessment.[14] Thus, the senses in which member C of our committee seems to have either equal or unequal power correspond to two different perspectives on his situation. In the first case, we are interested in the leverage provided by the committee's procedures, considered apart from any assumptions about the actual or probable distribution of preferences; thus, we consider whether there is any permutation of other peoples' preferences under which member C's vote would affect the outcome. In the second, we want to know how often this leverage might be expected to make a difference in the outcome, in view of what other people actually prefer; so we hold others' preferences constant and consider what the actual outcome is likely to be.

This shows that there is no real paradox in the observation that a system of representation might simultaneously treat people equally and unequally. These characterizations simply reflect two separate kinds of concerns that might be brought to bear on representation systems. One is a concern about the abstract leverage that procedures provide to each participant; the other, about the chances that participants with any particular set of interests will actually prevail. Whether, and to what extent, either kind of concern should influence judgments about procedural fairness are normative questions that any useful theory of political equality should answer. There is no need to resolve these questions now;[15] the point is that the simple view serves more to conceal than to clarify them.

THE POLITICAL AGENDA.   Different problems arise in connection with the composition of the range of alternatives presented to the voters. Rules governing access to the election ballot, and procedures through which political parties choose their candidates, can

[14] This is the truth behind the claim that power is an "essentially contested concept." See Steven Lukes, *Power: A Radical View* (London: Macmillan, 1974), pp. 26–33. Compare Barry, "Power: An Economic Analysis," p. 91.

[15] I discuss them in detail in chapter 7, below.

constrain the range of alternatives in ways that exclude widely held positions from the political agenda. At least some kinds of agenda constraints seem to treat those who favor the excluded positions unequally. Yet, from another point of view, equality is not offended at all by such exclusionary provisions, since they do not reduce the weight of the votes of those who would have supported the excluded candidates or positions.

The latter view strikes many people as implausible. One reason is that it rests on an identification of political power with voting power that is artificially narrow. We have said that power is the capacity to get what one wants despite resistance. Power is therefore a relationship between the desires and the capacities of an agent with respect to a specified outcome. Which *opportunities to act* are open to an agent who desires to realize that outcome (such as the right to vote, to have access to the ballot, or to participate in public debate) is an intermediate, not an ultimate, question. Obviously, in deciding whether someone has power over an outcome, we shall want to know which opportunities are available; but power ought not to be identified with these. What matters about power is its contribution to the realization of a possible desire, and this is only contingently related to the possession of any particular procedural opportunities. The idea that agenda constraints do not result in inequalities of power provided that voting weights are equal fails to appreciate this obvious fact.

Important as it is, however, this observation does not reach the heart of the matter. The real difficulty lies deeper; it concerns the adequacy of the principle of equal power itself as a characterization of political fairness. For consider: to understand the problem of fair access to the political arena as a problem about the distribution of power over outcomes, it would be necessary to imagine citizens as having fully formed desires from the outset. Agenda-structuring institutions would function merely as filters to narrow the range of alternatives to those enjoying widespread popular support, so that the final electoral choice would reflect popular preferences as accurately as possible. On this view, access restrictions represent the first stage of a continuous process of preference aggregation terminating in the election itself, and they are said to be unfair when they enable some preferences to count more heavily than others. But this reflects an unrealistic conception of democratic politics. Preferences do not exist independently of the institutions through which they are expressed; their formation is at least partially endogenous to the process of agenda formation, which must, therefore, be seen as a deliberative rather than as a purely aggregative mechanism.

A principal danger of access restrictions is that they could impair the process of public debate and reflection on which citizens rely in forming their views and in attempting to influence the views of others. The significance of this danger from the point of view of individual citizens is not easily conceived in terms of imbalances in the distribution of power as we have understood it. Power is a relationship between the desires and the capacities of an agent; but when an agent's desires are themselves in process of examination and, perhaps, revision, it would be wrong to characterize the agent's relative capacity to engage successfully in the relevant forms of political activity as an exercise of *power*, for those forms of activity do not usually consist in efforts to satisfy desires for substantive outcomes. Of course, the formation of political preferences may not *always* be endogenous to the process of public debate; one might be perfectly clear about one's *own* desires and engage in debate purely for strategic reasons. But even if the desires of one agent are taken as fixed, and attention is directed at that agent's capacity to influence the desires of others, it would still be unilluminating to characterize this capacity as a form of power. The means by which it can be exercised consist of education and persuasion, and although it may be no abuse of ordinary language to describe these as kinds of power,[16] it is enormously difficult, and perhaps impossible, to formulate any systematic analysis of power that would permit meaningful comparisons to be made among the capacities of different individuals to employ these means of influence.[17] It is true that the exercise of influence depends on the availability of various opportunities, such as access to the public forum; in a formal sense, the distribution of these opportunities could of course be measured and the extent of their availability to different people compared. Some

[16] Some would disagree, wanting to distinguish between *power* and *influence* on the grounds that only the latter involves persuasion. The canonical source is Talcott Parsons, "On the Concept of Influence" [1963], reprinted in *Sociological Theory and Modern Society* (New York: Free Press, 1967), esp. pp. 366ff.

[17] Perhaps this is why the literature of social choice is so remarkably silent on the subject of preference formation.

such comparisons might well be relevant to any plausible assessment of the fairness of political procedures. But they would not, themselves, be comparisons of degrees of *power*; and these reflections suggest that they are unlikely to be brought within the purview of any more general principle governing its distribution. If this is right, then understanding the subject of political equality as the interpretation of a principle of equal power would be unduly confining.

POLITICAL FINANCE.   The allocation of financial and other resources for political campaigning has become a subject of legislative and administrative regulation only recently, and there is still dispute about whether considerations of political equality should apply to it at all. In one view, the scope of political equality is limited to the distribution of political liberties themselves—that is, to institutionally defined (or procedural) opportunities to influence outcomes. In another view, this limitation is myopic, and no system containing great inequalities of campaign resources could be said to treat citizens equally even if *all* of the political liberties were evenly distributed.

The conflict between these views reflects a further tension within the concept of political power. There are many contexts (for example, the rules of order in a committee) in which it is natural to treat the distribution of power exclusively as a function of the distribution of political liberties. In these contexts what matters for normative purposes is the contribution of a set of procedures to people's capacities to attain their ends. This represents one familiar sense of power. On the other hand, the opportunities to act defined by a set of procedures are not the only factors that affect people's capacities to attain their ends. Associated with each of the institutionally defined opportunities to influence outcomes is a set of *enabling resources* whose presence or absence will affect, in varying degrees, the value of these opportunities as instruments for overcoming resistance. Power, in this second sense, is contingent on the availability of both the relevant opportunities and the associated resources.[18]

---

[18] It will not do to reply that the distribution of opportunities is determined by the institutional structure, whereas the distribution of resources is, at least to some ex-

Now, on the conventional view, the question whether a doctrine of political equality should concern itself with the distribution of resources depends on whether one accepts the more or the less limited of these interpretations of political power. This, in turn, must be seen as posing a normatively neutral analytical problem: what does equal power really mean? But it seems particularly clear in connection with the allocation of political resources that this question masks rather than states the substantive issue. Different interpretations of the concept of power correspond to different reasons for taking an interest in the arrangement whose procedures are being assessed. If it is appropriate for a theory of political fairness to be concerned about the distribution of political resources, the explanation must set forth a reason for taking an interest in that distribution that connects with the values that motivate concern about political fairness. Consider, for example, the understanding of democratic forms as an institutional means to counteract the political effects of inequalities of private wealth and power;[19] if one accepted this, one might say that an unregulated private market in political resources would treat people unfairly because it would predictably reinforce rather than mitigate the effects of private inequalities. One must ask why we should be concerned about political fairness in order to delineate the scope of that concern. But this question is foreclosed, or at least misrepresented, on the simple view of the subject matter of political equality.

Considered in connection with the allocation of resources, the conventional association of political equality with equal power faces a further difficulty. For the most part, financial resources are used to make possible political organization and expression and do not control outcomes directly. This complicates any attempt to conceive the allocation of resources as involving the distribution of power, not only because competing concerns associated with freedom of association and expression are implicated, but also because political campaigning is wrongly understood merely as a competi-

---

tent, independently fixed. For it is often within the competence of institutions to regulate this distribution or to make provisions to compensate for its undesirable elements.

[19] See, for example, T. H. Marshall, "Citizenship and Social Class" [1949], in *Class, Citizenship, and Social Development* (Garden City, N.Y.: Doubleday, 1964), pp. 65–122.

tion or a bargaining process.[20] Like the process of agenda formation, campaigning is also, and significantly, a process of argument, education, and opinion formation. The normative problem is not how a distribution of preexisting preferences or opinions should be aggregated into a social choice but rather what regulative framework is necessary to ensure conditions of fair deliberation. For reasons discussed earlier, a principle of equal power does not clearly apply, and may not apply at all, to this problem.

POLITICAL EQUALITY AND FAIRNESS

The simple view is deficient because it too readily identifies the abstract ideal of political equality with the more precise, institutional standard of *procedural* equality and because it wrongly portrays the latter as an unambiguous and univocal requirement. The view is insecure in its foundations and indeterminate in (some of) its applications.

Both kinds of difficulty reflect an unduly narrow conception of the subject matter of political equality. Any attempt to improve upon the simple view should begin with a reconsideration of this question. We must ask, What is the problem to which a theory of political equality provides a solution? What can such a theory be *about*?

A political system can be democratic in a generic sense without being egalitarian. Both Aristotle and Mill described political systems that were generically democratic but clearly not egalitarian. Every citizen was entitled to participate in the institutional mechanism that determined the policies of the government, but they were not necessarily entitled to participate on equal terms.[21] A re-

[20] Thus, it is a mistake simply to *identify* political power with the possession of "political resources," even for analytical purposes. For such an identification, see Robert Goodin and John Dryzek, "Rational Participation: The Politics of Relative Power," *British Journal of Political Science* 10 (1980), pp. 277–78.

[21] For Aristotle, see the description of the mixed constitution he calls *"politeia"*: *The Politics of Aristotle*, trans. Ernest Barker (Oxford: Clarendon Press, 1946), bk. 4, chap. 14 (1298b–1299a). For Mill, see the remarks on plural voting in *Considerations on Representative Government* [1861], chap. 8, in *Collected Works*, vol. 19, ed. J. M. Robson (Toronto: University of Toronto Press, 1977), pp. 473–79, and "Thoughts on Parliamentary Reform" [1859], in *Collected Works*, vol. 19, pp. 323–25.

quirement of equality adds something to the generic idea of democracy as self-government. This additional element is a constraint on the design of the mechanism that enables citizens to participate in public decisions, or as we might say, on the terms of democratic participation. At the most general level, what a theory of political equality should do is explain what must be true of the terms of participation if they can be said to reflect the equal public status of democratic citizens.

To be more precise, we might distinguish between the role or function of the egalitarian ideal in democratic theory and its content. Suppose we think of democracy as a kind of rivalry for control of the state's policy-making apparatus, with an electoral mechanism at its center in which all citizens are entitled to participate.[22] There is considerable room for variation in both the manner in which the rivalry itself might be regulated and the details of the electoral mechanism that determines its outcomes. The generic idea of democracy is indeterminate about these matters, but because not all of the possibilities are equally acceptable, some criterion is needed for selecting among them. This is the *role* of a requirement of political equality: it serves as the chief regulative principle of democratic political competition by defining fair terms of participation in it. Its *content* admits of a variety of interpretations, each corresponding to a particular understanding of "fair terms of participation." Thus, we might say that the main philosophical task of a theory of political equality is to identify the best interpretation of the content of this idea.

This conception of the subject of political equality reflects a further distinction between two levels—that of institutions and that of justifications—at which the idea of equality might operate within a theory. According to the simple view, equality enters at the first, or institutional, level and is expressed as a direct constraint on the structure of democratic processes themselves. What I have suggested instead is that the second level should be regarded as primary: the idea of equality is mainly constraining in its effects on the reasons that may be given to explain why we should accept

[22] This is not intended as a definition but only as a true statement about virtually all modern political systems we would normally call "democratic." As my earlier remarks suggest, the perennial dispute about the *definition* of democracy seems to me largely fruitless, and I hope to avoid it altogether.

one rather than another conception of fair terms of participation. At
the level of institutions, the sovereign regulative idea is not equality at all but rather fairness. Indeed, were it not for a desire to respect the canons of ordinary usage, one should simply abandon the
phrase "political equality" altogether, since it confuses matters of
institutional design with deeper questions about their justification.

Another way to formulate the point is this. The relation of a theory of political equality to political justice is analogous to the relation of a theory of economic equality to economic justice.[23] In both
cases, we are presented with a widely held egalitarian ideal whose
application to particular issues of public policy is unclear because
the content of the ideal is in dispute. Controversies about its application and content require for their resolution a more discriminating grasp of the ideal's philosophical foundations than the received
view provides. Now the ideal of economic equality is complex in
the following sense: its practical manifestation is typically to be
found in a set of institutional conditions, no one of which may be
overtly or obviously egalitarian, rather than in particular equal distributions or in a regular tendency toward them. For example, from
the point of view of economic equality, it is not a conclusive complaint about an economic system that it fails to produce at every
moment in time an equal distribution of wealth, or for that matter,
that it fails to produce equal expectations of satisfaction over complete lives. Indeed, any conception of economic equality that simply identified it with such a requirement would rightly be regarded
as naive; if this turned out to be the best interpretation of economic
equality, we would expect it to be the conclusion of an argument,
not its premise.

The distinction between the role and content of political equality
forestalls premature adoption of political conceptions that are naive
in an analogous sense, such as the simple idea that democratic institutions should be arranged so that each citizen has equal power
over political outcomes. Like their analogs in the theory of economic justice, such conceptions could be philosophically misleading in suggesting too close a connection between the ideal of equal-

[23] For this conception of the role of economic equality, see Ronald Dworkin,
"What is Equality? Part I: Equality of Welfare," *Philosophy & Public Affairs* 10
(1981), pp. 185–88.

ity and derivative principles for political institutions. As I shall eventually argue, there are several reasons for taking an interest in the manner in which democratic institutions organize public participation in political decisions; these reasons all have some relationship to the fundamental idea of equal citizenship, but the relationships vary, and their force can point in different practical directions. A theory of political equality should reveal rather than conceal the complexity of the interests that motivate concern about the structure of institutions for democratic choice and, if possible, show how these interests should be compromised when they come into conflict with each other. As with economic equality, if the naive view is the best view, this should be the conclusion of a philosophical argument, not its premise.

THEORIES OF POLITICAL EQUALITY

Understood in this way, a theory of political equality might be thought of as including an interpretation of the idea of fair terms of participation, together with an argument showing why *that* interpretation rather than some other should be accepted as a basis for the design or reform of democratic institutions. It might be possible to distinguish among the various possible views of political equality by referring to the contents of their interpretations of fair participation;[24] however, I believe it is more fruitful to proceed by distinguishing them according to the type of foundational considerations they appeal to in justifying the interpretations they provide. Certainly there are significant differences of view about the meaning or content of political fairness; but the more important divisions among theories of political equality, or at least those most worth attending to, involve differing conceptions of the reasons why we should care about it. For the most part, differences about the mean-

[24] Thus, for example, Jonathan Still has distinguished six meanings of political equality in "Political Equality and Election Systems," pp. 377–87. On the basis of their analysis of equality as a generic concept, Douglas Rae and his associates claim that it can have as many as 108 distinct senses (or more, counting all possible permutations), though not all of these could arise in the context of assessing political institutions. *Equalities*, p. 133.

ing of political equality derive from differences at this more basic level.

Many such theories can be imagined. The leading alternatives are *best result*, *popular will*, and *procedural* views.[25] We will consider these views at length in subsequent chapters; but it may help, to fix ideas, to explore their differences in a preliminary way here.

Best result theories hold that fair terms of political participation are those that are likely to produce the most desirable results. To clarify this idea, let us say that a *social welfare function* (swf) provides an ordering of social states according to their relative desirability. The aim is to generalize the notion of a social utility function as a criterion for ranking the various possible states of affairs from an impersonal point of view.[26] Then we might say that a best result theory regards institutions as fair when they are designed so as to maximize the expected value of an independently specified swf. Rousseau (on one interpretation) and both Mills held theories of this type (although of course they disagreed about the criterion of best results); a similar position can be found, as well, in some contemporary "economic" and "pluralist" theories of democracy. In best result theories, principled controversy about equality addresses the question of what characteristics the swf must have if it is plausibly to be construed as treating people's interests or their welfare equally.

Popular will theories are based on the idea that democratic institutions should realize the will of the people. Criteria of fairness are conditions that institutions must satisfy in order to realize this aim. Again, a technical conception will clarify the position. Say that a *social choice function* (scf) identifies one from among the possible political outcomes as the best, or most preferred, on the basis of the judgments or preferences about these outcomes held by the members of the community. Then we can say that a popular will theory

[25] I do not claim that these three kinds of views are mutually exclusive. Indeed, as we shall see, it not hard to imagine how the lines dividing them might be blurred. The distinctions are heuristic, not categorical: it suffices that the three views express familiar and reasonably distinct intuitive ideas about the place of egalitarian constraints in thinking about the fairness of democratic institutions.

[26] Thus, we aim at a conception like that of a Bergson-Samuelson social welfare function. See A. Bergson, "A Reformulation of Certain Aspects of Welfare Economics," *Quarterly Journal of Economics* 52 (1938), pp. 310–14.

is one that holds that the terms of participation are fair when their outcomes are those that would be identified by the appropriate SCF. Such theories require us to postulate a realm of political preferences existing independently of the institutions through which they are expressed and combined. The popular will is an abstract construction of these preferences, and institutions are assessed with reference to their success in picking out the outcomes it favors. Like best result views, these theories regard the definition of fair terms of participation as a derivative matter; here, however, principled controversy about equality arises at the level of the social choice function rather than the social welfare function. The issue in this case is what characteristics the social choice function must possess if it can plausibly be said to give equal weight to each person's preferences about the alternative possible outcomes.[27]

Best result and popular will theories are both outcome-oriented; because they share an instrumentalist approach to the evaluation of political procedures, they are easily confused. But there are fundamental differences. To illustrate, consider two contrasts between the ideas of a social welfare function and a social choice function.[28] First, the primary result of a social welfare function is an ordering of alternative social states; the ordering of alternative political outcomes (or government policies) is a secondary result, obtained from the primary ordering by assessing the impact of each possible outcome on the overall desirability of the resulting social state. On the other hand, the primary output of a social choice function is an ordering of political outcomes themselves; nothing is implied about the overall desirability of the resulting social state. (Of course, if

[27] Such a conception seems to stand behind what Coleman and Ferejohn refer to as the "proceduralist" approach to the justification of democracy. They write that such a justification "depends on the nature of the mapping from the original preference orderings of the collective to the outcome." I hope it will be clear from what follows why I regard this conception of proceduralism as misleading. Jules Coleman and John Ferejohn, "Democracy and Social Choice," Ethics 97 (1986), p. 7.

[28] The distinction has been clouded by Arrow's use of the phrase "social welfare function" in a nonstandard way, to describe something closer to what I refer to in the text as a social choice function. See Kenneth J. Arrow, Social Choice and Individual Values, 2d ed. (New York: John Wiley, 1963), esp. p. 23, where Arrow comments on the difference between the conception he adopts and that of Bergson, and pp. 104–5 (in the 1963 postscript) where he comments that a better term for his "social welfare function" would have been "constitution."

vox populi, vox Dei, things might be otherwise; but the appeal of popular will theories does not depend on accepting any such maxim.) The second contrast has to do with the basis of the ordering. The idea of a social welfare function is agnostic about this: there are no restrictions on the definition of social welfare. Thus, such familiar theories of social justice as classical utilitarianism and that set forth by John Rawls may be interpreted as conceptions of social welfare and represented as swfs. For the moment we need not be concerned about the merits of these and other possibilities. The important point is that social welfare judgments need not be based on or derived from individual judgments or preferences about alternative political outcomes. (Indeed, welfare need not be conceived individualistically *at all*.) Social choice functions, by contrast, are defined directly in terms of people's political preferences and hence are necessarily individualistic. On the assumption that a preference ordering over the alternative possible outcomes may be assigned to each individual in society, a scf represents a mechanism by which these individual orderings may be combined to yield a social ordering. It is true, of course, that there are similarities. Both conceptions bear on the question of which policies should be chosen, and both may (in the case of scfs, *must*) raise problems concerning aggregation. But these are superficial similarities that should not obscure the fact that these conceptions represent fundamentally different ideas.

Procedural theories stand in contrast to both of these instrumentalist views. Say that a *social decision procedure* (sdp) is a set of rules that describes an institutional mechanism through which social choices are actually to be made; more familiarly, we might think of an sdp as the political constitution of society. Although a procedural theory need not deny that there are substantive criteria for the assessment of political outcomes, it holds that assessments of outcomes are, if at all, only indirectly relevant to the fairness of the sdps that produce them. There are many kinds of proceduralism, each of which conceives of procedural fairness differently; later, we will consider several of these in more detail. What all of these views have in common (in fact, virtually the only thing they have in common) is the idea that the terms of participation in democratic procedures should themselves be fair; they should represent a division of political influence that would be appropriate among

persons regarded as equal citizens. Proceduralism holds that the definition of fair terms of participation in a democracy is a matter of
fundamental rather than derivative interest. The subject of principled controversy is the interpretation of the idea of equal citizenship itself. Fairness involves the equal treatment of citizens, but
this is not identified with (though it may be influenced by) equal
treatment of their welfare or their preferences.

To express these distinctions in a simple formula, one might say
that the three views express three conceptions of the object of political fairness. Best result theories are concerned with fairness to
people's *interests* or *welfare*; popular will theories, to their *political
preferences*; and procedural theories, to *persons themselves*, conceived as equal citizens.[29]

The view I shall set forth, as an alternative to these more conventional views, is a substantive variant of the procedural theory that
incorporates, albeit indirectly, certain result-oriented elements. To
distinguish it from simpler forms of the procedural view, we might
call this theory *complex proceduralism*. Like other forms of proceduralism, this theory holds that democratic procedures should treat
persons as equals; but it will not follow that the appropriate criterion for assessing procedures is the simple principle of equal power
over outcomes. Instead, complex proceduralism holds that the
terms of democratic participation are fair when they are reasonably
acceptable from each citizen's point of view, or more precisely,
when no citizen has good reason to refuse to accept them. To give
content to the idea of reasonable acceptability, I shall identify three
regulative interests of citizenship that democratic citizens may be
presumed to share;[30] and I shall say that it would be reasonable to
refuse to accept the terms of participation that institutions embody
when they offend any of these interests and when some less offensive alternative is available.

The analysis of fairness in terms of reasonable acceptability is an
application of the idea of the social contract to the problem of political equality; as with other applications of the contract idea, its dis-

---

[29] As with all simple formulas, this may be misleading. But nothing turns on this
expression of the contrasts; it is simply an expository convenience.

[30] These are interests in *recognition*, *equitable treatment*, and *deliberative responsibility*. They are discussed, together with the contractualist structure of complex
proceduralism, in chapter 5.

tinctive egalitarianism is to be found in the foundational requirement that fair terms of participation should be reasonably
acceptable to everyone. In contrast to the various forms of simple
proceduralism, this view allows that there may be circumstances in
which political fairness requires procedural inequalities; and it explains how considerations of fairness may apply even to institutional problems that are not plausibly understood as bearing on the
distribution of power, abstractly conceived.

NEGLECTED ALTERNATIVES

The three views I have distinguished hardly exhaust the possibilities.[31] Although I shall not discuss them in detail, it may help, if
only to clarify the conceptions already set forth, to distinguish two
other kinds of views about political equality that have been influential in democratic thought.

The first of these are *exchange* theories in the tradition of Wicksell.[32] Such theories presuppose a division of labor in society between the supply of private and of public goods; the former is the
domain of the market, and the latter, of the state. The chief problem
for *political* theory is to devise a choice procedure that ensures that
the state will limit itself to providing public goods and that it will
provide them in optimum amounts. Wicksell's principle of just taxation is a prototype solution to this problem. He proposed that the
political agenda be constrained so that voters are confronted with
choices over complete policies, including a description of the nature
and amount of the good to be provided and a taxation scheme (or
several alternative schemes) to finance it; assuming that the background distribution of resources is just, he argued that no such pol-

---

[31] The discussion in this section will mainly concern readers with particular interests in welfare economics and social choice. Others may prefer to skip to the beginning of chapter 2.

[32] See K. Wicksell, *Finanztheoretische Untersuchungen* (Jena, 1896), selections
translated and reprinted as "A New Principle of Just Taxation," in *Classics in the
Theory of Public Finance*, ed. R. Musgrave and A. Peacock (New York: St. Martin's
Press, 1967), pp. 72–118.

icy that fails to attract unanimous support can be an efficient use of social resources.[33]

Wicksell's view can be described as an exchange theory because it treats the political system as a mechanism through which each citizen reveals the amount of private resources she is willing to exchange (that is, the amount of private consumption she is willing to forgo) for the benefit she foresees deriving from the government's policies. The terms of participation—in this case including the constraints on the political agenda and the unanimity decision rule— are derived by asking what would be necessary to ensure that social resources will not be used inefficiently, as they might be, for example, if a policy were enacted that provided greater benefits to some than they were willing to pay for given their other consumption possibilities.

As it stands, Wicksell's proposal is unacceptable on its own terms because the unanimity rule fails to take account of distortions due to transactions costs and the possibilities for strategic voting. More recently, writers have sought ways to avoid these problems.[34] Considered as an approach to a theory of fair participation, however, the Wicksellian view faces a more serious difficulty. As Wicksell himself emphasized, the proposal assumes a just background distribution of income and wealth. Otherwise, policies adopted under the scheme may not be efficient and almost certainly will not be just: in particular, where the requisite background is absent, the unanimity rule will effectively exclude policies aimed at redressing distributive injustice.[35] Exchange theories that incorporate an assumption of background justice are doomed to irrelevance, since they depend on an essential counterfactual premise. Theories that set such an assumption aside,[36] on the other hand, will exclude from the polit-

[33] Although arguing that a unanimity decision rule is therefore the ideal, Wicksell noted that it would be impractical under most normal conditions and settled for "approximate unanimity" or a qualified majority instead. Ibid.

[34] For a brief survey, see Dennis Mueller, *Public Choice* (Cambridge: Cambridge University Press, 1979), pp. 68–89.

[35] "A New Principle of Just Taxation," p. 108. Actually, matters are even worse than Wicksell saw. Even where a just background distribution is initially present, there is no guarantee that it will be preserved over time.

[36] For example, that set forth in James M. Buchanan and Gordon Tullock, *The Calculus of Consent* (Ann Arbor: University of Michigan Press, 1962), and in James M. Buchanan, *The Limits of Liberty: Between Anarchy and Leviathan* (Chicago: Uni-

ical arena an important class of policies that are, in fact, the subjects of political controversy and that we have every reason to believe are appropriate objects—and perhaps the most important
objects—of political decision.[37] Either way, it does not appear that
exchange theories are likely to yield a conception of political equality that is both philosophically plausible and applicable to the institutional problems that need to be faced.[38] Thus, I shall not consider
exchange theories as a separate category of approaches to the definition of fair terms of participation.

It is worth noting, however, that on one interpretation such views
belong to the class of best result theories. The interpretation arises
in the following way. Theories in the tradition of Wicksell draw
their plausibility from an analogy with the market: the controlling
normative idea is that of efficiency. Now writers within the tradition differ about why efficiency should be counted as a virtue. For
some, it is because shifts from the status quo to a new, more efficient position (that is, Pareto improvements) represent changes that
no one has an interest in rejecting.[39] For others, it is because efficient outcomes are thought to possess greater social utility (in the
aggregate) than any alternative.[40] The criticisms sketched in the last
paragraph apply primarily to the former, which represents what is
today the orthodox ordinalist view.[41] The latter view, however, is

---

versity of Chicago Press, 1975). Elsewhere, Buchanan acknowledges that unequal
"starting positions" might undermine the justice of market distributions but apparently rejects adjustment of the political or constitutional structure to alleviate these
injustices. "Rules for a Fair Game: Contractarian Notes on Distributive Justice," in
Liberty, Market and State (Brighton, Sussex: Wheatsheaf Books, 1986), pp. 123–39.

[37] For a persuasive criticism of the Buchanan and Tullock view, see Brian Barry,
Political Argument (London: Routledge & Kegan Paul, 1965), pp. 242–59.

[38] This leaves open the possibility that a branch of government devoted to the provision of public goods *beyond* the requirements of justice might be organized according to Wicksell's principle, as Rawls suggests (*A Theory of Justice*, pp. 282–84). The
difficulties with this suggestion are different from those noted above; they involve
the feasibility of the procedures necessary to distinguish between policies aimed at
providing public goods beyond the requirements of justice (the concern of the Wicksellian exchange branch) and policies required by justice itself (the concern of the
other branches).

[39] See, for example, Buchanan and Tullock, *The Calculus of Consent*, pp. 265–81.

[40] The canonical modern statement of this view is Bergson, "A Reformulation of
Certain Aspects of Welfare Economics."

[41] As found, e.g., in the discussion of voting and representation in the standard

not necessarily subject to these criticisms, since it regards efficiency as a proximate rather than an ultimate goal, operating as a surrogate for social utility in circumstances in which complete cardinal utility information is unavailable. Exchange theories in which the importance of efficiency is accounted for in this way should therefore be seen as economic versions of best result theories; such views do not raise distinctive issues of political morality (relative to more traditional utilitarian theories of political equality), and so whatever criticisms apply to best result theories as a class will apply a fortiori to these theories as well.

Finally, there are views that found a requirement of political equality on a concern for what might be called *liberal stability*. If one were in the position to design political institutions, other things equal, one would want to find ways to encourage compliance with the laws and to promote social order with the least coercive interference in individual lives. One possibility—that pursued by Rousseau in *The Social Contract*—is to constrain the decision-making system so that its outcomes will be (and will be regarded as) in the interests of most of the people most of the time. But this is unrealistic in complex and diverse societies. Another possibility is to build into the system procedural requirements that will elicit popular support even when particular decisions disappoint some interests. Political equality might be regarded as one such requirement. What recommends egalitarian democracy, in this view, is that it is more likely than any other form of government, in the context of prevailing political attitudes, to elicit continuing popular support for liberal institutions.[42]

Views of this type are deficient in three ways. First, on their own terms they prove too little. The force of the argument for equality depends almost entirely on the empirical claim that egalitarian procedures are more likely than any others to elicit popular support for

---

welfare economics textbook by R. A. Musgrave and P. B. Musgrave, *Public Finance*, 3d ed. (New York: McGraw-Hill, 1980), pp. 106–21.

[42] Thus, as Barry writes, "[O]nce the idea of the natural equality of all men has got about, claims to rule cannot be based on natural superiority. Winning an election is a basis for rule that does not conflict with equality. Indeed, it might be said to flow from it. For if quality is equal (or, as Hobbes more exactly put it, quality must be taken to be equal as a condition of peace) the only differentiating factor left is quantity. . . ." "Is Democracy Special?" p. 193.

political decisions that are in substance unpopular. But it is hardly clear that this is true; at least, it is hardly clear that inegalitarian procedures, if they are well entrenched and their inegalitarianism is not too blatant, cannot serve the purpose as well.[43] Second, even if the general point is conceded, the view is too functionalist to settle questions about the interpretation and application of political equality. It yields insufficient grounds for discriminating among alternative procedural arrangements or for settling argument about which of several equally stable arrangements would be fairer. Finally, and most fundamentally, there are surely other reasons for taking an interest in how the terms of participation are arranged. A procedural arrangement might elicit popular support for liberal institutions yet still be objectionable for reasons like those often associated with political equality; for example, it might be demeaning to disadvantaged minorities or operate to deny them effective political influence. No plausible theory of political equality can ignore questions about stability, but any theory that takes stability, even liberal stability, as its only foundational concern must be seriously incomplete.

[43] Indeed, some political scientists believe that certain procedural inequalities, such as those that favor two-party as against multiparty (or no-party) systems, may make for *higher* levels of acceptance of political decisions, by creating incentives for compromise in the preelection stages of political competition. See, for example, Maurice Duverger, *Political Parties*, trans. Barbara and Robert North (London: Methuen, 1954), pp. 245–55, 328–37; and Gabriel A. Almond, "Introduction," in G. A. Almond and James S. Coleman, *The Politics of the Developing Areas* (Princeton: Princeton University Press, 1960), esp. pp. 33–45. For a discussion, see Leon Epstein, *Political Parties in Western Democracies* (New York: Praeger, 1967), pp. 73–76.

PART ONE

Theory

CHAPTER TWO

Results

We need a theory of political equality to answer two questions: what does the egalitarian ideal require of our institutions, and why should it matter to us whether our institutions satisfy these requirements? As I argued in chapter 1, there is no sense in trying to resolve these questions separately; for at some critical point, it will turn out that any answer to one of them depends on an answer to the other. Inquiry must therefore proceed more circuitously: we should explore various prominent ways of responding jointly to both questions and consider in each case the internal coherence of the view, the consistency of its elements with various settled elements of democratic political belief, and its adequacy as a basis for resolving disputed issues of institutional design. In this and the following chapters we undertake such an analysis of the three views about political fairness identified earlier. The hope is that a critical examination of these familiar views will illuminate conditions that a more satisfactory conception of political equality should embody.

We begin with best result theories, which identify fair terms of participation with those likely to produce the most desirable outcomes—that is, outcomes that maximize social welfare, however understood. The versions of this view with the greatest currency today arise in what is called the "economic" approach to democracy and in its "pluralist" cousins. However, I shall concentrate on the earlier (and, I think, more subtle) version set forth by John Stuart Mill. Although Mill's view might seem plausible enough in its structure, few people today accept its inegalitarian elements. It is important to understand the reasons why these elements are unacceptable, for these reasons cast doubt on the structure of best result theories considered as a class. My critical observations about best result theories suggest some general conclusions about the nature of political fairness, which I note briefly at the end.

MILL'S VIEW AND ITS DEFECTS

Mill argued that "the ideally best form of government" is "a completely popular government."[1] He meant to defend what I have called the generic conception of democracy: a form of government in which all citizens have an opportunity to participate in the institutions that determine political outcomes. Mill's famous argument rests on two points. First, popular government best achieves the "present well-being" of society by providing citizens with a mechanism for protecting their interests and by enlisting their energies in promoting the "general prosperity." Second, it encourages the formation of a "better and higher national character" by stimulating the faculties of self-help and self-reliance and by cultivating and enlarging the capacity to take and apply a public rather than a private point of view.[2] We may call these the "protective" and the "educative" arguments.[3]

The chief difficulty in grasping the form of Mill's argument involves the place of these points in his overall political theory. Within that theory, political institutions, like everything else, are finally assessed according to their contribution to "the aggregate interests of society."[4] But the connection Mill imagined between the advantages of popular government and this more fundamental concern might be interpreted in two different ways. According to the first (or "direct") interpretation, "the aggregate interests of society" are identified with a social ideal that includes a conception of human excellence; as Mill described it in *On Liberty*, this is "utility in the largest sense, grounded in the permanent interests of man as a progressive being."[5] Then the protective and the educative arguments may be seen as pointing to two separate respects in which popular government advances this end. According to the second (or

---

[1] *Considerations on Representative Government* [1861], chap. 3, in *Collected Works*, vol. 19, ed. J. M. Robson (Toronto: University of Toronto Press, 1977), pp. 403–4.

[2] Ibid., p. 404. The argument is presented in the whole of chapter 3, pp. 399–412.

[3] I adopt these labels from Dennis F. Thompson, *John Stuart Mill and Representative Government* (Princeton: Princeton University Press, 1976), p. 14.

[4] *Considerations on Representative Government*, chap. 2, p. 383.

[5] *On Liberty* [1859], chap. 1, in *Collected Works*, vol. 18, ed. J. M. Robson (Toronto: University of Toronto Press, 1977), p. 224.

"functional") interpretation, governments contribute to "the aggregate interests of society" by performing certain functions, such as legislation and the administration of justice. The protective and educative arguments might now be seen as identifying criteria of good government—characteristics that increase the probability that a government will perform its functions well.[6] The functional interpretation need not deny that Mill understood social utility "in the largest sense"; instead, it is distinguished by the insistence that the primary means by which a government contributes to this end is through the good performance of various well-defined legislative, administrative, and judicial functions.

The issue raised by this dispute is the status of the values appealed to in Mill's educative argument. Is the development of a vigorous and active national character important because it is itself a component of a desirable social ideal or because it is a necessary condition of good (and progressively better) legislation, administration, and adjudication? The question raises exegetical problems beyond our present scope; but it is worth observing that the first interpretation coheres better with Mill's more general moral and political theory, which undeniably includes an ideal of individual character that gives a prominent place to the virtues of autonomy, self-improvement, and sympathy that Mill claimed are promoted by popular government. Mill's description of his project in *Representative Government* also favors this interpretation. There, he wrote that one reason for taking an interest in "how far [political institutions] tend to foster in the members of the community the various desirable qualities, moral and intellectual" is that "[t]he government which does this best, has every likelihood of being best in all other respects, since it is on these qualities . . . that all possibility of goodness in the practical operations of government depends."[7] But he also claimed that in "its operation as an agency of national education" a government can contribute to the formation of social conditions conducive to "a higher level" of civilization.[8] The point

---

[6] Both interpretations may be found in the recent literature. For the first, see Thompson, *John Stuart Mill and Representative Government*, pp. 13–53; for the second, see William N. Nelson, *On Justifying Democracy* (London: Routledge & Kegan Paul, 1980), pp. 111–118.

[7] *Considerations on Representative Government*, chap. 2, p. 390.

[8] Ibid., pp. 393–94.

is that the influence of political institutions on character might have two parallel kinds of value: the people can be made more capable of good government, and they can be made better people. "A government is to be judged by its action upon men, and by its action upon things; by what it makes of the citizens, and what it does with them; its tendency to improve or deteriorate the people themselves, and the goodness or badness of the work it performs for them. . . ."[9]

Mill's theory is of interest here because it is a democratic theory that incorporates explicitly antiegalitarian procedural elements. The argument from best results to popular government is not simultaneously an argument to political equality: "though every one ought to have a voice—that every one should have an equal voice is a totally different proposition."[10] Mill argued that the interests of society will be advanced most effectively if the views of those with broader knowledge and higher intelligence are given greater weight in the political process. Accordingly, he proposed that those of greater "mental superiority" be entitled to cast plural votes in parliamentary elections.[11] The main advantage he claimed for such a scheme is that it would improve the quality of legislation, both by providing everyone's interests with the most competent representation and by "preserving the educated class from the class legislation of the uneducated."[12] In addition, he argued that "irrespective of any direct political consequences," plural voting would help, through its effect on the "tone" of "public feeling," to counteract the undesirable tendency of democracy to cultivate "a character of mind . . . which thinks no other person's opinion much better than its own."[13] The appeals to considerations of both interest and character correspond to the protective and educative arguments for representative government and show that Mill did not believe that plural voting implicated conflicts between them.

[9] Ibid., p. 392.

[10] Ibid., chap. 8, p. 473.

[11] Ibid., p. 475; see also "Thoughts on Parliamentary Reform" [1859], in *Collected Works*, vol. 19, pp. 323–28.

[12] *Considerations on Representative Government*, p. 476. For comments on the significance of the fear of "class legislation" for the interpretation of Mill's theory, see Fred R. Berger, *Happiness, Justice, and Freedom: The Moral and Political Philosophy of John Stuart Mill* (Berkeley: University of California Press, 1984), pp. 193–94.

[13] *Considerations on Representative Government*, chap. 12, p. 508.

Mill's defense of plural voting seems clearly to be consistent with the consequentialist structure of his justification of democracy; in this sense there is no doubt about its validity. The question is whether the argument is sound—or rather, since it is unlikely to be accepted by many readers today, where and how it goes wrong.

A conventional criticism holds that Mill's argument depends on implausible empirical assumptions and on a failure to anticipate the likely political effects of the scheme he recommends.[14] For example, he presumed that those of greater intelligence or education would be more effectively motivated to temper self-interest with consideration of the interests of others in deciding how to vote. But this is naive; it seems at least as likely that those granted procedural advantages will use them to secure more effective representation of their interests than they would receive under a scheme of equal votes. Thus, assuming that those with extra votes would disproportionately represent the higher income classes, the scheme would reinforce existing inequalities in the distribution of property, or, at least, diminish the prospects of desirable egalitarian reform.[15] Mill also presumed that more intelligent and educated voters would be likely to return representatives with superior legislative judgment and more publicly spirited motivation. But it is hardly clear today (and it was not much clearer in Mill's time) that there is such a simple or direct relationship between the intellectual characteristics of voters and those of the candidates who are most successful in attracting their votes. Distributive issues aside, plural voting may not improve the quality of legislation. If not, it would probably not improve the "tone" of public life either.

These criticisms are probably enough to defeat Mill's argument that plural voting would produce more utility, even as he understood it. But I do not believe that they constitute a fully adequate

[14] Berger, *Happiness, Justice, and Freedom*, p. 193.

[15] Notwithstanding Mill's protestations to the contrary (in *Considerations on Representative Government*, chap. 8, pp. 474–75), it is inconceivable that he could have failed to appreciate this. Indeed, writing about ten years later, he referred to the possible effects of plural voting on the distribution of wealth and economic power to explain his growing doubts about the wisdom of the proposal. *Autobiography* [1873], in *Collected Works*, vol. 1, ed. J. M. Robson and J. Stillinger (Toronto: University of Toronto Press, 1981), pp. 261–62. See also Thompson, *John Stuart Mill and Representative Government*, pp. 99–101.

response. What if Mill's empirical assumptions—or some appropriate surrogates—were true? Suppose that plural voting would, in fact, produce the best results. Someone who was entitled to cast only one vote might still feel unfairly treated by such a scheme. Mill himself disparaged this feeling. "No one but a fool," he wrote, "feels offended by the acknowledgement that there are others whose opinion, and even whose wish, is entitled to a greater amount of consideration than his."[16] But the prospect of greater overall social benefit is not enough to dissolve the impression that the scheme is unfair to those whom it disadvantages; and those among the disadvantaged who are offended by the scheme do not seem merely foolish.

Consider plural voting from the point of view of those whom it disadvantages. Mill believed that it would be unreasonable for them to refuse to accept a scheme of plural voting if the scheme would produce results that are better for society as a whole than any alternative. Why should this be? Suppose that the incremental benefit arising from better results accrued primarily to those who were advantaged by the scheme (the "winners"). For example, suppose that the superiority of the legislation likely to be produced under plural voting consisted mainly of greater encouragement of high culture and the arts. On Mill's assumptions, this would produce greater good for society in the aggregate, but because those unqualified for plural votes (the "losers") would for the most part be ill-equipped to enjoy it, they would derive no direct benefit for themselves from the overall benefit brought about by the scheme. It would be unreasonable for the losers to object to such a scheme only if they had some reason to concern themselves with the production of overall benefit to society, regardless of its effects on their own situation. But why should they concern themselves with that?

There would be an obvious reply if the Millian scheme were costless to the losers. The reply invokes the Paretian principle that it is unreasonable to oppose a change that produces benefits for others without imposing any additional burden on you. But plural voting is not costless to the losers. There are at least two kinds of costs. The first is the opportunity cost of forgoing the legislation that would be enacted under alternative voting schemes lacking the

---

[16] *Considerations on Representative Government*, chap. 8, p. 474.

preference for those of greater education. On Mill's assumptions regarding the propensity of the less educated to vote their own interests, it may be supposed that the interests of the losers under plural voting would fare less well than they would under a more egalitarian scheme. Of course, these interests might be frivolous, self-defeating, or even immoral; but, then again, they might not. The weight that the opportunity costs of plural voting should carry plainly depends on the nature of the interests involved; but nothing in Mill's scheme guarantees that even important interests would be looked after where there is insufficient voting power to back them up. The second type of cost is the effect on self-esteem likely to be produced when political inequalities reflect other natural or social distinctions that are the objects of invidious discrimination or are occasions of disrespect in society at large. These inequalities not only work to the detriment of the disadvantaged group but, on plausible assumptions about social attitudes toward intelligence and education, are also likely to be experienced by them as degrading. The visible dilution of influence will appear as an insult, conveying public approval of pre-existing, demeaning social practices. Moreover, this might be true even where there is reason to believe that those who are disadvantaged by the inequality will benefit from it in the long run: the inequality itself comes to symbolize the lesser merit or worth of those disadvantaged by it.

These costs—relating to foregone interest satisfaction and to predictable injuries to self-esteem—provide rationales for objections to plural voting. But the objections would not be conclusive against Mill; we can imagine several rejoinders. For example, a theory of individual good might be set forth to explain why it would be reasonable for people to want for themselves what is good for society as a whole. Thus, to return to our example, a defender of Mill might hold that the flourishing of high culture is good for everyone, at least in the long run, because it would help them cultivate more elevated tastes and thus enjoy pleasures of higher quality. More plausibly, perhaps, a social theory might be invoked to show that everyone would benefit indirectly from measures that would only benefit some people directly. Perhaps a society in which high culture flourishes is likely to be more innovative and productive, improving material conditions for everyone. (Such an argument would depend on empirical claims analogous to those found in *On Liberty*

about the beneficial social consequences of genius and eccentric-
ity.)[17]

Both of these rejoinders depend on dubious premises. But even if
the premises were granted, the objections mentioned earlier would
retain some force. The rejoinders do not so much defeat the objections on their own ground as bring forth different factors to be offset
against them. Considerations related to the self-esteem (and perhaps the material interests) of those disadvantaged by the scheme
are arrayed against considerations related to the benefits supposed
to flow from giving more power to the more intelligent. A further
argument is required to establish that plural voting represents the
least costly or most efficient reconciliation of these conflicting considerations from the point of view of those disadvantaged by the
scheme. But this does not appear to be true; alternative procedural
devices consistent with equal votes might be devised that would
have the same desirable features as plural voting. (Mill's later
doubts about plural voting suggest that he may have believed this
to be the case.)[18] It therefore appears that those who would be disadvantaged by plural voting would have good reason to refuse to
accept it.

But suppose that this last point is incorrect and that the defenses
of plural voting just suggested were convincing—or would be, if
they were more fully developed. What is interesting is *why* they
would convince. The reason, I believe, is that each involves a shift
of perspective, away from the point of view of society as a whole
and toward that of each person affected. In each case, plural voting
is said to have beneficial effects for those who regard themselves as
disadvantaged by it and in virtue of which *they themselves* would
have reason to accept it.

Mill offered a justification of plural voting of this general form;
he claimed, not only that the voting scheme would produce the
most utility for society at large, but, in addition, that it would benefit *everyone* in comparison to the alternative of equal votes.[19] As
he seemed to recognize, the fact that the scheme would be best for

[17] See *On Liberty*, in *Collected Works*, vol. 18, chap. 1, p. 224; chap. 3, pp. 266–75.

[18] *Autobiography*, pp. 261–62.

[19] In addition to Mill's account in *Considerations on Representative Government*,
chap. 8, see also Rawls's gloss in *A Theory of Justice* (Cambridge: Harvard University
Press, 1971), pp. 232–33.

society overall is not enough to explain why each citizen should accept it; it must be shown to be desirable from each person's separate point of view as well. Such an argument, of course, is characteristic of the social contract tradition in political theory;[20] and it differs significantly from the consequentialism of Mill's official argument from overall best results.

It is a telling fact that Mill felt pressed to shift to an implicitly contractualist justification of plural voting. For it calls attention to the especially intimate connection between the problem of institutional justification in democratic societies and the distinctive features of contractualist argument. This connection is of the first importance for the subject of political equality, and we will consider it at greater length in chapter 5. Here, we should note that the contract view of justification in democratic theory is consistent with a variety of normative positions regarding the design of institutions. It needs to be emphasized in particular that in adopting the point of view of contractualism one does not, without more, commit oneself to any general belief about the merits of procedural equality. Indeed, the Millian rejoinders imagined earlier suggest that plural voting might itself be provided with a contractualist defense, albeit perhaps not a very persuasive one. Such a defense would impute to the parties to a social contract interests corresponding to these rejoinders (for example, in higher quality pleasures or in the benefits of higher living standards resulting from greater innovation and productivity) and hold that plural voting serves these individual interests better than any alternative. I do not mean to claim that the defense would succeed. The point is only that, although Mill's official justification for plural voting lacks the appropriate form, it does not follow that procedural inequalities like those he advocates are unacceptable. To show this, more needs to be said; in particular, we need an account of the interests that determine the acceptability of political procedures from each person's point of view and an explanation of why, given these interests, it would be reasonable for some people, at least, to object to plural voting.

The critique of Mill that I have suggested supplies these require-

[20] I am indebted here to T. M. Scanlon, "Contractualism and Utilitarianism," in *Utilitarianism and Beyond*, ed. Amartya Sen and Bernard Williams (Cambridge: Cambridge University Press, 1982), pp. 103–28.

ments. However, while it yields the conclusion that the Millian scheme is unfair, it does not exhibit this as a derivation from any more general principle of procedural equality. According to this critique, plural voting is unfair because it would not be unreasonable for those disadvantaged by it to reject it. This is not because procedural equality has any morally privileged status; instead, it is because plural voting would undermine the self-esteem of those whom it disadvantages and because the political results it would be likely to produce would treat their interests inequitably. The idea of equality operates at a deeper level of the argument, in the structure of the justification that would have to be available if plural voting were to be adequately defended. The equal moral status of each person is represented by the fact that any scheme for registering political preferences should be acceptable from the point of view of each person affected. A scheme is counted as unfair if *anyone* has sufficient reason to refuse to accept it, taking into account the range of feasible alternatives and the need to have *some* scheme for registering preferences. Neither is the unfairness of plural voting a reflection of any special weight or priority accorded to the interests of those disadvantaged by it. Everyone's interests are taken into account; the interests of the disadvantaged are decisive because theirs are the interests that are harmed by the scheme, and the harm done, considered in comparison to its benefits, appears to be sufficiently important to justify a refusal to accept it.[21]

ENLARGED CRITERIA OF BEST RESULTS

The reason for considering Mill's scheme at such length is to show that his mistake derives from the structure of his official view about justification, which is generic to all best result theories, rather than from the content of his criterion of best results, which might be thought to be idiosyncratic. If my criticisms are correct, then no result-oriented view can provide an adequate account of political fairness, for in proceeding from the point of view of society at large rather than from that of each individual affected, all such

[21] Compare Scanlon's remarks in "Contractualism and Utilitarianism," p. 123.

views adopt a standpoint that is inappropriate to the subject of political fairness.

This conclusion, however, is vulnerable to the following challenge. The problem in Mill's view, it might be said, flows from a mistaken criterion of results rather than from its structure. His criterion is too narrow, because it excludes any reference to the kinds of interests I referred to in explaining why someone who was allocated only one vote would be justified in complaining. But surely these interests are relevant to the assessment of a procedure's outcomes. The criterion of results should therefore be enlarged, so that it takes account not only of the quality of legislation but also of the effects of the system of legislation, broadly understood, on individual contentment and character.[22] A procedural arrangement would be unfair if its overall effects were worse, assessed according to such a standard, than those that would be produced by some feasible alternative arrangement.

However, I do not believe that the challenge is likely to succeed; the argument against best result conceptions will survive even if an appropriately wider criterion is substituted for Mill's. There are two possibilities. Either the enlarged criterion will still be too narrow to rule out procedural arrangements we would recognize intuitively as unfair, or it will be so ambiguous or abstract that problems about fairness will reemerge as problems about the interpretation of the criterion. I cannot, of course, offer a conclusive argument for this hypothesis; I can, however, illustrate why it seems plausible, by discussing two possible revisions of Mill's criterion, which lead respectively to each possibility.

Consider first the theory set forth by William Nelson.[23] Its aim is to justify "the political institution[s] of modern constitutional democracy on the ground that they tend to produce just government, or, at least, to prevent serious injustice."[24] "Just government," in this view, is government that conforms with moral principles. Such principles constitute "a system of overriding constraints on action

[22] Such a view is suggested by Rawls's brief comments on Mill and plural voting in *A Theory of Justice*, pp. 232–34.

[23] In *On Justifying Democracy*, chap. 6. Nelson has proposed a somewhat different view in recent, and as yet unpublished, papers. I regret that these came to my attention too late to be considered here.

[24] Ibid., p. 129.

compliance with which tends to produce benefits or prevent harm and which could serve as the fundamental charter of a well-ordered society."[25] Of particular importance is the *public character* of moral principles: taken together, they must be the object of a possible consensus capable of enduring in a society over time as the basis on which conflicting claims are resolved. Nelson does not say anything about the *content* of principles of justice, except that they should be principles that "free and independent persons" could accept;[26] but this is enough for our purposes.

Nelson indicates that this conception is derived from Mill, but the view is perhaps more novel than this suggests. Since Nelson does not commit himself about the content of principles of just legislation, he cannot argue, as Mill did, that democratic institutions are most likely to produce legislation with any particular substantive characteristics (e.g., legislation that will maximize social utility). Instead, Nelson takes from Mill the idea that democratic government is distinguished by its "open" character. It is a system in which the advocates of legislation must be prepared to defend their proposals to those who would be affected by them, especially those whose interests would possibly be harmed. According to Nelson, to do so is necessarily to appeal to principles that could be accepted by everyone:

> [G]iven open institutions . . . public functionaries will attempt to formulate coherent justifications for their policies; and these justifications will have to be capable of gaining widespread public acceptance. Such justifications will have to represent a kind of possible consensus—a possible "fundamental charter of a well ordered society." But principles like this satisfy at least a necessary condition for adequate moral principles.[27]

In short, open government promotes just legislation by making the prospects of legislative initiatives depend on the political success of efforts to justify them in terms of principles that most people will have reason to accept.

Nelson provides no direct argument for any specific procedures.

[25] Ibid., p. 106.
[26] Ibid.
[27] Ibid., p. 117.

Indeed, since the theory is set forth as a generic justification of democracy, someone could accept the theory for that purpose yet maintain that the design of political procedures poses a separable normative issue: a consequentialist justification of democracy need not be associated with a best result doctrine of political fairness. However, Nelson holds that "it is not *necessarily* an objection to a specific system of representative government that it is unfair or unequal in some respect" provided that the system yields just legislation.[28] This suggests that procedures are to be chosen on the basis of a comparison of the political outcomes likely to be produced by the various alternatives. "Open government" is desirable because it normally produces the best results. Thus, "there is an argument against [procedures] that systematically prevent certain groups from making their concerns known. We need to encourage the development of principles acceptable to *everyone*, and of legislation justifiable in terms of those principles."[29]

Unfortunately, such an argument will establish too little in connection with procedures that are unfair for reasons unconnected with the dynamic of "open government" on which Nelson's theory relies. Again, plural voting provides a convenient example, for it would plainly not prevent anyone from making his concerns known; and, if Mill's empirical assumptions were correct, it might actually increase the probability that public political debate would take place at the level of principle rather than of possibly shortsighted self-interest. But this does not dissolve the impression of unfairness associated with procedures that embed in public political practice the belief that some people's opinions are worthy of less attention or respect than those of others.[30]

A plausible response to this difficulty yields an example of the other kind of problem—that of excessive ambiguity—mentioned earlier. One might argue that the defect of criteria of best results that apply only to the content of political decisions is that they fail

[28] Ibid., p. 123 (emphasis in original).

[29] Ibid.

[30] There are also many institutional issues about which such a theory would apparently be silent, including, for example, questions about the structure of representation and about regulations governing political finance. Yet these questions clearly implicate concerns about procedural fairness. (In chapter 6, I consider briefly an argument for proportional representation suggested by Nelson's view.)

to embody a concern for the manner in which the procedures that generate these decisions affect people's perceptions of themselves and of each other.[31] Accordingly, the outcomes of the political process should be conceived more generously than they are by theories of just or efficient legislation. In addition to the degree of improvement brought about by an act of legislation, we must also attend to the degree of improvement arising from the operation of the process of election and legislation. If a procedural device such as plural voting were experienced by some as demeaning or insulting, then that fact in itself should count against the procedure. Thus, the argument concludes, an adequate criterion of best results must include both a substantive and a procedural dimension. It might hold, for example, that fair procedures are those likely to produce the greatest average (or, perhaps, weighted average) of scores on these two dimensions of evaluation.

But this argument is not persuasive. Two-dimensional criteria are ambiguous about how conflicts between the dimensions of evaluation should be resolved. There is no reason to suppose that the substantive and the procedural dimension will always agree about any particular procedural choice. This may be true, for example, of plural voting: if Mill's empirical assumptions were right, then the substantive dimension would favor it, but the procedural dimension might oppose it. Some mechanism is required to resolve the conflict; but it appears that in the formulation and defense of any such mechanism, the initial difficulty about the fairness of procedures that yield the (substantively) best results will be reproduced. Thus, the shift to a more complex criterion of best results does not help, for it merely brings the initial difficulty into the formulation of the criterion itself.

Perhaps the difficulty could be avoided by invoking a more abstract criterion. At the limit, the criterion might simply be identified with social utility or perhaps with a (more perfectionist) conception of human development of the kind occasionally employed by Mill. It seems evident that the first alternative will not solve the problem, since there is no reason to believe that states of affairs that contain the most utility overall are most likely to be reached through procedures that could be defended to each person affected

[31] I am grateful to Dennis Thompson for suggesting this argument to me.

by them. The other alternative presents a more complicated problem, but it does not appear, in general, that a perfectionist principle, even if its procedural requirements conformed with ordinary intuitions about fairness, could provide a plausible systematic account of those intuitions; and the example of plural voting provides good reason to doubt that a perfectionist principle would normally justify only intuitively fair procedures.

We should observe parenthetically that two-dimensional views, or at least those of the kind I have been considering, are more than simply ambiguous. Such views locate the unfairness of practices like plural voting in the *fact* that those disadvantaged by them would experience the practices as demeaning. The unfairness of the practice is relative to the expectations and self-understandings of those affected. But such understandings are notoriously engendered and enforced by prevailing customs and institutions. Suppose (as Mill hoped) that social institutions actually succeeded in convincing, say, the uneducated that their political opinions were worthy of less consideration and that as a consequence they did not feel themselves demeaned by plural voting. The intuition that they were treated unfairly would not extinguish; indeed, it is an especially pernicious form of unfair treatment that cultivates the willing acquiescence of its victims.[32]

Perhaps it will help, by way of summary, to note how these conclusions differ from other criticisms of best result views that might seem attractive. I have not argued that such views are objectionable because they might sanction procedures that impose unequal levels of costs and benefits on their participants or ones that somehow fail to satisfy the Pareto criterion (for example, by producing outcomes that could be improved upon without reducing anyone's absolute position). The essential question is whether a procedural arrangement can be justified to everyone who is affected by it; thus, although either factor might be relevant to an assessment of the arrangement, neither, by itself, will determine its fairness, because other factors might be relevant as well. More basically, I have not argued that best result theories are unacceptable simply because

[32] As David Gauthier remarks about a similar point, "Feminist thought has surely made this, perhaps the core form of human exploitation, clear to us." *Morals by Agreement* (Oxford: Clarendon Press, 1986), p. 11.

they allow judgments about procedural fairness to depend on considerations about results. As I shall argue in chapter 4, no theory of political fairness that excludes result-oriented considerations altogether seems plausible. But these considerations might be brought into an evaluation of procedures in a variety of ways, of which best result theories represent only the most obvious. Thus, what I have argued is that these theories fail because they take account of results in the wrong way, not because they take account of them at all.

VARIETIES OF PROCEDURAL FAIRNESS

Best result constructions might recommend themselves in spite of these criticisms for a reason associated with an analysis of procedural justice familiar from Rawls.[33] He observes that there are some procedures whose outcomes can be judged according to standards that are independent of the procedures themselves, in the sense of being defined separately from and prior to the definition of the procedures. Some such procedures are sure to produce the desired outcome (Rawls gives the example of the common practice of having the person who cuts a cake choose her piece last); these represent cases of "perfect" procedural justice. Other procedures have some significant probability of producing the desired outcome but cannot be guaranteed to do so always (for example, the rules of criminal procedure); these are cases of "imperfect" procedural justice. Rawls holds that in both kinds of cases, questions about the justice of a procedure are settled by considering how well its outcomes satisfy the appropriate standard of desirability. Not all procedures are of these kinds, however; sometimes there is no independent standard governing a procedure's outcomes, but we are prepared to accept them provided that the procedure has been followed properly. This is "pure" procedural justice; Rawls gives the example of a fair bet. In these cases, judgments about the justice of the procedure depend upon the characteristics of the procedure itself, rather than on an assessment of its results.

[33] Rawls, *A Theory of Justice*, pp. 85–86. See also Brian Barry, *Political Argument* (London: Routledge & Kegan Paul, 1965), pp. 97–106.

The analysis encourages acceptance of a best result view of political fairness because there often *are* independent standards (such as principles of specifying individual rights and desirable social goals) to which we can refer in evaluating political outcomes. When political procedures regularly or systematically produce outcomes that violate these standards, we are inclined to consider them unfair. Thus, the question of political justice seems more similar to that of defining fair rules of criminal procedure than to that of describing the conditions of a fair bet; it appears to represent a case of imperfect procedural justice in which the independent standard is a criterion for evaluating the substantive outcomes of the political process.[34] Such an account, of course, would have the structure of a best result theory.

Although he does not say so explicitly, it appears that Rawls believes the three-part analysis exhausts the possibilities. If this were so, then some kind of best result theory of political fairness would indeed seem unavoidable. But the analysis is incomplete. A further possibility is suggested by cases in which there is an independent standard for assessing a procedure's outcomes, but there are also non-outcome-oriented criteria of fairness pertaining to the procedure itself. Consider, for example, affirmative action policies involving preferential treatment on the basis of race or gender. These policies might be recommended by the fact that they represent the best (or perhaps, the only) way to rectify past injustice or to promote a desirable distribution of some good; yet they may also come into conflict with the good-faith expectations of those whose aspirations the policies disappoint and who bear no responsibility for the past injustice or present inequity the policies seek to redress.[35] Analogous conflicts between outcome-oriented and process-oriented considerations arise in connection with many other problems of pro-

[34] As William Nelson writes, "an argument based on the notion of pure procedural justice will work only when there is no independent standard in terms of which the procedure's outcomes are to be evaluated." *On Justifying Democracy*, p. 23.

[35] For a discussion, see Thomas Nagel, "The Policy of Preference," in *Mortal Questions* (Cambridge: Cambridge University Press, 1979), pp. 91–105. Sidgwick described such a conflict as a reflection of the difference between "conservative" and "ideal" justice. *The Methods of Ethics*, 7th ed. (London: Macmillan, 1907), bk. 3, chap. 5, secs. 2–3, pp. 268–73. The conflict arises distinctively in nonideal contexts; one might be misled as a result of restricting attention to "ideal theory."

cedural design, such as rules of parliamentary debate involving the apportionment of speaking time, and even certain aspects of the rules of criminal procedure (consider, for example, the right of accused persons to be confronted by their accusers). In each case the propensity of the procedure to yield desirable results is *a* relevant consideration in determining the procedure's fairness without being the *only* consideration.[36]

The possibility of conflict between the various dimensions of fairness renders such cases uniquely problematic. Moreover, there does not appear to be any nonartificial way to combine the conflicting values within a single outcome-oriented criterion at a higher level of abstraction. An overall judgment about the fairness of such procedures requires us to reach some compromise among the divergent process-oriented and outcome-oriented considerations at stake. There is no need to consider generally how a compromise should be arrived at. Certainly one does not want to hold that the conflicts ought always to be resolved in favor of process-oriented factors; indeed, it may be that in most cases outcome-oriented considerations should win out. For the present, it is enough to see that this fourth category is not empty and that the three-part analysis may therefore mislead in concealing the possibility of conflict between outcome-oriented and other elements in judgments about procedural fairness. As our examination of plural voting illustrates, this kind of conflict is characteristic of controversy about political fairness; but it must either be ignored or distorted by any theory with the structure of best result conceptions. That is why no such theory can be adequate.

[36] For related comments, see Kent Greenawalt, "How Empty is the Idea of Equality?" *Columbia Law Review* 83 (1983), pp. 1171–73.

CHAPTER THREE

Preferences

The sovereign value in best result theories is the idea of an overall social good, which serves as the basis for judgments about procedural fairness (as for all other political judgments). People's preferences about the various outcomes that might be sought through the political process occupy a subsidiary position in these theories: preferences are not seen as having intrinsic importance, and their expression, in systems of voting, is treated only as a means for the production of political outcomes whose desirability could, in principle, be established independently.

By contrast, in popular will theories preferences themselves are sovereign. More exactly, what is sovereign is the collective preference of all the citizens, taken as a group—"the will of the people." The difficulty, of course, is that citizens' preferences are frequently in conflict, so that the meaning of "the will of the people" is typically not transparent. The idea of popular sovereignty expresses a substantive constraint on the content of political decisions, but the likelihood of conflict poses a problem about how this constraint should be interpreted. The distinctive conception of fairness found in popular will theories arises from the thought that when individual preferences are in conflict, the conflict ought to be resolved in a way that counts each person's preference equally.

Although the maxim of popular sovereignty is, of course, ancient, modern efforts to arrive at an illuminating analysis of the popular will have been confined almost entirely to the theory of social choice. The chief theoretical problem has been seen to be that of describing conditions in which a popular will can coherently be said to exist at all; the chief practical problem, that of describing systems of voting with a high probability of eliciting the sincere or faithful registration of individual preferences. In both respects the results have been disheartening. Arrow's "general possibility theorem" established that there is no social choice function taking only ordinal information about individual preferences as its arguments that conforms to several normative conditions rooted in the idea of popular sovereignty. And various writers have shown that there is, in general, no voting procedure that lacks incentives for insincere or "strategic" voting that would distort the identification of the social choice.[1]

For the most part I shall not question these findings. The important issue concerns their significance for the subject of political fairness. I believe that this has been widely misunderstood because the conception of political fairness on which popular will theories rely (usually implicitly) is faulty. It reflects an unwarranted generalization from the simple case of social choice among two alternatives to the general case where there may be more. The fairness of democratic procedures must consist in something other than their tendency to yield outcomes that give equal weight to the political preferences of citizens.

THE STRUCTURE OF POPULAR WILL THEORIES

It is critical to the integrity of popular will theories that "the people's will" be conceived independently of the outcome of any actual social decision procedure. Political procedures are regarded as instruments for the production of outcomes whose warrant does not derive from the details of the procedures themselves but rather from the array of preferences that constitute the popular will. There is a popular will, and the goal of decision-making institutions is to identify it as accurately as possible.[2] Accordingly, any popular will the-

[1] For the Arrow result, see Kenneth J. Arrow, *Social Choice and Individual Values*, 2d ed. (New York: John Wiley, 1963), discussed further below. On the impossibility of a strategy-proof voting procedure, see Michael Dummett and Robin Farquharson, "Stability in Voting," *Econometrica* 29 (1961), pp. 33–43; Allan Gibbard, "Manipulation of Voting Schemes: A General Result," *Econometrica* 41 (1973), pp. 587–601; and M. A. Satterthwaite, "Strategy-proofness and Arrow's Conditions: Existence and Correspondence Theorems for Voting Procedures and Social Welfare Functions," *Journal of Economic Theory* 10 (1975), pp. 187–217.

[2] Thus, for example, Michael Dummett holds that to determine "which is the fairest or otherwise best voting procedure" we need "both to have a means of judging, from the preferences of the voters, what would be the fairest outcome, and to deter-

ory must have two components: an abstract conception of the popular will (such as a social choice function) and a generalized description of a social decision procedure to identify it. Both components pose problems of combination. In both cases, some device is required to derive a social choice or political outcome from information about individual preferences. One might therefore be tempted to think that the combinatorial devices of the two components should be isomorphic. For example, if the popular will is the outcome (if there is one) preferred by the majority in comparison to every available alternative—that is, a "Condorcet candidate"—it might be thought that the best social decision procedure would be one requiring successive votes on each possible pair of alternatives. But this would be a confusion. The structure of a decision-making procedure need not mimic that of the conception of the popular will that it seeks to identify. The reason is that, in the construction of the popular will, one abstracts from various problems in practical political life that must be taken into account in the design of actual decision-making procedures but that are irrelevant to the definition of the people's will. These include, for example, the possibility of strategic voting and the transaction costs involved in participating in a society's decision-making institutions.[3] If conceptions of the popular will are represented as social choice functions, then the problem of *defining* the social choice function is distinct from that of *implementing* it. (The distinction is unimportant in some easy cases, such as that of majority decision between two mutually exclusive alternatives, in which practical problems like the possibility of strategic voting are not significant.) In deriving principles for institutions, we seek a "rough-and-ready test [that] will usually pick out the fairest outcome" in the face of the practical problems of political life, given an independent criterion for identifying fair out-

---

mine which voting procedure is the most likely to produce that outcome." *Voting Procedures* (Oxford: Clarendon Press, 1984), p. 50. See also Peter C. Fishburn, "Dimensions of Election Procedures: Analyses and Comparisons," *Theory and Decision* 15 (1983), pp. 371–97, esp. pp. 376–77.

[3] The greater portion of the literature on the theory of voting is devoted to these problems. The seminal modern work, which contains a historical survey, is Duncan Black, *The Theory of Committees and Elections* (Cambridge: Cambridge University Press, 1958). Also, see Robin Farquharson, *Theory of Voting* (New Haven: Yale University Press, 1969).

comes.[4] Popular will theories, as a class, are distinguished by the identification of the "fairest outcome" with the outcome that is selected by a function of people's preferences over outcomes. The main theoretical problem is how this function should be conceived. The design of a decision procedure is a secondary, although hardly a simple, problem.

This conception of popular will theories is more specific than may perhaps be apparent. To illustrate, consider Rousseau's theory, which has often been regarded as a theory of this type but which differs in an important way from the kind of theory I have described. Rousseau advanced the following four propositions:

1. The decisions of government should conform to the general will (or, equivalently, the common interest).[5]
2. The general will is *defined* independently of any social choice procedure. For example, it is not *as a matter of definition* to be identified with the outcome of a majority vote in the assembly.[6]
3. Legislation is to be enacted by a social choice procedure normally requiring a majority vote.[7]
4. Institutions are to be arranged so as to encourage citizens (a) to give priority to considerations of the common good in judging alternative government policies and (b) to conceive the common good as limited by respect for each person's rights to liberty and property.[8]

Conditions 1–3 are common to Rousseau's view and most popular will theories. Thus, for both theories, the chief problem in the design of institutions for social choice is to find the method that is most likely to yield decisions that accord with an independent standard of the general (or popular) will. Rousseau's theory differs with

[4] Dummett, *Voting Procedures*, p. 132.

[5] Jean-Jacques Rousseau, *The Social Contract* [1762], in *The Social Contract and Discourses*, trans. G.D.H. Cole (London: J. M. Dent, 1973), bk. 2, chap. 1, p. 182.

[6] Ibid., bk. 2, chap. 3, pp. 184–85; bk. 2, chap. 4, pp. 186–87; bk. 2, chap. 6, pp. 192–93; bk. 4, chap. 1, p. 248.

[7] Ibid., bk. 4, chap. 2, pp. 249–51.

[8] Ibid., bk. 2, chap. 4, pp. 188–89; bk. 2, chap. 5, pp. 189–91; bk. 4, chap. 2, pp. 249–50. My account is indebted to that given by Joshua Cohen in "Reflections on Rousseau: Autonomy and Democracy," *Philosophy & Public Affairs* 15 (1986), pp. 275–97. On the general will, see also Brian Barry, "The Public Interest," *Proceedings of the Aristotelian Society*, supp. vol. 38 (1964), pp. 1–18.

respect to both elements of condition 4. According to popular will theories, as I have described them, individual judgments are taken as given antecedently to the operation of the social decision procedure itself, and they are not constrained with regard to their motivation or content. The popular will is constructed from these judgments. For Rousseau, however, the social and political context within which individual judgments are formed is explicitly a matter of theoretical concern, since this bears on both the motivation of citizens in their political judgment (they should assess policies according to whether the policies advance the common interest rather than some particular interests) and the formation of their conceptions of the common interest itself (minimally, the common interest must respect individual rights to liberty and property). The general will can be derived from individual judgments only when these conditions prevail.[9]

Thus, although Rousseau's theory is similar to popular will theories in regarding the general will as a construction based on individual judgments, it differs in holding that the individual judgments on which the general will is based must be constrained as to both their motivation and content. One way to express the distinction is this. Popular will theories are actual-preference-based conceptions in the sense that the standard of legislation is derived from the preferences that people in society in fact have, regardless of their content. Rousseau's theory is ideal-preference-based in the sense that the standard of legislation is derived from the preferences that people in society *would* have under the ideal conditions specified by the theory. To put it another way, popular will theories take actual preferences as sovereign and regard the popular will as a legitimate standard for political decision just because it is thought to embody them. A fair social choice procedure simply transfers the sovereignty of individual preferences to the collective level. Whereas Rousseau's theory takes the common good as sovereign in its own right and regards a social choice procedure based on the aggregation of individual judgments as authoritative only under social condi-

[9] There are further conditions as well; e.g., the distribution of property must not be too unequal (Rousseau, *The Social Contract*, bk. 2, chap. 11, p. 204). In the text, I mention only those that bear directly on the comparison with popular will theories. For a further discussion, see Cohen, "Reflections on Rousseau," pp. 294–95.

tions in which there is a high probability that the procedure will correctly identify the common good.

The comparison with Rousseau also illuminates the distinctive role that popular will conceptions assign to the value of equality. Rousseau held that the conditions listed earlier (among others) would be the outcome of a hypothetical agreement or social contract identifying the principles that should govern the legitimate exercise of the state's coercive power. Equality enters his theory at this fundamental level. The parties to the agreement are conceived as having higher-order interests in liberty and property that they are unwilling to put at risk. Their equality is modeled by the requirement that the agreement be unanimous: it must embody conditions under which no one has reason to fear that his higher-order interests will be jeopardized. This is the justification, for example, of the constraints on the content of the general will implied by condition 4. By contrast, equality enters popular will theories at the level of the conception of the popular will itself: it is regarded as a condition on the relationship between individual judgments and collective choice. A decision procedure is fair just in case it normally produces outcomes that are ranked highest by a social choice function that depends equally on each person's judgment or preference.

Now it is hardly obvious how such an egalitarian constraint should be conceived, and many controversies within the theory of social choice can be understood as disagreements about its interpretation. (Consider, for example, the dispute about whether it is appropriate to restrict the arguments of the social choice function to ordinal preference information.)[10] Although we will return to some of these questions later, I pass by them for the moment. For in spite of their prominence in the literature of the theory of social choice, they serve to obscure a matter of more basic importance concerning

[10] This restriction provided the initial motivation for Arrow's impossibility theorem, whose significance for democratic theory I take up below. See Arrow, *Social Choice and Individual Values*, pp. 9–11. The restriction is reflected in Arrow's condition of "independence of irrelevant alternatives" (pp. 26–28), which has perhaps been the most widely criticized of his conditions. For critical commentary concerning the restriction to ordinal information, see Amartya K. Sen, "Personal Utilities and Public Judgements: Or, What's Wrong with Welfare Economics?" *Economic Journal* 89 (1979), esp. pp. 539–43; and Dummett, *Voting Procedures*, pp. 54–59.

the conception of political fairness that is distinctive of popular will theories. This conception is what requires attention.

THE POPULAR WILL
AND THE IDEA OF DEMOCRACY

From a viewpoint within the theory of social choice, the meaning of political fairness may appear to present no problem at all. It may seem obvious that the fairness of political procedures consists in their accuracy in identifying outcomes that correspond to some appropriate aggregation of individual preferences; indeed, there might seem to be no plausible alternative conception. The only theoretical problem of interest appears to be how an appropriate aggregation should be conceived. I begin with a brief comment on two related reasons why such a view might recommend itself.

First, this conception of political fairness might seem to be a self-evident implication of the definition of democracy. As Peter Fishburn writes, "[d]emocratic theory is based on the premise that the resolution of a matter of social policy, group choice or collective action should be based on the desires or preferences of the individuals in the society, group, or collective."[11] This "premise," which simply restates the idea of "rule by the people," is open to both weak and strong interpretations. In the weak sense, the resolution of a matter of social policy might be said to be "based on" individual preferences just in case there is some institutional connection between the expressed political preferences of the people and the policies carried out by the government. That the notion of "some institutional connection" is vague does not mean that it is empty; it rules out any system of social decision making (dictatorship is an obvious case; decision by some random process is another) lacking a procedural mechanism that provides opportunities through which the people (or a sufficient number of them) can bring about changes in leadership or policy.[12] In the strong sense, social choice is "based

[11] *The Theory of Social Choice* (Princeton: Princeton University Press, 1973), p. 3.

[12] For a similar view, see Brian Barry, "Is Democracy Special?" in *Philosophy, Politics and Society*, 5th series, ed. Peter Laslett and James Fishkin (New Haven: Yale University Press, 1979), p. 157. Also, see my "Democracy in Developing Societies,"

on" individual preferences only if the institutional mechanism will
predictably bring about the outcomes identified by a social choice
function having certain formal properties. These are clearly not
equivalent positions; the second introduces conditions on the relationship between individual preferences and social choice that are
missing from (and are not implied by) the first. The idea that a popular will conception of political fairness is implied by the definition
of democracy relies on the strong interpretation of "rule by the people." However, as a definitional matter, the concept of democracy,
or "rule by the people," embodies only the weak view. At least this
is true if the "definition" of democracy employed refers to anything
that might plausibly be seen as the plain or conventional meaning
of the term. To hold that it is true by definition or by linguistic
convention, or even by common consent, that rule by the people is
rule by the popular will in the technical sense of the term associated with the theory of social choice is to assert a normative thesis
that needs to be argued.

Relatedly, one might be drawn to a popular will conception by
the belief that there is some sort of fundamental individual right to
have one's political preferences counted equally with everyone
else's in the determination of the state's policies. In assessing such
a view, it is critical to distinguish it from the different view (associated with certain best result theories) that everyone has a right to
equal satisfaction, where satisfaction is understood, so to speak,
globally: a person's entire situation is taken into account and an
assessment is rendered indicating the person's score on some index
of overall happiness or preference satisfaction.[13] In such a view the
popular will cannot have fundamental political importance because
the satisfaction of *political* preferences cannot have fundamental
importance; preferences about political outcomes matter either as
proxies for individual utility or well-being (if overall happiness is
the ultimate aim) or as components of one's overall satisfaction (if
preference satisfaction is the aim). By contrast, on the present view,
the satisfaction of individual political preferences is itself seen as

---

in *Boundaries: National Autonomy and Its Limits*, ed. Peter Brown and Henry Shue
(Totowa, N.J.: Rowman and Littlefield, 1981), pp. 180–82.

[13] Such a view is set forth in Peter Jones, "Political Equality and Majority Rule,"
in *The Nature of Political Theory*, ed. David Miller and Larry Siedentop (Oxford:
Clarendon Press, 1983), pp. 165–67.

fundamental. One has a right to have one's *political* preferences counted equally regardless of the effect of satisfying them on one's global situation, whether that is assessed with respect to overall happiness or to overall preference satisfaction.

The precept that political preferences should be counted equally has been influential in recent democratic theory.[14] However, its plausibility dissipates once we consider the reasons why one might accept it. For example, it might be thought that this precept follows from the more general principle of equal satisfaction from which we have distinguished it; but the derivation would require heroic assumptions about the *ex ante* distribution of satisfaction, and even if these were true, it would run afoul of the possibility of unequal external costs and benefits arising from the choice of any particular political outcome. Alternatively, one might think the precept follows from a more basic commitment to respect the integrity of individual judgments; but here there is a non sequitur, perhaps resulting from a lack of clarity about the content of the more basic commitment. It might be intended that everyone is the best judge of his own good or that everyone has a right to his own view about the good for society; but it does not follow in either case that everyone has an equal right that these judgments be reflected in public policy. Or, it might be thought that equal respect for the integrity of individual judgments just *is* the precept of equal (political) satisfaction; but this is simply not true.

The preceding observations do not, of course, show that the conception of fairness implicit in popular will constructions is incorrect. Rather, they illustrate that the idea that fairness consists in an appropriate relationship between individual preferences and social choices represents a normative position that requires a justification; neither definitional nor prima facie moral considerations make it self-evidently true. I believe that there are strong reasons to resist this idea. However, since the position is rarely argued for explicitly, it is difficult to offer a straightforward critique. Instead, I shall proceed indirectly, by considering what appears to be a main reason why popular will constructions seem plausible to those who advocate them. This is a view about the fairness of majority rule in

[14] See, for example, Robert A. Dahl, *A Preface to Democratic Theory* (Chicago: University of Chicago Press, 1956), p. 37.

the simple case where there are only two alternatives. Popular will constructions emerge from the effort to generalize from the simple case to the general case where there are more than two alternatives. The latter has been the chief embarrassment of social choice theory, but if my comments about the simple case are correct, it will be seen that the consequences of this embarrassment have been overstated.

FAIRNESS AND SIMPLE MAJORITY RULE

Many people believe that the uniquely suitable method for resolving binary choices is the simple majority method. If there are only two alternatives, the best outcome is the one preferred by the larger number; and, given that voters are fully informed and that everyone votes, the method of majority voting will always succeed in identifying this outcome.[15]

How might this common belief be justified? One account is suggested by an elegant theorem due to Kenneth May.[16] May shows that the simple majority method is the only one that satisfies four conditions that he labels as decisiveness (or universal domain), equality (or anonymity), neutrality (or outcome indifference), and positive responsiveness.[17] May, who professes no direct normative concern, does not say why it should matter that a decision procedure satisfies these conditions, other than to suggest that they are "very weak" and so, perhaps, relatively unobjectionable. However, it is easy to see why the theorem might be thought to provide an account of the justification of majority rule: if the conditions are

[15] These assumptions, together with the fact that the majority method is strategy-proof (i.e., no one can expect to improve his chance of getting the outcome he wants by not voting for his most preferred alternative), mean that the majority *rule* and the majority *method* (respectively, a social choice function and a social decision procedure) may be treated equivalently.

[16] Kenneth O. May, "A Set of Independent Necessary and Sufficient Conditions for Simple Majority Decision," *Econometrica* 20 (1952), pp. 680–84.

[17] The labels supplied parenthetically in the text are those adopted by Bruce Ackerman in *Social Justice in the Liberal State* (New Haven: Yale University Press, 1980), p. 277. I consider his view further below. The conditions are labeled differently in the discussion in Amartya K. Sen, *Collective Choice and Social Welfare* (San Francisco: Holden-Day, 1970), p. 72.

ones in which we should take an interest, then the theorem shows that we have no alternative to accepting the majority method.[18]

The conditions of consequence are anonymity and outcome indifference. A decision rule satisfies anonymity if, when any two voters' preferences are interchanged, the social choice remains the same; each individual is treated "anonymously" in the sense that under the rule the identity of the person casting any particular vote is irrelevant to way the decision rule takes that vote into account. This condition rules out, e.g., schemes of plural or weighted voting. A decision rule satisfies outcome indifference if, when all voters' preferences are reversed, the outcome is reversed as well. This condition rules out, e.g., supermajority requirements. The conditions might be seen as representing two kinds of symmetry that could be exhibited by a decision rule: in the first case, it is symmetry with respect to voters, and, in the second, it is symmetry with respect to outcomes (or, perhaps, with respect to change). Taken together, these conditions embody an interpretation of the basic idea of popular will theories of political fairness—any fair method for aggregating individual preferences should treat each person's preference equally.

Are these conditions ones in which we should take an interest? Most writers in the theory of social choice who believe they are typically claim no more than that the conditions have prima facie or intuitive ethical appeal. Inquiry proceeds from the abstract question, What conditions ought the social preference relation to satisfy? The May conditions are then adopted either because they are thought to constitute an intuitively attractive response to this question or because they are thought to be necessary to eliminate apparently objectionable alternatives to the majority method.[19] However,

---

[18] There are, of course, many other reasons why people favor the majority method in simple cases. Most prominently, it is the only method that provides each person with an equal *ex ante* chance of affecting the outcome. For a formal statement of the argument, see Douglas W. Rae, "Decision-Rules and Individual Values in Constitutional Choice," *American Political Science Review* 63 (1969), pp. 40–56. For a critical discussion, see chapter 4, below.

[19] See, for example, P. K. Pattanaik, *Voting and Collective Choice* (Cambridge: Cambridge University Press, 1971), p. 51; Dennis C. Mueller, *Public Choice* (Cambridge: Cambridge University Press, 1979), pp. 208–10; William H. Riker, *Liberalism Against Populism* (San Francisco: W. H. Freeman, 1982), pp. 58–59.

there is cause for suspicion about any such rationale for the conditions. One reason is that there is cause for suspicion about the question itself, or rather, about the way in which it formulates the problem of evaluating decision-making procedures. The question is an
artifact of a technical conception of the problem of social choice
that does not reproduce any problem that arises in commonsense
reflection about political morality; indeed, by abstracting from contextual considerations specific to the environment in which a particular decision-making procedure operates, it deflects attention
from factors that ordinarily play an important, and sometimes a determining, role in commonsense reflection about the justification
of such procedures. These include both outcome-oriented considerations (e.g., the chances that the procedure will usually produce
substantively acceptable decisions) and considerations regarding
the context of preference formation (e.g., the extent and quality of
the information normally available concerning the feasible alternatives). The setting of the problem is artificially narrow. This is a
fundamental difficulty for popular will conceptions, to which I shall
return. But even if the setting of the problem is accepted, the excessive abstraction and artificiality of the question suggests that the
intuitions on which any response might be based cannot be regarded as having the kind of authority that attaches to intuitions
arising from reflection on moral problems that are more familiar
and less abstract. The conditions require a more satisfactory foundation.

Thus, it is significant, as Ackerman argues, that May's result can
be made use of in a more systematic argument for simple majority
rule.[20] Ackerman holds that the May conditions would be accepted
by rational citizens who were attempting to reach agreement on a
social decision procedure, provided that their deliberations were
subject to various constraints on the range of reasons on the basis
of which anyone could legitimately refuse to agree. Granting that
the theorem itself is correct, he argues that rational citizens would
agree upon majority rule as a social decision procedure, since (as the
theorem proves) it is the only social decision procedure for the case
of two alternatives that is consistent with the conditions. This account makes explicit a view about the connection between majority

[20] *Social Justice in the Liberal State*, pp. 277–85.

rule and considerations of equal treatment that is widely held, if not often articulated, and so is worth critical attention.

According to Ackerman, rational choosers would accept the May conditions as a consequence of their acceptance of the principle that each citizen's "opinion is at least as good as any others," which he holds to be implied by a more basic commitment not to treat anyone as "unconditionally superior" to anyone else or any conception of the good as better than any other ("the Neutrality constraint").[21] It is unclear precisely how the Neutrality constraint is supposed to compel acceptance of the May conditions. One possibility is that the conditions are implied by the constraint (or by the principle implied by it); another is that there is no plausible basis for objecting to the conditions that does not violate the constraint, so that they should be accepted, as it were, by default. I believe that the second possibility yields the more natural interpretation of Ackerman's text; either way, however, the argument fails.

Consider first the claim that the May conditions are implied by Neutrality. The difficulty is that the intermediate principle that each citizen's "opinion is at least as good as" anyone else's does not obviously follow from it. This is partly obscured by the ambiguity of the provision that no one is "unconditionally superior" to anyone else. Regarded as a maxim of political morality, one would ordinarily take this to be an elliptical formulation of the abstract principle that each citizen is equally deserving of respect and concern in the design of institutions or perhaps of the (even more abstract) principle that each person is to be regarded as having equal human worth. But these (and similar) principles are so abstract as not to yield any determinate implications without extensive interpretation and argument. In particular, without more they do not imply that each person's opinion is (or should be treated as being) "at least as good as" anyone else's. (It is possible to acknowledge that your opinion is better than mine, in the sense of providing a more reliable guide

---

[21] Ibid., p. 279; see also pp. 11–12, 44–45. For convenience, I abstract from the dialogic setting of Ackerman's account. Ackerman occasionally states the intermediate principle that each citizen's "opinion is at least as good as any others" in a different form, viz., that institutions should recognize "each citizen's standing as a statesman whose political judgments are entitled to equal respect" (p. 289). These formulations are plainly not equivalent, but Ackerman provides no explanation of their relationship.

to action, without claiming that you are "unconditionally superior" or denying that each of us deserves equal respect and concern.) Alternatively, the Neutrality constraint might simply be identified with the injunction not to treat any conception of the good as preferable to or more worthy of pursuit than any other, leaving aside the reference to the "unconditional superiority" of persons. But the intermediate principle does not follow from this either. (Your opinion could be better than mine for reasons unconnected to the superiority of your conception of the good. Perhaps you are better informed or have better political judgment.)

Moreover, other implications of the Neutrality constraint, or of the principle of equal treatment that Ackerman believes to be associated with it, might actually come into conflict with the procedural egalitarianism embodied in the May conditions. These fundamental moral considerations might, for example, license distributions of some substantive good that would not, at least in some circumstances, be likely to come about under political institutions that respected the conditions.[22] In Ackerman's theory, some such possibilities may be ruled out by the background assumptions that the political agenda has been purged of "exploitative" proposals and that citizens are motivated by a desire to achieve the most impartially desirable outcome (rather than by narrow self-interest).[23] But the need for background assumptions like these merely illustrates the difficulty of inferring determinate principles for institutions from abstract considerations of equal treatment taken by themselves.

But perhaps the view is that there is no plausible basis for objecting to the May conditions that does not violate the Neutrality constraint. Consider the condition of outcome indifference. It excludes decision rules that are asymmetrical with respect to outcomes, such as supermajority requirements that effectively favor the status quo. Given the background assumption that the agenda has somehow been purged of "exploitative" proposals (so that none of those remaining is "uncontroversially" inferior), Ackerman holds that "a

[22] Thus, a familiar complaint about majority rule is that it can yield systematically inequitable distributions of interest satisfaction, e.g., in the presence of "intense" or "permanent" minorities. See Dahl, *A Preface to Democratic Theory*, pp. 48–49; Jones, "Political Equality and Majority Rule," pp. 167–69.

[23] Ackerman, *Social Justice in the Liberal State*, p. 280.

rational decision procedure should not make either [alternative] easier to enact than the other."[24] This should not be taken too literally; the view is not that technical considerations of rationality alone require that the alternatives be treated symmetrically. Instead, the underlying thought is that when neither alternative can be ruled out as uncontroversially unjust or exploitative, then both are reasonably contestable, in which case the Neutrality constraint prohibits any decision procedure that gives a structural advantage to either alternative. Only an outcome-symmetrical decision rule gives equal weight to each citizen's judgment regarding reasonably contestable alternatives.

Now I do not wish to dispute the conclusion that under these (very) restrictive conditions simple majority rule, which treats the alternatives symmetrically, is the best, or anyway an acceptable, method of decision. The question is whether the fact that asymmetric decision rules violate the Neutrality constraint provides a persuasive reason for reaching this conclusion. The contrast with Rousseau is instructive. Like Ackerman, Rousseau held that simple majority rule is the best decision procedure, at least for ordinary matters of public business.[25] But he did not argue that there is any immediate or direct connection between this and the principle of equal respect for persons or for their conceptions of the good. Instead, he held that the majority method is most likely to yield the best social decisions, as these might be identified from the point of view of an independent standard of political morality (in this case, the general will).[26] As noted earlier, on Rousseau's view equal respect for persons is modeled by the unanimity requirement of the initial contract situation and is reflected in the standard for assessing political outcomes accepted there; it plays no direct role in justifying the decision procedure itself. It would be consistent with this reasoning to advocate asymmetrical decision rules in cases in which they seemed more likely than the simple majority method to yield the best outcomes; and, in fact, Rousseau recommended a

---

[24] Ibid., p. 280.

[25] *The Social Contract*, bk. 4, chap. 2, pp. 250–51.

[26] Assuming that voters have an average probability of judging correctly that is better than even, Rousseau was right, as Condorcet's jury theorem shows. See Black, *The Theory of Committees and Elections*, pp. 164–65; for the application to Rousseau, see Barry, "The Public Interest," p. 13.

decision rule requiring special majorities for "grave and important" measures.[27] Although he did not provide an argument for this, Rousseau probably believed that "important" changes in public policy require sustained, and perhaps repeated, examination to ensure that decisions are adequately informed and responsive to enduring changes in the environment and that a supermajority requirement would encourage this.[28] Rousseau's view illustrates that it is not necessary to violate the Neutrality constraint in order to justify adoption of procedures at variance with outcome indifference. Indeed, as we noted earlier, considerations associated with Neutrality could conceivably support such procedures. By a parallel argument, similar conclusions can be reached about procedures violating anonymity.

Ackerman's account is a particularly clear instance of the view that majority rule is a requirement of the more basic principle of equal respect for persons. The May conditions, on which his account relies, provide an interpretation of this requirement. But the conditions reflect an implausibly narrow understanding of the more basic principle, from which substantive concerns regarding the content of political outcomes and the context of public deliberation have been excluded (albeit perhaps not in an obvious way). Moreover, this narrowness is not defended within the account; it is forced on us by the mechanical way in which the question of procedural fairness has been conceived.

The negative conclusion we have reached is that considerations about the equal moral status of persons do not straightforwardly justify simple majority rule. The appealing elegance of May's theorem, regarded as an analytical result, is not easily transported to the normative realm. This is important for our larger purposes because it casts doubt on the effort to understand political fairness in the general case by analogy with the case in which there are only two alternatives. If the axiomatic analysis of simple majority rule inac-

---

[27] *The Social Contract*, bk. 4, chap. 2, pp. 249–51.

[28] If this was Rousseau's reasoning, it was consistent with an ancient tradition of thought about voting procedures, dating at least from medieval canon law, that held that the appropriate criterion for decisions was "intrinsic reasonableness, which may in ordinary matters of administration be ascertained, *prima facie*, by numbers," but which, in unusual matters, requires more than a simple majority. Th. Baty, "The History of Majority Rule," *Quarterly Review* 216 (1912), p. 11.

curately describes the reasons why we regard it as a fair means of decision making (at least in ordinary circumstances), then the fact that no decision procedure for the general case always satisfies similar axioms will have a different significance than that attributed to it in the social choice tradition.

Before turning to the general case, it is worth asking what a better explanation of the fairness of simple majority rule might be like. Intuitively, there are two points that such an explanation should incorporate. First, we do not consider the system of voting in isolation from the political framework in which it operates. Voting is the decisive stage in group decision making, but it is not the only stage. Various elements of the framework identify the alternatives to be made available for public consideration and establish the setting in which deliberation about them will proceed. Individual judgments about the merits of the alternatives will often be formed or revised (or at least confirmed) in the course of this process of public deliberation; it is unrealistic to regard them as formed extrinsically. These facts matter. For example, when voting takes place without suitable prior deliberation, we are less likely to regard the process as legitimate.[29] Second, it also matters how the particular issues set forth for electoral choice bear on individual interests. As Rousseau recognized, simple majority rule is more readily accepted for ordinary matters of public business than for issues that have possible outcomes that could work morally significant harms. Thus, we might adopt countermajoritarian devices such as bills of rights or requirements for "special majorities" in order to constrain the social choice mechanism so that results that could be severely damaging to some people's interests and rights will be less likely to occur. Without such constraints, there would be less reason for the minority (and perhaps for others as well) to accept the outcomes the political system produces.

The fairness of majority rule is not, therefore, to be found in its

---

[29] "Less likely," but not "entirely unwilling." Much depends on the character of the issue at hand, in particular, whether it involves public or private goods. When appropriate countermajoritarian constraints of the kind discussed below are in place, and the issue at hand involves provision of a private good of modest proportions, the absence of sufficient public deliberation may not cast doubt on the acceptability of the outcome. There is no need to deny that on some occasions not much is to be gained from extensive public debate.

mechanical capacity to aggregate preferences accurately, however that might be understood. A better explanation is that under normal circumstances it is the social decision procedure most likely to produce outcomes to which no one will have good reason to object. The judgment that simple majority rule has this property rests on complex, if usually tacit, premises regarding the structure of the overall decision process, including the means by which it may be constrained by countermajoritarian devices; the political culture of the society and the background of social values likely to influence individual voting decisions; and the dynamics the process is likely to exhibit in its normal operation, particularly in its deliberative aspects. Rousseau's theory represents a strong form of this idea: assuming that certain social background conditions prevail, he held that no one could have good reason to object to the majority method because it is more likely than any other to produce substantively correct decisions. But there are weaker forms of the idea as well; a decision procedure need not maximize the chances of producing correct decisions to be reasonably acceptable to all. The theory I shall set forth later is an example of such a view. In general, the defense of majority rule need not claim more than that, suitably constrained, it enables citizens to reach political decisions on the basis of adequately informed deliberation and in a way that avoids predictable forms of injustice.

These observations shed light on the common belief that the majority principle is defective in failing to take account of the intensity with which people hold their political preferences.[30] It is not hard to see how this idea might arise: if the satisfaction of preferences is what matters in democratic decision making, then if A regards her preferences as more important, in relation to her ends, than B regards his preferences, in relation to his ends, then presumably the satisfaction of A's preferences should matter more than the satisfaction of B's.[31] Indeed, the conception of political equality as

[30] See, for example, Dahl, *A Preface to Democratic Theory,* pp. 48–50; James M. Buchanan and Gordon Tullock, *The Calculus of Consent* (Ann Arbor: University of Michigan Press, 1962), pp. 125–30.

[31] Of course, it need not follow that the voting procedure itself should contain a mechanism giving greater weight to more intensely held preferences. It may be impossible to elicit sincere expressions of intensities of preference; and, in any case, other elements of the social decision procedure—for example, the process of public

equal respect for preferences seems to require such a view.[32] However, if the virtue of majoritarianism consists in something different than its accuracy in identifying the popular will, then its failure to attend to intensities seems far less damaging. Consider again Rousseau's view, in which the preferences expressed in the act of voting are conceived as judgments about the requirements of the general will (understood substantively, as the common good), and majority rule is regarded as the method ordinarily most likely to produce substantively correct decisions. In such a view, there is no point in allowing intense preferences to count more than others, for the strength with which one holds one's judgment about the public good, or the intensity of one's desire to see that judgment prevail, are plainly irrelevant to its truth and thus to its entitlement to count at all.[33]

THE POPULAR WILL WITH MORE THAN TWO ALTERNATIVES

Popular will theories in general, and the theory of social choice in particular, should be considered in light of these observations about the basis of majority rule in the simple case. Analytically, of course, there is an important difference. Whereas the May theorem shows that in the simple case there is a unique solution to the problem of social choice (as May defines it), the Arrow result shows that in the general case there is no solution.[34] The important question is

---

deliberation preceding the casting of votes—may allow intensities to be taken into account. Both points are recognized by Dahl. *A Preface to Democratic Theory*, pp. 48–50.

[32] As Peter Jones argues. "Political Equality and Majority Rule," pp. 162–63.

[33] Compare Rawls, *A Theory of Justice*, p. 361. See also J. Roland Pennock, *Democratic Political Theory* (Princeton: Princeton University Press, 1979), pp. 394–96 and 415–16, and the sources cited there.

[34] In fact, the conditions that Arrow imposes on an acceptable social choice function are in some respects weaker than May's; for example, none of the Arrow conditions self-evidently imports an egalitarian requirement on the aggregation of individual preferences. As Arrow remarks, majority rule in the simple case satisfies (though not necessarily uniquely) the weaker Arrow conditions. *Social Choice and Individual Values*, pp. 46–48. So although the Arrow theorem shows *a fortiori* that equality as May conceived it cannot be achieved in the general case consistently with various other apparently desirable values, it shows more as well.

whether this analytical difference has ethical significance for a theory of political fairness. Does it show, for example, that in general no ostensibly democratic decision procedure can be fair?[35]

The Arrow result is best seen as an abstraction from the well-known "paradox" of voting, first noticed by Condorcet and later characterized by C. L. Dodgson as the problem of "cyclical" majorities.[36] Where there are more than two alternatives, no one of which is the first choice of an absolute majority of the people, the method of sequential pairwise choices will not necessarily produce a final choice that ranks higher in the preference orderings of a majority of the people than one of the other alternatives. To illustrate, consider the array of preferences shown in the accompanying table. There are

The Voting Paradox (Condorcet's Paradox)

	Voter 1	Voter 2	Voter 3
First choice:	A	B	C
Second choice:	B	C	A
Third choice:	C	A	B

three voters and three alternatives, of which the voting procedure must select only one. Suppose that the voting procedure consists of successive pairwise comparisons; a vote is first taken between alternatives A and B, and a second vote, between the winner and the remaining alternative, C. Since two voters (1 and 3) prefer A to B, A would win the first round; and since two voters (2 and 3) prefer C to A, C would win the second and be declared the social choice—in spite of the fact that two voters (1 and 2) prefer B to C. Or, suppose instead that the alternatives are compared in reverse order: the first vote is taken between C and B, and the second, between the winner and A. In that case B would win the first round but lose to A in the second—in spite of the fact that two voters (2 and 3) prefer C to A. What this shows is that the paradoxical result is not an artifact of the order in which the alternatives were compared; instead, it is dictated by the preference orderings depicted in the table. The paradox can be avoided only if voter preferences satisfy certain conditions.[37]

[35] As Riker claims. *Liberalism Against Populism*, p. 243.
[36] For a discussion, see Black, *Theory of Committees*, chap. 7.
[37] Black showed that cycling can be avoided when voters' preferences are "single-

A consequence of this is that unless we know in advance that voter preferences have the appropriate profiles, the method of sequential pairwise comparisons cannot be guaranteed always to yield outcomes that are *stable* in the sense that no one could attain a result more favorable to herself by changing her vote. To return to our example, it is clear that voter 1, in whose preference ordering C ranks last, could produce a higher- ranking outcome by voting for B rather than A in the first round; for in that case, B would win against A in the first round and then against C in the second. However, analogous strategic calculations would then arise for voters 2 and 3, generating a continuous cycle. (Of course, no actual voting procedure could permit voters to change their votes *ad infinitum*; so the practical result of cycling under majoritarian procedures is likely to be the phenomenon of winning coalitions whose composition shifts from election to election.) The voting procedure cannot produce an equilibrium outcome, because, given the preference profiles illustrated, there is no equilibrium to be produced.

Arrow's theorem represents the voting paradox as only the most perspicuous form of a more general problem for any conception of the popular will based exclusively on ordinal information about the preferences of the individuals in society. Supposing that individual preference orderings satisfy certain standard canons of rationality, Arrow argues that any acceptable function mapping arrays of individual preferences onto social choices should conform to four normative conditions that he claims represent intuitively plausible value judgments about democratic choice.[38] The general possibility

---

peaked"—that is, roughly, when all voters' preferences can be depicted graphically along the same dimension so that the degree of each voter's preference is a decreasing function of its distance from that voter's most preferred alternative. Black, *The Theory of Committees and Elections*, pp. 14–32. Considerable effort has been devoted to refining this condition. For a discussion, see Mueller, *Public Choice*, pp. 40ff.

[38] The conditions are the following: (1) positive responsiveness: if A is preferred to B under some set of individual preferences, then if someone who favored B (or was indifferent) were to switch to A, the social choice should remain unchanged; (2) independence of irrelevant alternatives: if A is preferred to B when individual preference information concerning those two alternatives is considered, A should remain preferred to B when individual preferences about other alternatives are taken into consideration as well; (3) citizens' sovereignty (or nonimposition): there is no pair of alternatives A and B such that A is preferred to B regardless of the preferences of the individuals in society; (4) nondictatorship: there is no one person whose preferences determine the social choice regardless of the preferences of everyone else. *Social*

theorem shows that there is no social preference relation (or "social welfare function," in Arrow's nonstandard sense of the term) satisfying the conditions of rationality that also satisfies all four normative conditions. Hence, for some arrays of individual preferences, any actual process of social choice must violate at least one of the conditions.

I shall not discuss the validity of the theorem, which by now is well established, or the acceptability of Arrow's formulations of the normative conditions, which continue to elicit controversy.[39] The relevant question concerns the underlying conception of social choice and the interpretation of the theorem associated with this conception. Arrow regards the process of social choice as structurally analogous to the process of individual choice; thus, he insists that the social choice function should obey canons of rationality similar to those usually thought applicable to individual choice. This insistence is related to a reason why popular will theories might be appealing. In the case of individuals, we typically assess the rationality of a decision by asking how effectively it advances the individual's system of ends or goals. Where a decision advances these ends less effectively or at greater cost than an alternative decision that might have been taken but was not, we say that the actual decision is irrational. If the idea of rationality is viewed this way, then it is obvious that the question whether a decision is rational presupposes that the "ends" exist independently of the decision actually taken; if they did not, the question would be incoherent. Now if social choice is seen as analogous to individual choice, it seems that judgments about the rationality of social choices require some analogous conception of social ends. Such a conception is supplied by the idea of a popular will or a social choice function. But if as a general matter it is impossible to devise a combinatorial method that will yield a single social choice for each possible array of individual preferences, then, again as a general matter, it will be impossible to say that a policy or outcome chosen through any particular social decision procedure either does or does not accurately

---

Choice and Individual Values, pp. 23–31. There is an alternative formulation of the conditions in Sen, *Collective Choice and Social Welfare*, chaps. 3 and 3*.

[39] See, for example, Peter C. Fishburn, "The Irrationality of Transitivity in Social Choice," *Behavioral Science* 15 (1970), pp. 119–23; Mueller, *Public Choice*, pp. 188–201; Dummett, *Voting Procedures*, pp. 54ff.

register the social choice or popular will. As Riker puts it, such a "choice lacks meaning."[40]

If matters are seen this way, then the plausibility of the conception of political fairness found in popular will theories will depend on a prior acceptance of the analogy between individual and social choice. As many of Arrow's critics have observed, however, the analogy is suspicious: the collective entities that make social choices are aggregates of individuals, and, whereas we may grant that individuals have "wills" or systems of ends on the basis of which the rationality of their decisions can be assessed, there is no need to grant anything analogous in the case of collectivities. It is true that social wholes, if they are democratically organized, *make choices*; but it is not necessary to postulate that these choices reflect a "popular will" in the sense of a coherent social system of ends, and, consequently, the violation of canons of rationality need not be seen as objectionable or problematic in the way it would be in the individual case.[41]

This is, of course, a commonplace in discussions of the Arrow theorem; however, we should take care not to carry the point too far. The failure of the analogy of individual and social choice shows only that one conventional interpretation of the significance of the general result must be given up. If, for convenience, we say that procedures that violate the Arrow conditions are "irrational," then social "irrationality" is not objectionable or embarrassing for the same reasons as individual irrationality. To put it another way, the appearance that social decisions lack "meaning" is simply an artifact of adopting a conception of "meaning" that is inapposite in the social realm. However, this is not to say that the Arrow result is irrelevant to an appraisal of institutions for social choice. There may be a different explanation of its relevance, one that does not depend on importing into the social realm a conception of rational choice that is inappropriate there.

Here is such an explanation. The Arrow result may cause appre-

---

[40] *Liberalism Against Populism*, p. 136.

[41] An influential source of this criticism is I.M.D. Little, "Social Choice and Individual Values," *Journal of Political Economy* 60 (1952), pp. 422–32. Also, see the penetrating comments in Kurt Baier, "Welfare and Preference," in *Human Values and Economic Policy*, ed. Sidney Hook (New York: New York University Press, 1967), pp. 120–35.

hension because it seems to show that the intuitively desirable features of the simple case of majority rule where there are only two alternatives are unattainable in the general case, i.e., when this unrealistically restrictive assumption is relaxed. As I remarked earlier, in the simple case of two alternatives there is a widely accepted answer to the question, Which alternative do the people prefer? It is the alternative preferred by the larger number. The Arrow result shows that there is no similarly unambiguous answer to the question of what the people prefer in the general case. (The interpretation is natural enough if the Arrow theorem is seen as a generalization of the Condorcet "paradox.") Since, to avoid anarchy, *some* social decision procedure must be adopted, it appears that the choice among procedures must be based on considerations other than the procedure's tendency to yield outcomes that accord with the popular will. Consequently, it seems inevitable that the outcomes produced by any particular social decision procedure will be influenced by structural features of the procedure; they cannot be represented simply as "accurate amalgamations of voters' values."[42]

In the simple case the majority method might be thought to yield just this: an "accurate amalgamation of voters' values," not influenced by the structure of the decision procedure itself. But, of course, this is myopic. The method of majority rule is itself a decision procedure with a structure; a different procedure (say, a unanimity rule, or a two-thirds rule, or a rule of decision by consensus after thorough discussion) may produce different outcomes. In response, it might be insisted that the amalgamation produced by such procedures can be known to be inaccurate in the sense of not producing outcomes that accord with the popular will conceived as a social choice function satisfying the Arrow conditions. What this shows, however, is not that the general case differs from the simple case in that institutional factors influence outcomes in the first case but not in the second. It shows only that the considerations relied on to identify one outcome as the best, or correct, outcome in the simple case are insufficient to pick out a best outcome in the general case.

This would be important if it could be concluded that there is no further principled basis for choosing a social decision procedure for

42 Riker, *Liberalism Against Populism*, p. 236.

the general case.[43] However, nothing in the Arrow result compels this conclusion. There are two other possibilities. First, the simple case may not incorporate considerations that are necessary and sufficient for identifying a popular will in the general case; for example, the rationality conditions (requiring that the popular will be a consistent ordering of the alternatives) may be questioned. (For that matter, they may be questioned in the simple case as well; the fact that they *are* satisfied in that case obviously does not imply that it is *important* that they be satisfied.) Second, and more fundamentally, it might be argued that the choice of a social decision procedure need not be based exclusively (or at all) on its capacity to identify successfully the outcome specified by *any* social choice function (that is, by any "popular will" constructed from individual preferences over outcomes).

Much of the critical discussion of the Arrow result in the tradition of social choice theory can be seen as falling under the first possibility.[44] I shall not assess the results of this line of criticism, because, as our conclusions about the simple case suggest, the more important point is associated with the second possibility. The choice of a decision procedure is perhaps the central problem of democratic theory. A variety of values, which are not always easily reconciled, are implicated in such a choice. These include the predictable consequences of the procedures for the content of public policy and the conduct and quality of public political debate, the prospects for political stability and for the coherent administration of policy, the transparency of the procedure itself from the point of view of ordinary citizens, and the ease with which they may enter into it effectively. (Thus, for example, the fact that a system is *theoretically* unstable—in the sense that it produces cyclical majorities—might be seen as a virtue rather than a vice, because it reflects a capacity for adjustment in the face of conflict that enhances the

---

[43] Or, that it is therefore "to some extent a matter of taste which [voting] system anybody regards as 'best.' " Iain McLean, *Public Choice: An Introduction* (Oxford: Basil Blackwell, 1987), p. 167.

[44] For some prominent examples, see Little, "Social Choice and Individual Values"; A. Bergson, "On the Concept of Social Welfare," *Quarterly Journal of Economics* 68 (1954), pp. 233–52; Steven Strasnick, "The Problem of Social Choice: Arrow to Rawls," *Philosophy & Public Affairs* 5 (1976), pp. 241–73.

system's *political* stability.)[45] As a basis of public confidence in the efficacy of political participation, it also matters that outcomes normally bear some predictable and consistent relationship to the array of individual preferences about outcomes that come to exist in society and that are actually expressed in the political process. But to regard some variant of this last condition as the sovereign requirement of democratic theory, and to consider the others as matters which are either subordinate or without ethical significance, is no more than dogmatic belief, induced by unreflective acceptance of a technical conception of social choice that has no clear normative justification.

Some such belief is a necessary element of the view that the Arrow result shows the choice of a social decision procedure for the general case to be arbitrary or without foundation in considerations of fairness. This is sometimes seen to be the truth that emerges when what common sense regards as a simple problem of preference aggregation is understood in its full complexity. However, if the foregoing is correct, then what is excessively simple is not common sense but the technical conception of social choice that has been substituted for it. Political fairness implicates a wider range of concerns than this conception allows.

[45] There is an interesting discussion in Nicholas R. Miller, "Pluralism and Social Choice," *American Political Science Review* 77 (1983), pp. 734–47.

CHAPTER FOUR

Procedures

According to best result and popular will theories, political procedures have only instrumental significance: we should value them only to the extent that they are more likely than the feasible alternatives to produce outcomes that treat people's welfare or their preferences equally. Procedural theories differ from these in being directly process-oriented; they identify equal treatment with the provision of equal opportunities to influence outcomes, whatever these outcomes turn out to be like.

To understand the impulse that leads to proceduralism, consider the case of the railway car that the conductor has neglected to designate either "smoking" or "no smoking." Each of the passengers either wants to smoke or objects to others smoking in the car. The option of leaving the car is not available: all the other seats on the train are occupied, no standing is allowed in the corridors, and so on. Everyone would prefer some agreement to none at all (feelings are running high and without agreement there might be violence). Now although one might think there are good reasons why one or the other decision should be reached, it seems likely that any such reasons would be disputed by those on the other side. The passengers need some mechanism for reaching a decision that would resolve the conflict. Brian Barry, who invented the example, observes that where there are "no presumptions as to merits," the natural solution seems to be a voting procedure based on procedural equality: each person casts one (equally weighted) vote and the majority rules.[1]

[1] *Political Argument* (London: Routledge & Kegan Paul, 1965), p. 312. Barry reconsiders the example in "Is Democracy Special?" in *Philosophy, Politics, and Society*, 5th series, ed. Peter Laslett and James Fishkin (New Haven: Yale University Press, 1979), pp. 161–72. I have taken some liberties in adapting the story for present purposes.

Why would anyone think of this procedure as fair? It may be that none of the passengers believes there are decisive reasons why one or the other decision ought to be reached, each regards his preference simply as an arbitrary taste, and none believes that much harm would be done by either possible outcome of the decision process. There are "no presumptions as to merits" in the sense that *no individual passenger* has a view about which decision would be best on the merits. Upon reflection, each recognizes that he has no good reason to hold the preference he finds himself with rather than some other. In that case, each might think that majority rule with one person, one vote is a fair way to resolve the issue because it is the simplest way of reaching a determinate outcome, which everyone desires, and because, since no preference has more to be said for it than any other, no one could have any substantive basis for complaint about the outcome, whatever it turns out to be.

In this interpretation of the story, the passengers are trying to solve a pure coordination problem: they seek a determinate outcome, and while recognizing that their preferences may conflict, each is indifferent, upon reflection, about which outcome would be best on the merits. Certainly the majority method is a reasonable solution to this problem (though hardly the only one; why not agree to toss a coin?). But of course, interpreted this way the case has few interesting political analogs (and it is clearly not the interpretation Barry intends). However, if we elaborate the facts so as to make the story more realistic, the conclusion that everyone has reason to accept procedural equality grows more problematic. Suppose that each passenger does have a reasoned belief about which decision would be best, but these beliefs conflict. Each has presumptions as to merits, but there are insufficient *shared* presumptions to generate agreement. Here it is harder to see what moral significance attaches to the fact that majority voting yields a determinate outcome, particularly when we consider the question from the point of view of those who turn out to be in the minority. Lacking the means to coerce more favorable outcomes, perhaps they have no other choice but to suffer their fate quietly. However, the argument demands more than acquiescence in the face of greater force: it must provide a reason why the parties to the arrangement should regard it as *fair*. Why should the minority endorse an arrangement favoring the satisfaction of preferences that are unreasonable from their own point of view?[2]

Proceduralism is a response to this kind of problem. It is motivated by the thought that although we might disagree about how any particular dispute should come out, there may be procedures for resolving conflict on which we have reason to agree. Recognizing the prospect of disagreement about outcomes in particular cases, proceduralism seeks an account of the reasonableness of accepting the procedures it counts as fair in the characteristics of the procedures themselves, rather than in considerations about the merits of the decisions they are likely to yield. The challenge for any procedural theory is to explain what considerations are relevant to procedural fairness and why these considerations should carry weight with those who are disappointed by the outcomes produced by procedures that satisfy the theory's requirements.

The challenge might be met in several ways, each representing a distinct form of proceduralism. We shall consider three approaches. The first regards fair procedures as those that would emerge from a bargaining process in which persons who recognize the likelihood of disagreement about particular decisions attempt to reach a procedural compromise that it would be rational for all to accept, in view of the political interests they actually have. We will call this "fairness as a compromise." The second is similar in structure, but imposes information restrictions on the parties to the bargaining process. Fair procedures are the result of an *ex ante* agreement among persons who do not know what their own and each other's interests will turn out to be. This is "fairness as impartiality." The third approach abandons altogether the attempt to conceive fair procedures as the outcome of a hypothetical bargain and concentrates instead on what might be called their expressive or symbolic function in giving public recognition to the equal status of citizens. This is "fairness as equal respect."

---

[2] This thought is the source of Wollheim's "paradox" of democracy. Richard Wollheim, "A Paradox in the Theory of Democracy," in *Philosophy, Politics, and Society*, 2d Series, ed. Peter Laslett and W. G. Runciman (Oxford: Basil Blackwell, 1962), pp. 71–87.

FAIRNESS AS A COMPROMISE

As an example of the first approach, consider a view set forth by Peter Singer in the course of a criticism of the plural voting scheme advocated by Mill. Singer proceeds from a distinction between "absolute fairness" and "the paradigm of a fair compromise." Absolute (or "perfect") fairness requires an equal division unless sufficient reason for inequality can be provided. Arguably, Singer holds, Mill was right that differences in intellectual capacity or education could provide sufficient reason for inequality of power. Therefore plural voting may be "perfectly" fair. But people would probably not agree about who was to get the extra votes. Thus, "it would be wise to put aside beliefs about what would be perfectly fair, and settle for the sort of compromise represented by 'one man, one vote.'. . ."[3] Agreement on egalitarian decision procedures represents a fair compromise that is reasonable when some decision procedure is needed and agreement on the merits of conflicting claims is unlikely to be reached. In the absence of such a compromise, there would be no alternative to a " 'fight to the finish' over each issue."[4]

How does the compromise character of the egalitarian principle explain its fairness? In view of the likelihood of disagreement about the allocation of extra votes and the desirability of reaching some agreement as to procedures, equality might recommend itself simply as a strategic accommodation to the threat of chaos. However, as in the railway car case, no agreement of this kind can carry much moral weight. For the criterion of fairness is simply that the agreement is accepted all around: the features in virtue of which a procedural arrangement is fair are set by what those who will be bound to its results will accept, given that everyone prefers *some* decision procedure to none at all. There is no account of the reasons that motivate the parties other than the desire for some determinate solution; there is no independent standard of fairness that can be invoked to persuade or criticize someone who refuses to accept procedural equality; and there is nothing in principle to prohibit dispensing special favors or procedural advantages to such a holdout

[3] Peter Singer, *Democracy and Disobedience* (New York: Oxford University Press, 1973), p. 35.
[4] Ibid.

if that were the only way to get him to go along. Moreover, there is nothing to prohibit procedural inequalities that yield desirable results if the compliance of those affected could somehow be guaranteed.

Accordingly, Singer suggests a further consideration in favor of the egalitarian principle: by accepting it, everyone can "refrain from acting on his own judgement about particular issues *without giving up more than the theoretical minimum* which it is essential for everyone to give up in order to achieve the benefits of a peaceful solution to disputes."[5] Offhand, it is not clear how this argument should be understood. One possibility is this. Say that a bargaining process involving a number of parties has a set of *possible outcomes*. When the bargaining begins, each party's *initial demand* is the possible outcome that she has the greatest reason to favor. If the initial demands of all the parties coincide, then the bargaining process ends with agreement on the outcome represented by the initial demands. If not, then a compromise is necessary: at least some of the parties must make concessions. They must agree to accept an outcome that promises them less than their most-favored outcome. A compromise is *feasible* just in case every party has reason to accept it in preference to no agreement. A compromise is *fair* if, of all the feasible compromises, it is the one that requires each party to concede the least. Call this, provisionally, the *minimum concession rule*.

Some form of this rule is a plausible criterion for identifying a fair compromise in certain kinds of bargaining situations. I say "some form" because matters are more complicated than our provisional formulation suggests. First, the idea of a concession needs clarification. In the political context, for example, one might think of a concession in relation to a bargaining outcome conferring less power than initially demanded, or in relation to one with less expected utility (or, perhaps, less expected preference satisfaction). Singer appears to adopt the first interpretation, whereas the second yields the more plausible construction of the argument. If the idea is that there should be some parity among the concessions made by the parties, then presumably what matters is the significance of the concession to the conceding party. This is not necessarily what

---

[5] Ibid., p. 32 (emphasis added).

would be reflected by a measure of power, since other factors could also affect the utility to a person of her procedural opportunities. But this raises the further problem of how the significance of the concessions made by various parties should be compared. It will not do to compare interval measures of individual utility or satisfaction, since we have no way of establishing a basis of comparison. Instead, we might relativize each party's concession to the amount she would gain from acceptance of her initial demand, or to the extent to which her situation would be improved by acceptance of that demand in comparison to what it would be if there were no agreement. In other words, we might concentrate on each party's *relative concession*—the ratio of the concession she makes in accepting a compromise to her expectation if her initial demand had prevailed.[6] A second complication is that in the general case the optimal outcome is not always attained when everyone makes an *equal* relative concession (or, presumably, the *minimum* equal relative concession, when concessions of different amounts would identify different outcomes in the feasible set), because there may be solutions involving unequal concessions that are Pareto superior to equality. Instead, the *maximum* relative concession should be minimized: when this condition is satisfied, no one must make a greater relative concession than that necessary to reach agreement. These observations lead us to the principle of *minimax relative concession*—a bargain is fair if it minimizes the greatest relative concession required of any party.[7]

Singer's critique of the fairness of plural voting can be reformu-

---

[6] For this idea, see David Gauthier, *Morals by Agreement* (Oxford: Clarendon Press, 1986), pp. 134ff. Gauthier differs from the formulation in the text about whether each party's initial demand should be identified with that which each party thinks would be best on the merits. Instead, he holds that each should begin by asking for more. Gauthier's remarks on this matter (pp. 142–43) are problematic, but I cannot pursue the point here. There is a helpful discussion in Alan Nelson, "Economic Rationality and Morality," *Philosophy & Public Affairs* 17 (1988), pp. 153ff.

[7] An equivalent principle would be *maximin relative benefit*. See Gauthier, *Morals by Agreement*, pp. 133–46; and "Justice as Social Choice," in *Morality, Reason and Truth*, eds. David Copp and David Zimmerman (Totowa, N.J.: Rowman and Allanheld, 1985), pp. 258ff. Gauthier's principle is a variation on the view set forth in E. Kalai and M. Smorodinsky, "Other Solutions to Nash's Bargaining Problem," *Econometrica* 43 (1975), pp. 513–18. See also Alvin E. Roth, *Axiomatic Models of Bargaining* (Berlin and New York: Springer Verlag, 1979), pp. 105–7.

lated in terms of this principle. Each party's initial demand (or most-favored outcome) is a voting procedure in which votes are weighted in order to maximize the chances of yielding the best results. But the parties disagree about which weights would accomplish this. Since their initial demands do not coincide, a compromise is necessary. Procedural equality—in the sense of "one person, one vote" with simple majority rule—is a "fair compromise" because, of all the feasible outcomes, it requires each party to make the minimum concession (to "give up" the "theoretical minimum") necessary to generate agreement. Since plural voting is inconsistent with procedural equality, it is not fair.

One problem in this argument is that procedural equality is not necessarily the bargaining outcome that would be identified by the minimax concession rule; "fairness as a compromise," as interpreted here, may therefore have counterintuitive results. Recall that the extent of anyone's relative concession is a function of the difference between the value to him of his initial demand and that of the compromise, *relative* to the most he would have gained if his initial demand had prevailed. The nature of a fair compromise depends on the context of the bargaining, including the initial demands of the parties, the values they attach to achieving agreement on these demands, and the (dis)value they attach to no agreement. Equality would be the fair compromise if, for example, the values attached to the initial demands were symmetrically opposite and if the parties attached the same (dis)value to no agreement. But in the general case we are not entitled to make such assumptions. Suppose, for example, that half of society favors equal votes and half favors giving three votes to each university graduate and one to everyone else. The maximum concession would be minimized by some intermediate scheme (perhaps university graduates should each get 1.5 votes). The fair compromise view of political fairness may not justify procedural equality. Indeed, on some assumptions about the initial dispositions of the parties, it might even vindicate the Millian scheme that Singer sets out to criticize.

Of course, the fact that the account can produce counterintuitive results does not show that it is incorrect. So it is important that there are further difficulties. They involve its adequacy as an interpretation of procedural fairness. "Fairness as a compromise" is one kind of fairness—that appropriate in bargaining situations meeting certain special conditions. In particular, it should be reasonable to allow the context of bargaining (including the parties' initial demands and their valuations of the possible outcomes) to determine the outcomes. There are many situations in which this is the case. The choice of political procedures, however, is not one of them. Suppose the integrationists favor a voting system giving everyone one vote; the segregationists favor a system giving whites one vote and blacks no votes. Given suitable hypotheses about individual utility functions, the maximum concession might be minimized by some intermediate arrangement—say, one giving each white a full vote and each black three-fifths of a vote. This may be a "fair compromise." But it would not be *fair*, since the initial demands that determine the outcome are not (or not all) ones to which we have any reason to give moral weight.

This is a relatively obvious objection, so it is worth asking why the analysis of political fairness as a compromise might seem even initially plausible. I believe that the answer has to do with the point of view from which a justification of democracy—and, relatedly, a conception of political fairness—is sought. Suppose we were to approach the question of justification from the point of view of a self-interested citizen. Then we would be led to consider what reasons there are for such a citizen to obey the laws, and in particular, whether the fact that the laws issued from democratic institutions provides any special reason for obeying them.[8] If the likelihood of disagreement about the structure of decision-making procedures is accepted and everyone is assumed to prefer general acceptance of some procedure to none, then the conception of fairness as a compromise would be a natural result.

Although it serves some theoretical purposes to consider why a self-interested citizen should obey the laws of a democracy, I do not believe that this question provides an appropriate formulation of the problem of justification or of the point of view from which a doctrine of political fairness should be worked out. This can be seen by considering how the three-fifths compromise might be defended to those who favor equal votes for everyone:

This compromise is the best outcome available under the circumstances. Any arrangement more favorable to you would re-

[8] For this formulation of the problem, see Barry, "Is Democracy Special?" pp. 155ff.

quire the segregationists to concede more, relative to their initial demands, than the compromise requires you to concede, relative to yours. But no one should expect anyone else to go along with an arrangement that could only be reached on the basis of disproportionate concessions, for that would merely invite noncompliance and, hence, the collapse of the agreement. If you want to enjoy the benefits of a peaceful mechanism for settling disputes, you would do better by accepting the fair compromise. Refusing to accept it would be self-defeating.

The question we should consider is what kind of reason this provides for accepting the compromise. The reference to disproportionate concessions may seem initially to be an argument of fairness; the disproportion is, after all, a kind of inequality. However, it is difficult to say why it should *matter* that a bargain can only be achieved when some people concede relatively more than others; not *every* kind of inequality is morally objectionable. In fact, the role played by disproportionality in the argument is really quite different: it serves as a basis for predicting noncompliance by the other side with any arrangement giving them less than the "fair compromise." On the assumption that the segregationists would not adhere to any such agreement, what is being said is that the *rational* course for the integrationists (given that they prefer general acceptance of some procedural arrangement to none) is to accept the compromise. It is true that this might be a forceful reason for acceptance, or more precisely, for acquiescence; for under some circumstances, at least, one's interests are better served by accepting what others are willing to offer than by holding out for more desirable alternatives that can be attained, if at all, only at great cost. But this does not show that the terms of participation identified by the compromise are *fair*. (What if the segregationists could be successfully compelled, at acceptable social cost, to adhere to an arrangement that was less favorable to them? Would it be unfair to do so?) By assimilating the concept of political fairness to the idea of an equilibrium point in a bargaining game, the analysis of fairness as a compromise collapses the distinctive normative content of the concept of political fairness into different, though not always unimportant, considerations of collective rationality. Rationality is frequently a virtue, but it is surely a mistake to identify procedural principles that would be accepted by a group of rational and self-interested individuals, under the constraints of prevailing patterns of power and preference, with fairness. We would have little use for the concept of fairness if it amounted to no more than this.

FAIRNESS AS IMPARTIALITY

Fairness as a compromise allows judgments about procedural fairness to be influenced by the initial demands and power relations of the parties. Perhaps this is the source of its deficiencies. We are seeking an account of fairness that can explain what demands we are justified in making on each other. But conceiving fair terms of participation as those that would be accepted, as a compromise, by persons whose initial claims are influenced by their social positions, prejudices, and interests, seems to introduce a kind of circularity into the account.

The second kind of procedural theory is an attempt to avoid this kind of circularity. It is best described as a hypothetical agreement theory in which the parties to the agreement meet behind a "veil of ignorance" that deprives them of information about their individual interests and the distribution of interests throughout the community. Fair terms of participation are seen as ones that would be agreed to by parties so conceived. Thus, in the railway car case, perhaps we should suppose that the passengers were required to come to agreement on a decision procedure without knowing their attitudes toward smoking; or, in the racial voting case, that the integrationists and segregationists were required to do so without knowing their race or their beliefs about its political significance.

Before examining the outcome of such a hypothetical agreement, we must pause to consider a preliminary question about the rationale of the information restrictions on which it is based. Any theory employing the idea of a hypothetical agreement faces the problem of explaining why real persons should care about its provisions. Hypothetical agreements are not like actual ones in the sense of being voluntary engagements whereby one binds one's will or restricts one's freedom of action; their force in practical reasoning, if any, must be explained differently. If we regard the "fair compromise" view as a hypothetical agreement theory, we can see that it yields a relatively uncomplicated answer to this question. Since the parties are conceived as representatives of real people, endowed with full knowledge of their actual interests, it can be said that acceptance of any agreement the parties might reach would be in the interests of the real people they represent. *Our* motivation for accepting the hypothetical agreement derives from the fact that we identify with the interests of the parties; the use or value of the hypothesis to us is simply that it helps to clarify how best to advance our interests under conditions of strategic interaction. No similar explanation is available, however, for hypothetical agreement theories in which the interests of the parties are conceived counterfactually, for in that case an agreement that satisfied *their* interests would not necessarily satisfy *ours*. Suppose, for example, that parties who are deprived of information about their interests are thought of as representing "anyone in society"; then the problem might be stated by asking why we should identify our own interests with those of "anyone." Without an answer, there might be no reason to care about any agreement the hypothetical parties were supposed to reach.

One kind of rationale for restricting the knowledge of the parties is pragmatic. It reflects an association of the problem of defining fair political procedures with the historical process of constitutional choice.[9] If we were in the position of devising a constitution for our own society, it would be shortsighted to choose a set of procedures on the grounds that they were more likely than others to result in outcomes that satisfied our present preferences. For those preferences might change; and even if they did not, the distribution of preference in society at large might shift, so that today's majority would become tomorrow's minority. Either way, we would wish to choose procedures that would be acceptable to us whatever the distribution of preference turned out to be. The best advice might be to proceed as if in ignorance of our actual preferences, assuming instead that we are equally likely to find ourselves with any set of preferences represented in society.

However, this would not always be good counsel. According to the pragmatic rationale, if we were choosing a constitution, we

[9] For such a view, see Douglas W. Rae, "Decision-Rules and Individual Values in Constitutional Choice," *American Political Science Review* 63 (1969), p. 41.

should choose as if in ignorance of actual preferences because, being unable to anticipate our own or others' future preferences, we could not say for sure how our actual interests would fare under the procedures we are to choose. Choosing as if we might turn out to be anyone seems to be the best way to safeguard our interests, whatever the future course of events. But it is an empirical matter whether future preferences can be accurately predicted, and the assumption that they cannot be might be incorrect. Prevailing patterns of social cleavage might make it easily predictable that certain forms of political conflict would recur and would be resolved differently under different procedures. (Reflection about real instances of constitutional choice suggests that this is more likely to be the case than artificial examples like that involving the railway car might indicate.)[10] In that event, rational choosers would be ill-advised to make constitutional choices as if they did not know their interests; for example, such a choice could be catastrophic for an entrenched minority, for whom it would pose the risk of being permanently excluded from participation in government. Self-interested choosers of decision-making procedures have reason to presume ignorance about their own interests only where certain empirical conditions are known to be met in their society.[11] When these conditions do not hold, the choices that would be made under informational constraints would be of little concern for actual people.[12] The pragmatic rationale, therefore, will not yield a plausible *general* explanation for conceiving fair procedures as those that would be chosen in ignorance of information about individual interests.

It would be better to adopt another explanation of the information constraints, which interprets them as a means of ensuring the *impartiality* of the agreement. This yields a different reason why

[10] The complicated political conditions in which the framers of the U.S. Constitution reached the three-fifths compromise provide a good case in point. See Staughton Lynd, "The Compromise of 1787," in *Class Conflict, Slavery, and the United States Constitution* (Indianapolis: Bobbs-Merrill, 1967; reprint, Westport, Conn.: Greenwood Press, 1980), pp. 200–205.

[11] For example, there should be no intense or permanent minorities. These conditions are discussed in Barry, "Is Democracy Special?" pp. 176–77. See also my "Procedural Equality in Democratic Theory: A Preliminary Examination," in *Nomos XXV: Liberal Democracy*, ed. J. Roland Pennock and John W. Chapman (New York: New York University Press, 1983), pp. 77–79.

[12] For a further discussion, see Brian Barry, "Is it Better to be Powerful or Lucky?" *Political Studies* 28 (1980), pp. 344ff.

actual persons should care about it, for now it can be said that because the agreement was not biased by information about anyone's individual interests and preferences, it treats people fairly regardless of their substantive aims. This rationale does not depend on contingent assumptions about the accuracy of predictions of future preferences; instead, it denies that predictions would be relevant to procedural choice even if they could reliably be made. One might say that the change of rationale moralizes the account by converting it from one motivated by considerations of self-interest to one that embodies a normative conception of the role that political procedures should play in public life. The main idea is that this role should be neutral: procedures should provide a mechanism for adjudicating among contending views of the social good without presupposing the truth of any.

To avoid misunderstanding, we should recall that the view we are considering is a *procedural* theory of political fairness, and it regards the choice of procedural principles as a problem to be resolved without regard to the results that any particular procedures might produce. Thus, it differs from what Rawls calls the "constitutional convention" stage of reasoning in the "original position." There, principles of social justice have already been identified, and the main problem is to decide which procedural rules are most likely to yield outcomes that accord with the principles.[13] A theory of political fairness with such a foundation is not a procedural theory in our sense, for its appeal does not derive from desirable features of "fair" procedures taken by themselves but instead from their conduciveness to just outcomes, or perhaps the extent to which they support a just social order. The choice of procedural rules is framed by a prior choice of ends for the political process and so can be impartial, if at all, only derivatively. Here, by contrast, there are no such ends in the background to serve as a benchmark in evaluations of alternative procedural rules. This kind of theory aspires to provide an account of procedural fairness whose impartiality is intrinsic rather than derivative: fair procedures should be rationally acceptable to all persons even if they disagree about substantive standards for evaluating political decisions.

Recognizing that more complex formulations are possible, I shall

[13] John Rawls, *A Theory of Justice* (Cambridge: Harvard University Press, 1971), pp. 221ff.

restrict myself to a relatively simple version of the view.[14] (I believe that analogous remarks apply to more complex variants.) Let us say that fair procedures are those that treat their participants impartially, and let us model this idea by conceiving principles of procedural fairness as those that would be agreed to by parties whose impartiality is reflected by restrictions on the information they are allowed to bring to bear on the choice. In particular, they must choose in the absence of knowledge about the likely course of future political events, the range of issues on the political agenda, their individual political interests, and the distribution of political interests throughout the community. Although they do not know their interests, they do know that whatever these turn out to be, it will better for them to win than to lose any political struggles in which they might engage. In appraising alternative procedures, they are motivated by a desire to minimize the frequency (over a sufficiently long time span) with which any of them can expect to be in the minority. In the face of ignorance about their interests, the parties suppose that each person's preferences are independent of everyone else's and that on any issue each person is equally likely to be on either side.[15] As Rae has shown in connection with the problem of selecting a decision rule, the optimal choice under such circumstances (assuming that the agenda consists only of binary choices) is simple majority rule.[16] This is a special case of the more general proposition that parties aiming to minimize their losses in conditions of uncertainty would choose a principle under which each person has an equal capacity to influence outcomes; or, in the terms adopted in chapter 1, under which each person has equal (abstract) power.

This account of procedural fairness has a superficial appeal. How-

[14] The view I shall describe is an interpretation of that set forth in Rae, "Decision-Rules and Individual Values in Constitutional Choice," pp. 41–49.

[15] Each supposition is an application of the principle of insufficient reason. On some views about the rationality of risk aversion, this might appear to be objectionable. Perhaps it is. It would be interesting to consider the consequences for a doctrine of procedural fairness of substituting suppositions reflecting a more conservative attitude to risk than the neutral attitude reflected in the suppositions in the text. I shall not do this here; the view as sketched is a more faithful reconstruction of the conception of fairness I wish to examine.

[16] Rae, "Decision-Rules and Individual Values in Constitutional Choice," p. 49.

ever, its appeal conceals an important difficulty concerning the conception of impartiality that the account embodies. One way to approach the problem is to consider the import of the claim that in the circumstances imagined, our hypothetical choosers would insist on equal power. Suppose this is true; why should it matter to actual persons in society? In the absence of information about the actual distribution of interests, there is little we can conclude from a description of the formal properties of decision-making procedures about the substantive character of political decisions. For example, we cannot conclude that egalitarian procedures guarantee outcomes that satisfy everyone's interests equally, even in the (very) long run. Nor can we conclude that such procedures protect against any particular kind or degree of deprivation. Now if we were members of a society governed by procedures that were fair according to this conception, yet found ourselves consistently on the losing side of issues bearing on the satisfaction of our important interests or the success of our projects, what would be the significance of the fact, if it were a fact, that we would have chosen the procedures if we were ignorant of our interests? Why should that *matter* to us?

This is the question to which the rationale of impartiality is supposed to provide a reply. It says that we should accept procedures that we would have chosen in ignorance of our interests because they treat everyone impartially. But now we must wonder whether it is right to interpret impartiality in so formal a way. Impartiality is sometimes thought to require giving equal weight to the interests of everyone involved, and perhaps there is a sense in which the account of fairness we have sketched incorporates this conception. However, the conception is deficient. To adapt an example from Scanlon, impartiality does not require us to give the same weight to the claim of someone who wants help in building a monument to his god as to the claim of someone else who needs aid in getting enough to eat, even if the claims are of equal extent and are pressed with equal intensity.[17] What counts as impartial treatment depends on the character of the interests involved; impartiality is not, so to speak, content-neutral. Though the subject is complicated, it does

[17] T. M. Scanlon, "Preference and Urgency," *Journal of Philosophy* 72 (1975), pp. 659–60.

not appear, in the general case, that we violate impartiality by giving greater weight to interests of greater urgency.[18] Indeed, the truth seems to be more nearly the opposite: we violate impartiality, at least in ordinary circumstances, by giving equal weight to interests of significantly different degrees of urgency.

Fairness as impartiality falls into this error in an attempt to arrive at criteria of procedural fairness in abstraction from any consideration of the substantive characteristics of the results that procedures are likely to produce. By modeling impartiality by means of information restrictions on procedural choice, it excludes categories of information that would be necessary to identify procedural principles that treat persons in a genuinely impartial manner. Such principles would have to be sensitive to differences in the importance or urgency of the interests at stake in politics, so that, for example, a majority would not be enabled to secure a trifling interest held by many at the cost of the urgent interests of a few. (Thus, fair procedures ought not to allow the more or less permanent exclusion of an entrenched minority from effective participation in politics—at least where there are alternative feasible procedures that would avoid this.) But fairness as impartiality cannot allow such substantive considerations to enter into judgments about procedural fairness without losing its character as a procedural view.

How, then, can we account for the superficial appeal of the view? Perhaps the best explanation is that the view succeeds in exhibiting a *kind* of impartiality, albeit one without much ethical significance. *Within* the contract situation—that is, once the information restrictions are in place—the reasoning of the parties is necessarily impartial; the parties are conceived as aiming to minimize their losses, and since an outcome that realizes this aim for one realizes it for everyone else as well, the outcome of the agreement is impartial with respect to the parties to it. Assuming that procedural equality would be the outcome of the agreement, we might say that it is facially or formally impartial. What I have argued is that this kind of impartiality would properly not be of much importance to the actual persons the parties are supposed to represent; it is certainly not enough, by itself, to explain why impartiality as it is understood

[18] There is a discussion of some complications in Thomas Nagel, *The View from Nowhere* (New York: Oxford University Press, 1986), pp. 172–73.

here should trump other considerations in the assessment of democratic procedures.

Another way to put the point is this. The effect of the assumptions on which fairness as impartiality is based is to portray the parties as if the only interest that informs their assessment of procedural principles is an interest in finding a peaceful means for resolving disputes that maximizes the abstract power reserved to each citizen. The view elevates the conservation of (abstract) power to a sovereign position in determining the parties' procedural choices. The question I have raised is why the interest in power should eclipse the other concerns it would be natural to bring to bear on the selection of a mechanism for dispute settlement, such as the interests in conditions of responsible deliberation or in protecting the capacity to satisfy one's urgent needs. As we have already observed, in any but the smallest of groups, the contribution to individual well-being of an equal procedural opportunity to affect outcomes is likely to be relatively small in comparison to the other manipulable factors that determine outcomes. Under the guise of a mistaken understanding of impartiality, this view artificially restricts the range of considerations taken into account in assessing political procedures to a concern for the conservation of power whose importance it inflates far beyond what is reasonable.

THE EXPRESSIVE FUNCTION OF PROCEDURAL FORMS

We have been considering versions of proceduralism in which procedural equality is portrayed as the outcome of a hypothetical agreement among members of society concerned to find a peaceful means of making social decisions in the face of inevitable dispute about how particular matters of public policy should be resolved. We have seen that there is a range of interpretations of such an agreement, differing according to the assumptions made about the entitlements and preferences in the background. With respect to interpretations in which actually existing entitlements and preferences are allowed to constrain the outcome, I have argued that there is no reason to think of the outcome as *fair*: it is simply the equilibrium point of a bargaining game, with nothing to recommend it morally. With respect to interpretations that attempt to avoid this difficulty by substituting counterfactual assumptions about preferences, I have suggested that the assumptions required to generate agreement on procedural equality arbitrarily exclude considerations that it seems natural to take into account but that, if taken into account, draw the procedural character of the view into question.

At this point, someone might object that the attempt to portray criteria of political fairness as the outcome of a hypothetical bargain was misguided from the start. For any such attempt must take one or another kind of instrumental view of political procedures: hypothetical choosers must base their choice of principles on something, and it seems inevitable that they would consider the desirability or acceptability of the results anticipated from procedures that satisfy the principles. However, the objection continues, this misconstrues the moral significance of procedural forms. The structural characteristics of political procedures do not so much matter because they conduce to acceptable outcomes as because they give public expression to each person's status as an equal citizen.[19] This thought suggests a third kind of procedural theory, which locates the importance of the formal properties of political procedures in their expressive or symbolic function rather than in their consequences for legislation and policy.

It is not clear what "each person's status as an equal citizen" can mean. Plainly, it cannot be simply that each citizen should have equal power over outcomes, since this would yield a trivially circular argument. Some deeper conception of equal status is needed. For example, we might consider the idea that fair institutions should express public recognition of the equal worth of persons, conceived as autonomous centers of deliberation and action: such

---

[19] Such a view is suggested by the some of Rawls's remarks about political liberty. For example: "The idea [of the guarantee of fair value] is to incorporate into the basic structure of society an effective political procedure *which mirrors in that structure the fair representation of persons achieved by the original position.*" John Rawls, "The Basic Liberties and Their Priority," in *The Tanner Lectures on Human Values*, vol. 3, ed. Sterling McMurrin (Salt Lake City: University of Utah Press; Cambridge: Cambridge University Press, 1982), p. 45 (emphasis added); compare Rawls, *A Theory of Justice*, pp. 233–34. This line of thought is different from, and might not even be consistent with, the more instrumental view of procedural fairness suggested elsewhere in Rawls's discussion of principles for political institutions.

institutions should avoid interfering with, and when possible should contribute to, their members' respect for themselves and for one another as persons equally capable of making deliberate choices about their own situations and of carrying out these choices in action.[20]

I concentrate on this formulation of the idea of equal status because something like it is frequently appealed to in the justification of generically democratic institutions. In that context the idea has several aspects, each of which connects with democratic institutions in a different way. Most obviously, the fact that opportunities to influence political decisions are available to everyone ensures that those so motivated will be enabled to defend their interests and to promote their ideals. They will understand themselves as agents who have a capacity to exercise some degree of control over aspects of their lives affected by political decisions rather than as passive victims who must accept those decisions as *faits accomplis* that are beyond challenge. Further, since democratic politics requires public discussion and debate, it supports a political culture with incentives for investigation and criticism of government and for the public presentation of opposing political views. Such a culture both encourages and enables the exercise of the faculties of judgment and choice. Finally, democratic politics creates an environment in which persons confront each other not only to manipulate but to persuade and so must take seriously each other's nature as a rational being. In this sense, public recognition of rights of participation provides grounds for the belief that one is regarded by others as a person whose opinions and choices deserve respect.[21]

No doubt these considerations furnish strong reasons for preferring democratic to other kinds of institutions. However, they do not also determine the question of institutional fairness; indeed, they leave open significant room for variation. In particular, they do not establish that fair institutions should have egalitarian procedures. First, procedural equality is not evidently necessary to ensure that citizens will regard themselves as sharing in control rather than as

[20] Thus Meiklejohn: "Whether it be in the field of individual or social activity, men are not recognizable as men unless, in any given situation, they are using their minds to give direction to their behavior." *Political Freedom* (New York: Harper & Brothers, 1960), p. 13.

[21] Jack Lively, *Democracy* (Oxford: Basil Blackwell, 1975), pp. 134–35.

objects of manipulation by an alien power. As Mill observed, this consideration requires that everyone have *some* opportunity to participate in political decision making; but it is not obvious that these opportunities must be equal, particularly if other considerations making for inequality are widely accepted. Similarly, the distinctive political culture of democracy seems to be consistent with some amount of political inequality. The essential condition is that political competition should be extensive enough to generate a continuing interest in having available independent sources of information and criticism regarding a government's activities and to create recurring situations in which engagement in argument and persuasion will be necessary to compete effectively for power. In both cases, institutions must be sufficiently open to allow conflicting positions to be represented, but every citizen need not have an equal opportunity to influence outcomes.

Some forms of inequality are clearly objectionable for other reasons related to equal respect as we have construed it. Consider, for example, the white primary or exclusion of women from the franchise. Such inequalities not only work to the detriment of the disadvantaged group but will also be experienced by them as demeaning. But not every procedural inequality has this effect; few, for example, feel insulted or degraded by the patent inequality of representation in the U.S. Senate. So it does not appear that there is any very direct inference from the idea that institutions should express equal respect for persons to an institutional requirement of equal power or influence. In fact, these reflections suggest that an account of political fairness that proceeds from a concern about the expressive functions of procedural forms will produce an important asymmetry that is not reflected in simple proceduralism: procedural inequalities will be objectionable when they express or reinforce objectionable inequalities elsewhere in society, but not (or not necessarily) when they are, in this respect, benign. Moreover, there are some procedural choices to which considerations of *fairness* are plainly relevant, but which cannot intelligibly be described as expressing equal respect for individual citizens—for example, choices regarding the structure of the political agenda. Thus, while in some cases expressive concerns may prove to be pivotal factors in judgments about procedural fairness, they will not always (or perhaps even usually) determine these judgments, and other considerations will be needed to resolve the indeterminacy.

THE TRUTH IN PROCEDURALISM

Perhaps there are other ways to derive criteria of procedural fairness from non-result-oriented considerations; if so, there are reasons to doubt that they would be successful. Assertions that some procedural arrangements are fair invite the question of why *those* arrangements should have a special claim on our support. If one wishes to maintain a procedural view, this question must be answered by showing that the favored procedures have a characteristic whose value is both overriding and independent of considerations about the political results that the normal operation of these procedures would produce. But then the further question arises of why we should accord that characteristic overriding value. When the choice among alternative procedures makes a difference in the expected results and there are independent standards for evaluating these results, the response that procedural equality is *intrinsically* fair seems insufficient. This is particularly true when the requirements of procedural fairness are themselves in dispute. The value of fairness should be susceptible to some more compelling explanation than is provided by the claim that its value is intrinsic. But any other response—including the effort to bring to bear a principle of equal respect for persons—seems to be question begging or underdetermining, or to bring to bear considerations about results of the kind that proceduralism is an attempt to avoid.[22]

None of this provides any reason to doubt the contractualist impulse that seems to motivate proceduralist theories. If my earlier remarks are right, then we must still maintain that fair procedures should be justifiable to each person affected by them. What these criticisms suggest is that no such justification is likely to be persuasive if it excludes considerations about results entirely. The political outcomes to be expected from the operation of a set of procedures are simply too important to be left out of account. On the

[22] For a helpful further discussion of this last point, see William N. Nelson, *On Justifying Democracy* (London: Routledge & Kegan Paul, 1980), pp. 17–33.

other hand, as the discussion of fairness as equal respect illustrates, in some circumstances considerations about the expressive function of procedural forms provide a reason to be concerned about their formal characteristics independently of the substantive outcomes likely to be produced. An adequate doctrine of political fairness should make a place for both kinds of considerations.

CHAPTER FIVE

A Theory of

Political Fairness

As Hobbes recognized, the members of political society occupy two distinct roles: they are both the "makers" and the "matter" of government, its agents and its objects, its producers and its consumers.[1] Each role constitutes a point of view from which political arrangements can be judged. Hobbes's innovation was to relegate persons conceived as "makers" to a hypothetical act of "authorization" establishing a form of government where there is no place for participation in the choice of leadership or policy, no occasion for political deliberation, no sharing of information, no compromise, no voting, indeed no organized *public* life at all. The measure of a government's success, according to Hobbes, is its ability to induce its people to accept the conception of their political identity implicit in this vision—to accept, that is, the legitimacy of institutions designed to replace the desire to participate in public life with a desire to enjoy a felicitous private one. A government that succeeds in protecting the lives and promoting the satisfaction of the private desires of its people does all that they can reasonably require of it.[2]

[1] Thomas Hobbes, *Leviathan* [1651] (New York: Collier Books, 1962), pp. 19, 229 (the passages occur in the "Author's Introduction" and chap. 28). The centrality of the distinction in Hobbes's thought was first made clear to me by Michael Walzer in a lecture presented in Princeton in 1973.

[2] This is reflected in Hobbes's conception of the social contract as an undertaking in which people surrender their power to a sovereign (an "alienation" contract), rather than as one in which their power is merely "loaned," subject to certain conditions on its use (an "agency" contract). For this distinction, see Jean Hampton,

The democratic ideal stands in contrast to Hobbes's vision. Its aspiration is a form of government continuously justifiable from both points of view. That political decisions take fair account of each person's prospects is not enough; for, in theory at least, this could be the case in a perfectly impartial dictatorship. As a generic form, democracy is distinguished from the other traditional forms of government by provisions for the regular participation of its citizens in political decisions. The "making" of policy is a shared function of the many, not the exclusive province of one or a few. The uniqueness of democratic forms lies in the fact that the set of rulers and the set of the ruled—the "makers" and the "matter" of politics—for the most part coincide.

This fact defines the philosophical problem to which a theory of political equality is a response, and it explains why any adequate theory must be complex. Popular participation in political decisions is possible only within an institutional framework that organizes and regulates it. But many such frameworks can be imagined, and the basic idea of democracy—that the people should rule—is too protean to settle the choice among them. A theory of political equality must resolve this indeterminacy by identifying the features that institutions for political participation should possess if they can truly be said to treat citizens as equals.

An adequate solution to this problem must be complex because the status of democratic citizenship is complex. The terms of participation in democratic politics should be fair to persons conceived as citizens. However, as both the "makers" and the "matter" of politics, citizens occupy multiple roles and so can judge their institutions from more than one point of view. We must not suppose that the interests of citizens conceived from one of these points of view will always harmonize with their interests conceived from the other or that an effort to secure one kind of interest will not put the other in jeopardy. For example, we can hardly assume a priori that the conditions of participation that would be optimal for the making of responsible judgments about public affairs will be the same as those that would generate political outcomes that would be best for those to whom they apply. Indeed, we must not suppose that

Hobbes and the Social Contract Tradition (Cambridge: Cambridge University Press, 1986), pp. 3–4, 256–79.

either of these points of view, taken separately, defines a single consistent set of aims; either could dissolve on examination into a series of disparate, and potentially conflicting, concerns. It would be a mistake to assume (though in the end, it may prove to be true) that fairness to persons conceived as citizens names a simple, univocal criterion. We may understand it better as a complex criterion that brings together a plurality of values corresponding to both the active and the passive dimensions of citizenship.

OUTLINE OF THE THEORY

These remarks summarize the lessons to be learned from the criticisms of conventional conceptions of political equality presented in earlier chapters. I turn here to the more constructive task of formulating an alternative theory that takes account of these lessons. In form, the theory I shall set forth is a hybrid version of the procedural theory; thus, it differs not only from best result and popular will theories but also from simple versions of proceduralism that identify fair participation with procedural equality. To distinguish it from these other views, I call this theory *complex proceduralism*.

The central idea is this. Institutions for participation should be justifiable to each citizen, taking into account the interests that arise from both aspects of citizenship. We should be able to regard the terms of participation as the object of an agreement that it would be reasonable to expect every citizen to accept. Institutions that satisfy this condition can be said to be egalitarian in the deepest sense: being equally justifiable to each of their members, they recognize each person's status as an equal citizen.

The notion of reasonable agreement is an application of the idea of a social contract to the subject of political equality. As we shall see, this idea has normative consequences: it will rule out any arrangement for participation in political decisions for which no justification of the appropriate form is plausibly available. However, this is not likely to be enough to settle many practical disputes about the structure of democratic institutions. Often, what is at issue is not the *form* of the justification but its *content*; various reasons might be advanced to show why some arrangement is acceptable to all, and the question is whether these reasons ought to be seen as compelling. Hence, the formal conception of contractualist justification needs to be supplemented by a generalized account of the kinds of reasons we are prepared to recognize as grounds for refusing to accede to any particular arrangements for participation.

In complex proceduralism, this account is provided by a doctrine of *regulative interests of citizenship*. These are higher-order interests that represent within the theory the plurality of regulative concerns that arise in connection with the complex status of democratic citizenship. Paramount among these are interests in *recognition*, *equitable treatment*, and *deliberative responsibility*. Each defines a category of interest it would be reasonable to take into account in assessing the arrangements for participation. Taking the formal and the substantive elements of the theory together, complex proceduralism holds that *the terms of participation are fair if no one who had these ("regulative") interests and who was motivated by a desire to reach agreement with others on this basis could reasonably refuse to accept them.*

Unlike best result and popular will theories, complex proceduralism does not seek criteria for identifying the uniquely best or most desirable institutions; its aim is to identify grounds on which some of the feasible arrangements might reasonably be ruled out. To put it somewhat differently, it seeks criteria that any procedural arrangement should satisfy in order to be regarded as acceptable. Moreover, unlike the simpler versions of proceduralism considered earlier, complex proceduralism does not embrace any single value (such as the conservation of power) as definitive of political fairness; it recognizes a plurality of reasons why a procedural regime might be judged to be unfair. Its main concern is to devise a method for characterizing these reasons more precisely and for guiding judgment when they conflict.

The Idea of a Social Contract

A more detailed account of complex proceduralism should provide an explanation of both its formal and its substantive elements and of the important relationship between them.

Beginning with the social contract framework, there are three questions. First, in view of the variety of interpretations of the contract idea, why adopt so informal a conception as that employed in complex proceduralism? For example, why not impose informational constraints (a "veil of ignorance") on the parties to the agreement? Second, why should we take any interest in the contract idea, so understood? In particular, how is it connected to the traditional aspirations of democratic reform? Third, what is the normative force of this idea? What difference does it make that our conception of political fairness is based on contractualist reasoning rather than on reasoning of some other kind?

There are many ways to understand the idea of a social contract, each importantly different from the others. Later we will note some of the differences; for the moment we concentrate on the common elements. The social contract doctrine is first of all a view about the form that the justification of political principles should take. Like other moral conceptions, contractualism holds that principles should be justifiable from the perspective of everyone affected by them. What is special in contractualism is the attempt to understand this perspective as that of several distinct individuals, combined so that the separateness of each person's point of view is retained. In the classical social contract theories, this idea was expressed metaphorically in the requirement that the original agreement be unanimous. To remove the metaphor, we might say, following Scanlon, that contractualism regards moral principles as principles that "no one could reasonably reject as a basis for informed, unforced general agreement," provided they were moved by a desire to reach such an agreement.[3]

The requirement of unanimity reflects what might be called a distributive conception of justification: contractualist principles should be reasonable from each individual point of view. By way of comparison, views in the tradition of classical utilitarianism embody an aggregative conception: the perspective of everyone affected is interpreted as that of society at large, and principles are held to be justified when they are shown to be better, for the community as a whole, than any others, even if from some individual perspectives they appear less reasonable than some alternatives.

[3] T. M. Scanlon, "Contractualism and Utilitarianism," in *Utilitarianism and Beyond*, ed. Amartya Sen and Bernard Williams (Cambridge: Cambridge University Press, 1982), p. 110. My interpretation of the social contract idea is greatly indebted to this article throughout.

Thus, although aggregative conceptions hold that principles should be acceptable from the perspective of society, this does not imply that they should be acceptable from the perspective of everyone, taken seriatim. In contrast to contractualist conceptions, utilitarian views might therefore be seen as an application of the idea of rule by the majority.[4]

It may help to compare this understanding of the essentials of the contract idea with a different one, which sees the idea of reciprocity rather than that of reasonable agreement as the central feature. According to this view, the unity of the social contract tradition, and what distinguishes it from utilitarianism, is (roughly) the insistence that the net benefit that social institutions confer on each of their members should be greater by a similar amount than what each could expect in a nonsocial "state of nature."[5] When this condition is met, people can regard the sacrifices their institutions call upon them to make as justified by the advantages they may expect to derive, in turn, from the sacrifices of others. The basis of political justice is the reciprocal expectation of benefit. This conception of the contract idea is natural enough if the description of society as "a cooperative venture for mutual advantage" is taken literally.[6] However, I believe the conception is too narrow. As a historical matter, it is inapt: none of the writers in the tradition, arguably (although implausibly) with the exception of Hobbes, regarded the original agreement as justified by considerations of parity of benefit.[7] Their views converge, instead, on the notion of reasonable consent.[8] As a philosophical matter, the conception confuses species and genus. Under some circumstances, reciprocity may not be necessary to show that a social arrangement is reasonably acceptable

[4] Thomas Nagel, "Equality," in *Mortal Questions* (Cambridge: Cambridge University Press, 1979), p. 112.

[5] For such a view, see David Gauthier, *Morals by Agreement* (Oxford: Clarendon Press, 1986), pp. 8–13.

[6] John Rawls, *A Theory of Justice* (Cambridge: Harvard University Press, 1971), p. 4.

[7] Indeed, the characterization fits Hume, the great opponent of contractualism, better than it fits anyone within the contract tradition as it is normally understood. See David Gauthier, "David Hume, Contractarian," *Philosophical Review* 88 (1979), pp. 3–38.

[8] Jeremy Waldron, "Theoretical Foundations of Liberalism," *Philosophical Quarterly* 37 (1987), pp. 135–40.

from all points of view, and under other circumstances it may not be sufficient: an agreement could be reasonable from each person's perspective without conferring equivalent net benefits, and it could confer equivalent net benefits without being reasonable on all sides. A condition of reciprocal benefit imports a specific normative criterion into the notion of a social contract that the form of that notion does not require. The core idea is better conceived as that of reasonable agreement.

So understood, the contract doctrine describes a conception of justification that is particularly compatible with the aspirations of modern democratic culture.[9] The Leveller defense of an expanded suffrage was perhaps the first important attempt to invoke these aspirations on behalf of political reform.[10] Commenting on Colonel Rainsborough's famous words, Lindsay wrote: "The poorest has his own life *to live*, not to be managed or drilled or used by other people."[11] The poorest and the richest are equally responsible for the conduct of their own lives and the choice of an individual good and should have equal authority over the public decisions that affect them. Of course, this aspiration would be fully realized only if

[9] The contractualist formula has also been advanced as a general characterization of the subject matter of morality, or of the grounds of moral truth (most influentially by Scanlon in "Contractualism and Utilitarianism," esp. pp. 110–15). Whether this is correct is a question I cannot consider here. Our concern is the more traditional conception of the social contract as a basis of *political* justification.

[10] Quoted on page 3, above. On the character of the Leveller position as it was represented at Putney, see Austin Woolrych, *Soldiers and Statesmen: The General Council of the Army and Its Debates, 1647–1648* (Oxford: Clarendon Press, 1987), esp. chap. 9. On the Levellers' conception of democracy, see J. C. Davis, "The Levellers and Democracy," *Past and Present*, no. 40 (1968), pp. 174–80; and Keith Thomas, "The Levellers and the Franchise," in *The Interregnum: The Quest for Settlement 1646–1660*, ed. G. E. Aylmer (London: Archon, 1972), pp. 57–78. There is an accessible survey in Brian Manning, *The English People and the English Revolution* (London: Heinemann, 1975), pp. 286–317.

[11] A. D. Lindsay, *The Essentials of Democracy*, Lectures on the William J. Cooper Foundation of Swarthmore College (Philadelphia: University of Pennsylvania Press, 1929), p. 13 (emphasis in original). Although historians of the Leveller movement have been particularly concerned with the question of the franchise, it does not appear to have been central to the Leveller program; what was more important—and more radical—in their thought was the idea that the legitimacy of the political order derives from the agreement of the people (by which they meant adult males who had not forfeited their birthright). Woolrych, *Soldiers and Statesmen*, pp. 221, 236.

unanimous consent were required for political decisions and then only if there were grounds for supposing that the status quo ante were itself unanimously accepted; otherwise, someone might find himself coerced to accept, or at least to accommodate himself to, political decisions affecting the conduct of his life that were taken without his consent. Contractualism arises in democratic theory once it is acknowledged that this degree of agreement will not normally obtain on political matters; indeed, it will not normally obtain even at the level of constitutional choice. The most that can be hoped is that institutions will be compatible with principles that no one could reasonably reject, supposing that they were motivated by a desire to find principles that each could justify to everyone else. Then, when someone complains that a procedural arrangement may disappoint her interests, it can be replied that this is the unavoidable result of acting on principles that her fellow citizens could reasonably expect her to accept. Institutions that can be justified in this way come as close as possible to the ideal of respect for each person's final authority over the conduct of her own life.[12]

There are many ways of interpreting the contract idea for normative purposes consistently with this understanding of the source of its appeal. For example, there are more and less formal conceptions, which differ according to the degree to which the background and setting of the original agreement are constrained by counterfactual assumptions about the knowledge, interests, and motivation of the parties. Rawls's theory is an instance of a relatively formal view, which proceeds by offering an account of the circumstances of agreement with sufficient normative content to enable principles to be derived, ideally, by deduction. On the other hand, the theory described by Scanlon is considerably less formal; the parties are imagined to be motivated by a desire to come to agreement but are otherwise conceived as having the knowledge and interests of the actual persons whom they represent. The theory consists of a generalized description of the point of view from which the justification of principles is to be sought and invites substantive argument about the reasons that would be sufficient to justify someone who took up

---

[12] This interpretation of the appeal of contractualism derives from Kant. See "On the Common Saying: 'This May be True in Theory, but it does not Apply in Practice' " [1793], in *Kant's Political Writings*, ed. Hans Reiss and trans. H. B. Nisbet (Cambridge: Cambridge University Press, 1970), pp. 77–81.

this point of view in rejecting any particular principle. Because the structure of the theory incorporates less normative content than more formal views, it is less determinate in its consequences.[13]

In this sense, complex proceduralism is a relatively informal conception. One reason for adopting such a formulation is that any theory that included sufficient constraints to resolve the main institutional problems concerning political fairness would seem excessively artificial. Another is that the more informal view facilitates a clearer presentation of the considerations relevant to various interpretations of fair participation, and it forces the resolution of conflicts among these considerations into the open, so to speak, rather than allowing them to be concealed within the structure of a more formal theory.

Complex proceduralism is not, however, without significant normative content. We stipulate that the parties have certain regulative interests, that these are higher-order interests in the sense of being controlling in matters of procedural choice, and that the parties are motivated by a desire to reach an agreement that no one who had *these* interests would have sufficient reason to reject in preference to any feasible alternative. These assumptions are clearly significant additions, for they limit the range of considerations that the parties can be imagined to bring to bear on the choice of political procedures. Later, we will consider the basis of these constraints. For the moment, the point to stress is that complex proceduralism is nonetheless an informal view in at least two respects. First, in the construction of the contract situation we do not attempt to correct for the influence of knowledge of people's natural endowments or social situation by imposing informational limitations like the "veil of ignorance."[14] It is true that the regulative interests have a similar effect but only to the extent of preventing the parties from seeking procedural advantages for themselves that conflict with these interests which all are assumed to share. Counterfactual assumptions are made about the motivation of the parties but not about their knowledge of individual circumstance and so-

[13] Scanlon, "Contractualism and Utilitarianism," pp. 123ff. See also Scanlon, "Liberty, Contract, and Contribution," in *Morals and Markets*, ed. Gerald Dworkin, Gordon Bermant, and Peter G. Brown (Washington, D.C.: Hemisphere, 1977), pp. 63–64.

[14] As in Rawls's theory. See *A Theory of Justice*, pp. 136–42; and "Kantian Constructivism in Moral Theory," *Journal of Philosophy* 77 (1980), pp. 515–72.

cial context, which is allowed to influence judgments about procedural fairness from the start. Second, no attempt is made to frame the contract situation so that the technical devices of the theory of rational choice can be brought to bear. Thus, for example, there is no claim that the interests of the parties can be represented as individual utility functions or that their reasoning can be meaningfully described as maximizing the satisfaction of these interests. Whereas the first point shows that in complex proceduralism the interests that explain agreement function as substantive constraints on the deliberations of the parties rather than as structural elements of the model itself, the second indicates that the problem of combining these interests to yield a decision on any particular issue of procedural design must be treated as a freestanding moral issue to be worked out more or less intuitively in a way that takes account of the historical circumstances in which the procedures are to operate. By leaving so much to be worked out by moral reasoning of the ordinary kind, we forbear from representing the agreement, so to speak, as the output of an axiomatic decision procedure or from claiming that the model is capable of generating by its own rules determinate decisions in the choices facing the parties.

These remarks provide answers to the first two of our questions about the contract idea—why we should interpret it so informally and why, so interpreted, its consequences should matter to us. However, the effect is to make the third question—about the normative force of contractualism—more pressing. For in view of what I have said thus far, the following objection will arise. The substantive elements of the theory—that is, the regulative interests—appear to do all of the normative work. These interests furnish the main basis for resolving disputes about procedural design; the contractualist framework seems not to contribute anything of its own. One might therefore wonder why it should not be seen as empty: a mere formality serving only to rationalize conclusions that would be fully determined by the regulative interests alone.

The answer to this objection has two parts. First, there is no need to deny that the doctrine of regulative interests has normative content. However, to grant this is not also to agree that the contract idea is empty. As a contractualist view, complex proceduralism holds that institutions should be justifiable to *each* person who comes under their sway; it should be possible to say to each person that the terms of participation are acceptable from her own point of view, given her social and historical circumstances, when this point of view is conceived as that of an equal citizen of a democratic society. As I have argued, it may be relevant, but it cannot be enough, that institutions yield outcomes that are best for society at large or that they generate decisions that accord with a technical construction of the popular will. For neither condition ensures that each citizen would have reason to accept the institutions when they are regarded from her own point of view. This would be true even if what is "best for society at large" could somehow be interpreted as a function of the regulative interests: complex proceduralism does not seek to maximize the aggregate, societywide level of satisfaction of these interests. It is true that by postulating a set of higher-order interests that motivate the choices of the parties, we restrict the bounds of possible agreement. But what is being restricted are the bounds of possible *agreement*: it is the set of procedural arrangements one could reasonably expect each of his fellow citizens to accept. There is no reason to believe that arrangements that satisfy this requirement will normally, if ever, yield the highest level of interest-satisfaction in society at large.

Second, and more basically, the regulative interests themselves stand in need of justification. Otherwise, the claim that they should be assigned a privileged position in reasoning about political fairness would seem arbitrary: we would have provided no special reason to care about them. I have said that these interests represent within the theory various elements of an ideal of democratic citizenship. But this ideal is not, so to speak, imposed on the theory from the outside; as we shall see, the theory seeks to provide an account of its appeal by connecting it with values we are prepared to accept as reasonable grounds for objecting to a procedural arrangement. The regulative interests themselves have a contractualist justification. Their prominence within the theory is not, therefore, an indication that the contractualist framework is normatively empty; indeed, it is only by accepting the framework that their prominence can be accounted for.

Regulative Interests of Citizenship

An explanation of the interests in recognition, equitable treatment, and deliberative responsibility should specify their content and show why it is reasonable to regard them as furnishing grounds for refusing to accept a procedural regime.

Imagine that citizens could meet to establish the terms of participation that their institutions should embody. We assume that the institutions are generically democratic; the question is not whether people should be entitled to participate in political decisions but how the mechanism of participation is to be arranged. What kinds of considerations would it be reasonable to take into account in assessing the alternatives?

It would be convenient if a catalog of these considerations could be exhibited as a systematic deduction from some more abstract and widely accepted conception of democratic citizenship. As no such deduction presents itself, we must proceed inductively, attempting to construct such a conception from more particularistic judgments. Thus, we might reflect on various procedural arrangements that would be widely agreed to be objectionable. We may regard such cases as *paradigmatic*[15] of procedural unfairness; they are ones about which most people's judgments converge. They might include, for example, weighted voting by race, systems of representation that favor certain minority interests (say, those of the landed gentry), unrestricted majority rule and the idea of majority tyranny, ballot access regulations that exclude popular candidates or positions from consideration, or imbalances in election campaign resources that give a decisive advantage to incumbents.

In considering each case, we should try to explain at a general level the reasons that would justify someone in objecting to the procedural arrangement in question. Any such explanation must be *constructive*. That is, we do not aim for a description of the actual basis of people's objections to the kinds of unfairness found in the paradigmatic cases; instead, we seek an account that seems maximally plausible in view of the characteristics of the case at hand, keeping in mind the desire to produce a more general conception of political fairness that coheres with the accounts that can be provided for the other cases as well. Accordingly, judgments about the reasonableness of objections to paradigmatic cases of unfairness will normally have a two-level structure. First, a weight must be

[15] The term is used this way by Ronald Dworkin: *Law's Empire* (Cambridge: Harvard University Press, 1986), p. 75.

assigned to the interest motivating the objection (the "harm"), reflecting its objective importance or urgency. By "objective" I mean, roughly, that the weight of the harm should reflect the degree of importance or urgency one could expect others in society to accord to it. It is not sufficient to rely on an agent's own subjective valuations; someone who detests being awake while the sun shines should have less weight attached to his objection to daytime voting hours than someone whose fourteen-hour-a-day job keeps him at work from dawn to dusk, even if each attaches equal subjective importance to his objection.[16] Second, the harm must be compared with the harms to other interests that might be anticipated under the feasible alternative arrangements, again taking into account their objective importance. For, clearly, supposing that everyone is moved by a desire to reach *some* agreement, it would not be reasonable to refuse to accept an institutional arrangement, even if it would do harm, if the alternatives would be even worse.

The three categories of values I have identified as regulative interests arise from reflection about paradigmatic cases of procedural unfairness. Each interest represents a type of reason that would justify someone in refusing to accept a procedural arrangement.

The interest in *recognition* involves the public status or identity that procedural roles assign to those who occupy them.[17] Political procedures define the terms on which citizens recognize each other as participants in public deliberation and choice. In the extreme case, when some people are excluded entirely from any public role (as, for example, with the wholesale denial of the franchise to blacks in the antebellum South), it has been said that those excluded "are not publicly recognized as persons at all" and might be described as "socially dead."[18] Something similar occurs when pro-

---

[16] For a more general argument that social judgments should be based on objective rather than subjective valuations, see T. M. Scanlon, "Preference and Urgency," *Journal of Philosophy* 72 (1975), pp. 655–69. On the idea of objectivity, see also Thomas Nagel, *The View from Nowhere* (New York: Oxford University Press, 1986), pp. 138–63.

[17] On procedural roles as a basis of status, see T. H. Marshall, "Citizenship and Social Class" [1949], in *Class, Citizenship, and Social Development* (Garden City, N.Y.: Doubleday, 1964), pp. 84ff.

[18] John Rawls, "Justice as Fairness: Political not Metaphysical," *Philosophy & Public Affairs* 14 (1985), p. 243. For the idea of "social death," see Orlando Patterson, *Slavery and Social Death* (Cambridge: Harvard University Press, 1982).

cedural roles are assigned in a way that conveys social acceptance of a belief in the inferiority or lesser merit of one group as distinct from others—as, for example, with racially weighted voting or efforts to dilute the votes of racial minorities through the use of gerrymandering techniques. Those singled out as less worthy are demeaned and insulted; they are encouraged to feel that patterns of disrespect that exist in society at large enjoy official sanction. It would be reasonable for anyone to object to procedural arrangements that had this effect. This is not simply because, from a subjective point of view, it is unpleasant or painful to be assigned a demeaning role in public procedures, although this is certainly true. The objection has a more objective foundation—not because it rests on some transcendent or immutable standard of value, but rather because it is a fixed point in a democratic culture that public institutions should not establish or reinforce the perception that some people's interests deserve less respect or concern than those of others simply in virtue of their membership in one rather than another social or ascriptive group. The political roles defined by democratic institutions should convey a communal acknowledgment of equal individual worth.[19]

Because it bears so directly on the definition of the procedural roles in which people participate in public decisions, the interest in recognition corresponds to the point of view of citizens as "makers." The interest in *equitable treatment* corresponds instead to that of citizens as "matter." The basic idea is that citizens might reasonably refuse to accept institutions under which it was predictable that their actual interests—that is, the satisfaction of their needs and the success of their projects—would be unfairly placed in jeopardy, at least if there were alternatives that would avoid these effects without imposing even worse risks on others. Normally we rely on democratic mechanisms themselves to guard against the oppressive use of state power; however, recognizing that these may not always be sufficient, we are prepared to supplement them with further constraints such as a bill of rights, judicial review, and the

[19] For the idea of communal acknowledgement of individual worth, see Jack Lively, *Democracy* (Oxford: Basil Blackwell, 1975), pp. 134–35. The connection between institutional roles and self-respect is clearest in Rousseau. *The Social Contract* [1762], in *The Social Contract and Discourses*, trans. G.D.H. Cole (London: J. M. Dent, 1973), bk. 1, chaps. 8–9; bk. 2, chaps. 2–3.

like. Without these further protections, democratic forms might reasonably be seen as so dangerous as to be unacceptable.

The idea of equitable treatment is difficult to render more precisely, primarily because it is uncertain how the notion of an interest's being "unfairly placed in jeopardy" should be interpreted. It seems clear that procedural interpretations will not suffice; one ought not to say, for example, that a person's interests are unfairly jeopardized when institutions accord the person less than an equal share in power or influence over the relevant class of decisions. This follows from our earlier observations about power: many manipulable factors can affect a person's prospects in a procedural regime; the extent of his power is only one (and ordinarily not the most important) of these. As the example of entrenched minorities illustrates, one's interests might be placed in great jeopardy even when power is equal. The interest in equitable treatment needs a more substantive interpretation.

One possibility is to identify equitable treatment with the principle that political decisions should aim to generate equal increments of preference- or interest-satisfaction. However, here we face a familiar difficulty: whereas any such principle must presuppose that the *ex ante* distribution was morally satisfactory, as a general matter we have no reason to believe this. People would not necessarily be justified in objecting to participatory mechanisms that lead to unequal increments in preference- or interest-satisfaction if the inequalities worked to the benefit of those whose most urgent needs would otherwise be placed in jeopardy. Suppose, for example, that a choice was to be made between two systems of legislative representation, each of which guaranteed everyone equal procedural opportunities to influence the choice of representatives. If those with the greater or more urgent needs would tend to do better in one system than in the alternative, those who would fare worse in that system could not reasonably complain simply because another system would be better for them.[20] Since what is at issue is the contribution of particular decisions to each person's global situation rather than the distributive characteristics of individual political decisions viewed in isolation, there seems to be no alternative to

[20] I discuss issues about the structure of representation at greater length in chapter 7.

relying on substantive views concerning social justice to render a complete account.[21] Political decisions could then be said to satisfy the interest in equitable treatment when, over time, they promote (or do not systematically detract from) a distribution that accords with the requirements of justice, which are themselves to be worked out from a point of view in which each person's prospects are taken equally into account.

It may be surprising that a theory of political fairness should incorporate a concern for the substantive characteristics of political outcomes. For people's conceptions of equity differ; if the present view were widely accepted, then disagreement about the meaning of political fairness would be endemic. But this hardly seems consistent with the notion that a main function of the idea of fairness is to regulate the social processes through which substantive disagreements are adjudicated, or at least compromised.

In response, there are two points. First, it is no misrepresentation of our pre-theoretical views about political fairness to hold that result-oriented considerations sometimes play a role. Consider, for example, the traditional democratic concern about the dangers of majority tyranny and the protection of minority rights.[22] The idea that fair institutions should contain safeguards against the oppressive use of state power by popular majorities would be incomprehensible unless the concept of oppression had some substantive content. Moreover, as a matter of descriptive accuracy, it does not seem wrong to characterize some procedural disputes as reflections of underlying disagreements about the nature of the outcomes that procedures should produce.[23] The account I have offered recognizes this by relativizing the requirements of fairness to underlying views about acceptable results. (To say this is not *also* to say that the underlying disagreements are incapable of principled resolution.)

Second, the direction of political decisions is determined by a great variety of factors, among which the structure of the system of

[21] As William Nelson argues. See *On Justifying Democracy* (London: Routledge & Kegan Paul, 1980), chap. 6.

[22] See, e.g., Giovanni Sartori, *The Theory of Democracy Revisited* (Chatham, N.J.: Chatham House, 1987), vol. 1, pp. 131–37, esp. the references to Madison, Jefferson, and Tocqueville.

[23] We will consider some examples in part 2 in connection with legislative districting and political finance.

political participation plays at best a subordinate role. It is unrealistic to think that, by a series of fine manipulations of this structure, small improvements in the distributive characteristics of political outcomes could often be guaranteed. Hence, the interest in equitable treatment is likely to operate more selectively and at a greater remove. It will justify a refusal to accept an institutional scheme mainly when it seems likely that the scheme will give rise to (or perpetuate) serious and recurring injustices and when there is an alternative available that would be less likely to do so without introducing countervailing harms of other kinds. Thus, in the context of reasoning about political procedures, the interest in equitable treatment will normally appear as an interest in safeguarding one's urgent or vital interests in the face of the threat that they might be systematically subordinated to the competing but less urgent claims of others. While there may be considerable disagreement in society about conceptions of social justice and the common good, it seems likely that the prospects of convergence are greatest in connection with the most vital of human interests. So, although the chances that substantive disagreement will generate procedural controversy cannot be ruled out, they need not pose too great a difficulty.

Now the central virtue of democratic forms is that, in the presence of a suitable social background, they provide the most reliable means of reaching substantively just political outcomes consistently with the public recognition of the equal worth or status of each citizen.[24] Democratic forms succeed in achieving this aim, when they succeed at all, less because they aggregate existing preferences efficiently than because they foster a process of public reflection in which citizens can form political views in full awareness of the grounds as well as the content of the (possibly competing) concerns of others.[25] It is a mistake to conceive democracy as a crude hydraulic device, moving society in the direction of the

---

[24] This is a comparative judgment; it need not presuppose any very optimistic non-comparative view about the tendency of democratic institutions to produce just outcomes.

[25] As Pericles famously (if, perhaps, self-servingly) put it, ". . . instead of looking on discussion as a stumbling-block in the way of action, we think it an indispensable preliminary to any wise action at all. . . ." Thucydides, *The Peloponnesian War*, trans. John H. Finley, Jr. (New York: Modern Library, 1951), II.40, p. 105.

greater power. Instead, we must understand it as a deliberative mechanism that frames the formation and revision of individual political judgments in a way likely to elicit outcomes that treat everyone's interests equitably. The characteristics of preference-aggregating devices are clearly significant for an assessment of the fairness of the system as a whole, but they should be seen as parts of a larger deliberative framework.

These observations illustrate the significance of the third regulative interest, in *deliberative responsibility*: democratic institutions should embody a common (and commonly acknowledged) commitment to the resolution of political issues on the basis of public deliberation that is adequately informed, open to the expression of a wide range of competing views, and carried out under conditions in which these views can be responsibly assessed. This is important for reasons connected with both of the points of view characteristic of citizenship. Citizens conceived as participants in public decisions (Hobbes's "makers") will wish to regard their judgments as the most reasonable ones possible under the circumstances; such judgments should be formed in light of the relevant facts and should be defensible in the face of the conflicting views held by others in the community. If individual judgment could not be seen as justifiable in this way, it would be indistinguishable from prejudice; and this should be intolerable for anyone who takes seriously her responsibility for her own beliefs. On the other hand, for citizens conceived as the objects of public policy (its "matter"), the awareness that institutions encourage responsible deliberation is a necessary basis of confidence in the integrity of political decisions and, indeed, of the system of participation itself. Without this, the supposed tendency of democratic mechanisms to elicit equitable outcomes would be no more than a pious hope, and an important ground of the stability of democratic regimes would be lacking.

The interest in deliberative responsibility has two elements, which may be in conflict. The first is openness: deliberation should not be constrained by the exclusion of positions that would gain substantial support if they were sufficiently exposed to public scrutiny.[26] Thus, someone might reasonably object if widely supported

---

[26] This is a preliminary formulation of a complicated idea. For a further discussion, see chapter 8.

candidates or positions were excluded from the political arena by such mechanisms as restrictive ballot access regulations or a distribution of campaign resources that gave some parties or positions a decisive advantage in access to the principal fora of public debate. Such an objection would be reasonable partly because exclusionary provisions could prevent people from representing their own interests in public deliberation; but even if this were not the case, exclusion of positions widely held by others would be objectionable because it would suppress information and points of view that would be essential for all citizens in reaching responsible judgments about the public good. The other element involves the quality of the deliberative process itself: the conditions of public deliberation should be favorable to the thoughtful consideration and comparative assessment of all of the positions represented. Citizens should be enabled to reach political judgments on the basis of an adequately informed and reflective comparison of the merits of the contending positions. Only then will they have reason to conduct themselves as cooperating members of a public deliberative enterprise, to exercise the capacities for judgment and choice in the public realm, and to regard others as similarly equipped and motivated.

Both elements are part of the nature of responsible deliberation. The potential for conflict arises from the fact that the conditions of public deliberation may be maximally favorable to the thoughtful assessment of the alternatives only if the number of alternatives to be considered is not too large. There is no guarantee that the range of alternatives that elicit nontrivial numbers of adherents will always fall within this limit. The interest in seeing a wide range of positions represented argues for openness, but the interest in conditions of public deliberation in which political judgments can be adequately informed and reflective argues, at least under some circumstances, for constraint. It is not easy to generalize about how such conflicts are most appropriately to be reconciled. In practice, as we shall see, any reconciliation will be heavily influenced by local considerations concerning the context in which the conflict arises and the impact that one or another way of resolving it seems likely to have on satisfaction of the other regulative interests. However such conflicts are resolved (and they may of course not arise at all), the interest in deliberative responsibility clearly expresses an important requirement on the choice of institutions for political participation and one which is distinct from those embodied in the other regulative interests.

The interests I have identified function within the theory as the criteria by which political institutions and procedures are to be assessed when they are regarded from each person's point of view. Although it would be surprising if things were otherwise, there is no claim that all citizens, in fact, conceive themselves as having these interests or are motivated to accord them a controlling position in actual political deliberation. This fact gives rise to an objection we have already anticipated: why not regard the regulative interests as no more than an arbitrary selection from the much wider range of values reflected in people's actual aims and preferences? And why endow them with a higher-order status, so that they eclipse people's more particularistic concerns in informing judgments about procedural design?

The answer is that these interests give theoretical expression to certain aspects of a normative conception of democratic citizenship, which is implicit in our ordinary judgments about political fairness and which we are prepared to accept as determining in matters of procedural choice. The list of regulative interests, and their interpretations, is derived from a consideration of cases of procedural unfairness that we may regard as paradigmatic. The diversity of the interests reflects the complexity of the status of membership in a democratic society, and the desire to realize this status on terms compatible with a similar realization by everyone else is taken to be the fundamental motivation for concern about procedural fairness. If the distinctive egalitarianism of the view is found in its contractualist framework, its distinctive idealism lies in this motivational aspect.

Finally, as I have suggested, a choice among institutions must rest on a consideration of how the alternatives affect all three kinds of interests. However, there is no reason to believe that the regulative interests will always coincide; indeed, it would be surprising if they did not occasionally conflict. A possible response would be to deny that, under the circumstances, *any* institutions could be fair. Perhaps there are cases so extreme that this is what we must say. However, this need not always be true: a degree of sacrifice in one interest may be a reasonable expectation, particularly when it is made up by gains in another. Because the regulative interests are irreducibly plural, it is unlikely that any systematic mechanism can be set forth for reconciling conflicts; one is forced to rely on an intuitive balancing of competing values. This is not an insuperable difficulty, particularly when the range of interests that enter at the foundational level is restricted and the grounds of their importance are reasonably clear. In part 2, I shall illustrate this by considering how complex proceduralism applies to several controversial problems of institutional design. Here, I note a related point. One must recall that we are driven to adopt a theory like complex proceduralism by a recognition of the diversity of the considerations it seems natural to take into account in assessing political institutions. It is neglect of some of these, and excessive concentration on others, that gives rise to the critical defects of more conventional theories of political equality. The need to rely on intuitive comparisons of conflicting and irreducible interests may seem less than satisfactory from a theoretical point of view, but it is an unavoidable reflection in democratic theory of the variety of ways in which political institutions touch people's lives.

CONTRASTS WITH OTHER VIEWS

Complex proceduralism differs from the views discussed in earlier chapters in several respects. First, unlike best result and popular will theories, the form of proceduralism I have sketched is not in any straightforward sense instrumentalist. Fair terms of participation are not conceived as those most likely to succeed at producing outcomes that strike some independently identified target, whether this is described in terms of the substantive characteristics of desirable political decisions or the relationship of the decisions actually taken to the political preferences held by the people. Of course, both types of concerns may play a role in complex proceduralism, but this role is neither definitive nor morally basic; there are always further questions about why a given kind of outcome-oriented concern should matter and how it should be balanced against the other regulative concerns with which it may conflict.

Moreover, as I have emphasized, there is no a priori reason to assume that these interests will always be complementary, and it may be necessary to balance them against one another. Now the weights it would be appropriate to assign to these interests when they conflict may depend in part on a society's historical circumstances. For example, the interest in protecting against the political effects of racial bigotry and prejudice will be more weighty where its legacy is more pronounced. Hence, the theory contains some residual indeterminacy. Of course, the application of any abstract conception of political fairness will require some reference to the circumstances of the society in question. What is different about complex proceduralism is where, within the theory, historical considerations play a role: here they may enter at the foundational level of the theory—in judgments about appropriate weights for the regulative interests—as well as at the level of application. In other words, the theory's conception of fairness may itself remain partially indeterminate until the context of its application is taken into account. This does not seem to me to be objectionable; in fact, it might be seen as a virtue of a theory of political equality that it takes account of historical considerations in a way that more faithfully represents their actual effects on intuitive judgments about fair participation.

Third, this theory is primarily negative. It does not attempt to describe ideal conditions that institutions should strive to satisfy; rather, it seeks an account of the forms of unfairness that they should strive to avoid. (Of course, it need not follow that considerations of fairness *operate* only negatively, for example, by ruling out institutions with this or that objectionable feature; sometimes the avoidance of unfairness requires institutional provisions that might be characterized as affirmative.) I believe this feature of the theory is consistent with the characteristic role of political equality in controversy about the structure of democratic institutions: it is invoked more often to support criticism of the established order than as a description of a constructive ideal. Moreover, I believe that it accords with our intuitions about a variety of questions of policy: when a particular procedure is uncontroversially unfair, it is frequently possible to give an account of the reasons for the unfairness without committing oneself to a view about the nature of a uniquely preferable alternative.

This points to a fourth contrast to other theories.[27] According to

---

[27] I am grateful to Thomas Scanlon for pointing this out.

at least the more familiar versions of the best result and popular will theories, there is always a uniquely best solution (or, in the case of indifference, class of solutions) to the problem of social choice. Thus, the fact that under certain circumstances a decision procedure operating on the same utility or preference information might produce either of two (or more) inconsistent outcomes must be deeply embarrassing: it shows either that there is some deficiency in the theory or that under those circumstances the ideal of fair participation is unattainable.[28] As we noted earlier, some such reasoning explains the unease with which the Arrow result is viewed in the theory of social choice. A consequence of the negative character of complex proceduralism is that its requirements may be satisfied in more than one way; several institutional structures, each perhaps likely to have different or even inconsistent political results, may be equally fair. But this need not be cause for concern. Because institutions are not evaluated simply with respect to the outcomes they are likely to produce, it is no occasion for unease, for example, that institutions that are equally fair according to the theory might generate inconsistent outcomes given identical information about people's preferences. This is not to say that it will never be occasion for concern *within* the theory: if, for example, considerations of stability indicate that institutions should normally produce outcomes that bear a predictable relationship to the political preferences in society, then the possibility that a particular decision procedure may give rise to inconsistency will count against that procedure. It will be one among many factors to be taken into account in comparing that procedure with the feasible alternatives. Moreover, the fact that several institutional configurations may be equally fair does not mean that they will be equally desirable overall; for example, considerations relevant to the vitality of political culture might incline toward one or another alternative. What complex proceduralism requires is that these considerations operate within the range of equally fair alternatives. It is no reason for embarrassment that there may be more than one of these.

[28] The latter view is advanced in William Riker, *Liberalism Against Populism* (San Francisco: W. H. Freeman, 1982), chap. 4 and pp. 233–41.

PART TWO

Applications

CHAPTER SIX

Proportional Representation

A theory of political equality should satisfy two desiderata, one theoretical and the other practical. It should provide a persuasive philosophical interpretation of the ideal of democratic equality, and it should be capable of illuminating controversial matters of institutional design and reform. Thus far we have been concerned with the first point; I turn now to the second. We shall consider several issues concerning the structural features that fair democratic institutions should possess, including problems about the system of legislative representation, the composition of the political agenda, and the distribution of the financial resources needed for effective participation in electoral politics. I hope to show that complex proceduralism is more successful than its rivals in characterizing the central normative questions that arise with respect to each of these problems. *Inter alia*, we shall see how the theory brings order to the unsystematic, and frequently conflicting, conceptions of political equality found in more specialized studies of these problems.

The problem of fair legislative representation, which we take up in this and the next chapter, is surely the leading issue of institutional design in any modern democratic state. I begin with the question whether considerations of political fairness provide a general argument for proportional representation (PR) as against systems based on single-member territorial constituencies. This requires an explanation, since proportional representation is not a subject of much practical controversy, or even interest, in the United States today; certainly there is no significant chance of its being adopted in the foreseeable future, either at the national level or in most of the states.[1] The explanation has two parts.

---

[1] In this respect the U.S. is an anomaly. In most industrial democracies that have not come under British influence, and in some that have, some form of PR is prac-

First, many people believe that a fully realized system of proportional representation would be more faithful to the ideal of political equality than any system of district representation. For example, as Mill remarked, "In a *really equal* democracy every or any section would be represented, not disproportionately, but proportionately. A majority of the electors would always have a majority of the representatives, but a minority of the electors would always have a minority of the representatives. Man for man they would be as fully represented as the majority."[2] Similar views are held even by some who oppose proportional representation, all things considered; while accepting that PR is the most fully egalitarian method of representation, they may think that it imposes dangerous risks of political instability or discontinuity of policy and that in view of these risks a final judgment must rest on a compromise between equality and the competing values of stability and continuity.[3] The fact that PR is thought to be connected especially closely with an ideal of political equality provides a convenient means of exploring how equality bears on the choice among representation systems generally.

The second reason for beginning with proportional representation is that if considerations of equality favor it, then some further problems about institutional design might be settled as well, including those concerning "qualitative" fairness in representation and access to the ballot. When fully realized, PR automatically achieves representation of groups in proportion to their size (at least if groups vote their interests), and it guarantees access to the ballot for all willing and qualified candidates. Even if one's final judgment is that a dif-

---

ticed. In the U.K. itself, where PR has never been adopted, it has nevertheless figured prominently in several generations of election reform movements. For the U.K. case, see Vernon Bogdanor, *The People and the Party System* (Cambridge: Cambridge University Press, 1981).

[2] *Considerations on Representative Government* [1861], chap. 7, in *Collected Works*, vol. 19, ed. J. M. Robson (Toronto: University of Toronto Press, 1977), p. 449 (emphasis added). Proportional representation is endorsed, apparently for similar reasons, by Joshua Cohen and Joel Rogers in *On Democracy* (Harmondsworth, Middlesex: Penguin Books, 1983), pp. 156–57. See also Robert Dixon, "Representation Values and Reapportionment Practice," in *Nomos X: Representation*, ed. J. Roland Pennock and John W. Chapman (New York: Atherton, 1968), p. 178.

[3] For such a view, see Giovanni Sartori, *The Theory of Democracy Revisited* (Chatham, N.J.: Chatham House, 1987), vol. 1, p. 54.

ferent system of representation would be preferable, or if one favors PR on the merits but thinks there is no realistic hope of attaining it, the ideal of PR may still guide efforts to solve these further problems.[4]

I will argue that these beliefs are incorrect: considerations of political equality or fairness do not necessarily require adoption of proportional representation. In the general case, one would not be justified in refusing to accept a system of representation *simply* because it is not PR. Representation by single-member territorial districts may satisfy the requirements of fairness, leaving issues involving the representation of groups and access to the ballot to be resolved separately. We need not deny that PR might be the most desirable mechanism for the election of legislators under various kinds of historical circumstances or even that, under those circumstances, it might be a requirement of political fairness. However, such cases would be special in the sense that the prevailing circumstances render it unlikely that any feasible alternative system would be equally fair. Because we may not assume that circumstances of this kind always or usually prevail, no general argument that considerations of fairness require adoption of PR can succeed.

VARIETIES OF REPRESENTATION SYSTEMS

In the discussion that follows, I shall contrast one type of proportional representation with one type of representation by territorial district. Both need preliminary comment.

Beginning with proportional representation, it is important to stress that there are several forms and that both their principles of construction and their operational characteristics can differ significantly from one another. The system proposed by Thomas Hare and popularized by Mill is perhaps the most familiar.[5] The Hare system

---

[4] For one such effort, see John R. Low-Beer, "The Constitutional Imperative of Proportional Representation" [Note], *Yale Law Journal* 94 (1984), pp. 163–88.

[5] Thomas Hare, *The Election of Representatives: Parliamentary and Municipal*, 4th ed. (London: Longmans, Green, Reader, and Dyer, 1873). Hare was not the first to conceive of such a system. Its main elements were worked out in 1821 by Thomas Wright Hill (Enid Lakeman, *Power to Elect: The Case for Proportional Representation* [London: Heinemann, 1982], p. 46). A similar system was proposed in the U.S.

is distinguished by its use of the single transferable vote (STV), a form of preferential voting with multimember constituencies. (In the version advanced by Hare, the nation was, in effect, one constituency, as voters could choose candidates regardless of their home district; but permutations of the system can be imagined with multiple multimember territorial constituencies.) The ballot invites the voter to rank-order her preferences. Ballots are tallied according to a procedure aimed at ensuring that each successful candidate will have been elected by the same number of affirmative votes and that every ballot (if it contains sufficiently many preferences) will contribute to the election of one candidate.[6]

Hare called this system "personal representation," and the phrase serves well to emphasize its distinctive individualism. Under its rules, constituencies are self-defining, or in Hare's term, "voluntary."[7] Since, under the tallying procedure, nearly every vote is ultimately counted in favor of a successful candidate, each such candidate may be said to be the unanimous choice of (and thus, to represent) those whose affirmative votes contributed to his election. Moreover, because votes are cast preferentially for individual candidates rather than categorically for parties or slates, the system

---

by Thomas Gilpin in "On the Representation of Minorities of Electors" (Philadelphia: American Philosophical Society, 1844), reprinted in part in C. G. Hoag and G. H. Hallett, Jr., *Proportional Representation* (New York: Macmillan, 1926), pp. 457–64.

[6] The details are complex; here is a rough summary. First, the top-ranked candidate on each ballot is credited with one vote. Those candidates who attain a sufficient number of votes (a quota expressed as a proportion of all ballots cast) are declared elected. (The formula most often used is the "Droop quota": to be elected, a candidate must win a number of votes equal to $[b/(s + 1)] + 1$, where b is the total number of valid ballots cast and s is the number of seats to be filled.) If all seats are filled, the process terminates. If not, the surplus votes of the successful candidates (those in excess of the quota) are transferred to the next-ranked candidate, the unsuccessful candidate with the lowest number of votes is eliminated, and his votes are transferred to the next-ranking candidate who is still in the running. Candidates who have now attained a quota are declared elected, and the process is repeated until all seats are filled. There is an accessible description, including refinements not considered by Hare, in Michael Dummett, *Voting Procedures* (Oxford: Clarendon Press, 1984), pp. 268–73.

[7] Hare, *The Election of Representatives*, p. 23. In contrast, Bagehot referred to territorial constituencies as "compulsory." *The English Constitution*, 2d ed. [1871] (London: Oxford University Press, 1928), p. 133.

enables individual voters, in their choice of candidates and order of preferences, to form coalitions of opinion or interest and to indicate their views regarding the relative significance of various issues that may come before the legislature. There is no need for primary elections to narrow the field of intending candidates to those whose names are to appear on the final list nor for party organizations to define in advance the contending coalitions and policy programs among which voters are allowed to choose. The legislature will mirror the population in the sense that each voter will be represented by a delegate of her choice, and the distribution of opinion in the legislature will reflect that found in the electorate at large, undistorted by filtration devices like primaries or the political judgments of party elites.[8]

Contrast this with forms of proportional representation employing the system of party lists. Voters cast ballots for parties rather than for individual candidates, and seats are allocated to the candidates listed (or nominated) by the respective parties in proportion to their shares of the total vote. (A minimum share, or threshold, is sometimes imposed, below which a party is denied representation altogether.) The main idea is to transfer the functions of selecting candidates, composing platforms, and forming coalitions from the voters themselves (as under STV) to party organizations. Because voters vote for parties rather than for candidates, it cannot be said that each member has a distinct constituency or that each voter is represented by a member of her own choice. More importantly, perhaps, the party list system reduces the capacity of individual voters

---

[8] Indeed, as a historical matter, it would not be misleading to describe early advocates of PR as having been motivated in large part by the desire to reduce, or even to eliminate, the political influence of elite-dominated mass parties. See, for example, Simon Sterne, *On Representative Government and Personal Representation* (Philadelphia: J. B. Lippincott, 1871), pp. 58–59; Hoag and Hallett, *Proportional Representation*, pp. 98–102; and M. Ostrogorski, *Democracy and the Organization of Political Parties*, trans. F. Clarke (New York: Macmillan, 1902), vol. 1, pp. 104–13; vol. 2, pp. 536–37, 701–9. Ostrogorski frankly hoped that under PR "electors will no longer be forced to choose between the two candidatures, both equally odious" and that parties would be reduced to "simple political groups within the nation" (vol. 2, p. 536). Although experience with STV systems is extremely limited, it does not appear that this hope has been borne out. Vernon Bogdanor, "Introduction," in *Democracy and Elections: Electoral Systems and Their Political Consequences*, ed. Vernon Bogdanor and David Butler (Cambridge: Cambridge University Press, 1983), p. 10.

to employ the ballot to register their views regarding the relative significance of the issues before the legislature; instead, they must choose among the limited range of positions set forth in party programs. Thus, whereas STV aims at the proportional representation of persons, the list system is more accurately said to aim at the proportional representation of parties. It is not individualistic in the same way as STV.

As a consequence of these differences, it cannot be assumed a priori that any list system employing a form of preferential voting or a proportional method of seat allocation will yield a proportional relationship of seats to the partisan division of the popular vote. In fact, some familiar variations of list PR may actually be less faithful to the proportionality principle than some district systems.[9]

Primarily for these reasons, proportional representation with the single transferable vote (or some other procedure enabling voters to indicate which candidates are acceptable to them)[10] appears to be the form in which the underlying egalitarian impulse is best realized.[11] Accordingly, in what follows I shall concentrate on proportional representation substantially in the form in which Hare imagined it. (This does not imply a criticism of list PR; I mean only to suggest that considerations of egalitarian principle of the sort I wish to take up are more clearly applicable to personal representation. List PR, where it is appropriate at all, will most likely be supported by more instrumental and strategic considerations.)

The system of representation by territorial districts (*district representation*) is less well defined and is open to a wider range of variation. In what I shall call its simplest form it employs single-member districts and the "first-past-the-post" voting system: ballots permit voters to indicate only their first preferences among the

[9] Douglas W. Rae, *The Political Consequences of Electoral Laws*, rev. ed. (New Haven: Yale University Press, 1971), esp. chap. 9; Bogdanor, "Conclusion: Electoral Systems and Party Systems," in *Democracy and Elections*, pp. 247–51; and the papers collected in *Choosing an Election System*, ed. Arend Lijphart and Bernard Grofman (New York: Praeger, 1984). For an analysis, see Scott L. Feld and Bernard Grofman, "On the Possibility of Faithfully Representative Committees," *American Political Science Review* 80 (1986), esp. pp. 865–66.

[10] Such as approval voting. See Steven J. Brams and Peter C. Fishburn, *Approval Voting* (Boston: Birkhauser, 1983), esp. pp. 143–46, for the contrast with STV.

[11] As Lakeman argues. *Power to Elect*, chaps. 4–5, pp. 54–103.

candidates listed, and the winner is selected by a plurality rule. In elections where there are more than two candidates, this clearly means that the victorious candidate might be elected with less than an absolute majority of the votes. Even when there are only two candidates in each district, and assuming that each is the nominee of one of two national parties, it means that the victorious *party* (the one winning a majority of seats) might have won less than a majority of the total number of votes cast in all districts. From the point of view of the individual voter, it means that a vote may turn out to have been "wasted" by having been cast for a candidate who would have been successful anyway; not every vote counts in the sense of contributing to the election of a successful candidate.

These possibilities—none of which can arise with PR—are inherent in district systems; however, the likelihood that they will actually occur will be significantly affected by three contingent features of these systems that might be varied without abandoning the territorial basis of constituencies. These are the plurality decision rule, the system of ballot access, and the method of composing constituencies. For example, if the plurality rule were replaced with preferential or approval voting, then where there are more than two candidates the chances of one of them attaining an absolute majority of affirmative votes (though not, of course, of first preferences) would be increased. If ballot access were restricted to the nominees of two recognized parties, then the candidate selection and coalition formation functions would be relegated to internal party processes and primary elections, and the possibility of a nonmajority winner at the final stage would be completely eliminated. If the geographical distribution of party strength were taken into account in drawing the boundaries of constituencies, the discrepancy between the winning party's share of the total vote and its share of seats in the legislature could be minimized (just as, with gerrymandering of the traditional kind, it could be maximized).[12] These contingencies must be kept in mind in assessing systems of district representation.

As I suggested earlier, much of the dispute about the merits of proportional versus district systems has historically involved the relative weight to be given to the presumably greater fairness of pro-

---

[12] The last point is discussed further in chapter 7.

portional representation, on the one hand, and to certain alleged operational deficiencies, on the other. Thus, advocates of district systems have argued that proportional representation tends to be
associated with a proliferation of increasingly fragmented political
parties, which results in an absence of stable majorities in the legislature and, in parliamentary systems, in frequent changes of government. District systems, by contrast, are said to favor stable two-
party competition, to discourage the emergence of minor parties
and (owing to the tendency of district systems to transform popular
pluralities into legislative majorities) to promote more responsive
government.[13] Without pursuing these matters in detail, it can
safely be said that empirical investigation has shown both points to
be overdrawn. Historical, cultural, and social factors appear to be
more important than electoral laws in determining the nature of the
party system likely to develop in any particular society. These factors also appear to be more important determinants of the responsiveness of governments with district representation.[14] Thus, for
example, district systems are likely to be less stable, and to accommodate minority interests less successfully, in societies marked by
pronounced and overlapping ideological, class, and ethnic divisions
than in societies in which these divisions are more muted and
crosscutting.[15]

[13] The leading source for both points is Maurice Duverger, *Political Parties*, trans.
Barbara and Robert North (London: Methuen, 1954), esp. pp. 245–55, 328–37. See
also Duncan Black, *The Theory of Committees and Elections* (Cambridge: Cambridge University Press, 1958), pp. 81ff; and William H. Riker, "The Two-party System and Duverger's Law," *American Political Science Review* 76 (1983), pp. 753–66,
and the sources cited there. The argument that district representation with the plurality rule promotes more responsive government is found in J. A. Chandler, "The
Plurality Vote: A Reappraisal," *Political Studies* 30 (1982), pp. 87–94.

[14] For a review of the evidence, see Riker, "The Two-party System and Duverger's
Law." See also Michael Taylor and V. M. Herman, "Party Systems and Government
Stability," *American Political Science Review* 65 (1971), pp. 28–37; and the essays
in *Democracy and Elections*, ed. Bogdanor and Butler, which are summarized in Bogdanor's "Conclusion: Electoral Systems and Party Systems," pp. 247–62. The most
comprehensive statement of the argument that the nature of the party system is
mainly determined by the underlying social structure is in Seymour Martin Lipset
and Stein Rokkan, "Cleavage Structures, Party Systems and Voter Alignments: An
Introduction," in *Party Systems and Voter Alignments*, ed. Lipset and Rokkan (New
York: Free Press, 1967), pp. 1–64; also see Stein Rokkan, *Citizens, Elections, Parties*
(New York: David McKay, 1970).

[15] Bogdanor, "Conclusion: Electoral Systems and Party Systems," in *Democracy*

Another way that the structure of a representation system might affect political stability is through its effects on the characteristics of political parties and of party competition. Thus, it has been argued that proportional representation creates incentives for ideological posturing among parties and candidates that produces both a greater need for parliamentary compromise and greater obstacles to it. This dynamic, moreover, is independent of the supposed tendency toward party fragmentation. District systems, which lack these incentives, are thought to encourage compromise and moderation. On the other hand, where there are deep or enduring conflicts of interest in society, these systems are more likely to exclude them from the arena of legislative debate, substituting issues of more particularistic or local concern.[16]

Proportional representation (with either the single transferable vote or party lists) and district representation are hardly the only alternatives. There are also various hybrid forms, including, for example, systems with small multimember districts each of which operates according to the proportionality principle,[17] multistage systems employing a second ballot when the first fails to produce a majority winner, and "additional member" systems in which part of the legislature is elected from single-member constituencies and part from party lists, with a provision ensuring overall proportionality between the partisan division of the vote and the allocation of seats. In view of the diversity of possibilities and the empirical uncertainties concerning the interaction of electoral laws and social structure in determining the behavior of any particular system, it may be that the simple distinction between proportional and district representation is not the most illuminating way to classify representation systems, particularly for the purposes of empirical research. Nevertheless, it is a fundamental question of democratic

---

and Elections, pp. 251–52. It is worth noting that list-PR, which is *not* our subject here, is not generally vulnerable to charges of instability like those that apply to the Hare system. For a discussion, see Ronald Rogowski, "Trade and the Variety of Democratic Institutions," *International Organization* 41 (1987), pp. 209–12, and the references cited there.

[16] Richard S. Katz, *A Theory of Parties and Electoral Systems* (Baltimore: Johns Hopkins University Press, 1980), pp. 120–22.

[17] For this idea, see Rein Taagepera, "The Effect of District Magnitude and Properties of Two-Seat Districts," in *Choosing an Electoral System*, ed. Lijphart and Grofman, pp. 91–102.

theory whether political equality compels adherence to the proportionality principle, and the comparison of the Hare system with district representation in its simplest form frames this question in the clearest possible way.

POLITICAL EQUALITY AND
PROPORTIONAL REPRESENTATION

To vindicate the claim that considerations of equality favor proportional representation, two premises must be made good: first, that proportional representation treats people equally in a sense that district representation does not; second, that there are significant reasons to take an interest in equality in this sense.

The main difference we have observed between PR and district systems is that under proportional representation constituencies are "voluntary" rather than "compulsory." What is the importance of this? Suppose we regard an election system as a bargaining game in which voters try to form coalitions of sufficient size to affect the membership of the legislature. We should not say that the aim is to elect the candidate of one's choice: if one's first preference is not supported by sufficiently many others, this aim will be disappointed. Rather, the aim is to become a member of a coalition large enough to control the allocation of a seat. Now, the fact that proportional representation leaves voters free to choose their constituencies means that each voter is in a position to vote in the way that maximizes his chances of becoming a member of such a coalition. Moreover, these chances will be equal, or as nearly so as possible.[18] Clearly, this will not normally be true in district representation; since it employs a winner-take-all decision rule and denies voters the opportunity to form constituencies through voluntary bargaining, it will concentrate power in the hands of a majority or plurality and exclude electoral minorities within districts from a share in control over the membership of the legislature. Thus, the traditional argument in favor of proportional representation—that it re-

[18] I add the qualifier because, strictly speaking, *everyone* may not have an equal chance of voting for a winner. Even in a perfectly constructed scheme of proportional representation a voter might be unlucky enough to vote only for candidates who turn out to accumulate fewer votes than the quota required for election.

spects the principle of free association in the composition of constituencies—can be seen to express a distinctive conception of
political equality.[19] Because it affords every voter an equal share of
control over legislative seats, proportional representation treats voters equally in a way that district representation does not.

However, the idea of a "share in control" is vague, and the point
might better be expressed in terms of the distinction between
"power" and "prospects of success" introduced in chapter 1. Assuming that in each type of system, each voter is entitled to cast
one vote, and that, in the district system, districts are of equal size
and return one member each to the legislature, both systems will
satisfy equal power: each voter's procedural opportunities enable
her to overcome the same amount of resistance as any other voter.
However, only proportional representation satisfies equal prospects
of success as well: unlike district representation, it confers on
nearly every voter an equal chance of voting for a winning candidate, regardless of the distribution of preferences in the electorate.
This is the sense in which PR might be thought to embody a special
kind of fairness.

Are equal prospects of success a feature whose absence would justify someone in refusing to accept a system of representation? Suppose we consider this question in connection with the regulative
interests in recognition, equitable treatment, and deliberative responsibility. Beginning with the interest in recognition, not much
appears to be gained by ensuring that each voter has an equal prospect of voting for a winning candidate. Assuming that equal power
is already satisfied, then even if prospects are unequal, public
expression will be given to the equal status of all voters as participants in decision making: each will have procedural opportunities
to overcome exactly the same amount of resistance. There is no
general reason to believe that this would provide an inadequate institutional expression of the equal worth of citizens or of equal respect for their ends.

At least, this seems clear in the general case. It is possible to
imagine historical circumstances in which proportional represen-

[19] For a recent statement of this argument, together with the analysis of voting as
a game of coalition formation, see Robert Sugden, "Free Association and the Theory
of Proportional Representation," *American Political Science Review* 78 (1984), pp.
31–43.

tation might recommend itself as a means for ensuring representation for significant positions otherwise unlikely to be represented at all or for groups that have been the objects of particularly invidious treatment. Even here, however, proportional representation may not be the only means available; districting systems might be manipulated (in ways discussed more fully below) to accomplish substantially the same ends. In any event, the interest in recognition combined with considerations arising from a society's peculiar circumstances obviously will not underwrite any general conclusion about the relative fairness of proportional representation.

Both Hare and Mill advanced a different argument that might be thought to embody an appeal to the interest in recognition. They held that proportional representation, because it requires voters to appraise a larger number of candidates and because it confers on nearly every voter the maximum chance of casting a successful vote, is more likely to engage the political energies of citizens, to promote the spread of civic virtue, and to encourage the exercise of the powers of judgment and choice. District systems, on the other hand, because they limit political activity to territorial constituencies and encourage the growth of parties, tend "to the mental and moral deterioration of both the electors and the elected."[20] This argument has the required form, and if its empirical premises were true it would surely yield a strong reason to reject district systems. But there does not appear to be any systematic comparative evidence in its favor, either regarding the elevating effects of PR or the dulling effects of district systems.

Turning now to the interest in equitable treatment, advocates of proportional representation hold that because every vote contributes to the election of a candidate, popular minorities of sufficient size will be guaranteed legislative representation. Their political preferences may therefore be expected to be treated more equitably than in an electoral regime in which they were not represented in proportion to their numbers.[21] In response, the main point is that

[20] Hare, *The Election of Representatives*, p. 19; compare Mill, *Considerations on Representative Government*, pp. 456–60.

[21] See, e.g., Hoag and Hallett, *Proportional Representation*, pp. 93–94. The core of this argument—though, without the explicit endorsement of PR—was anticipated by the antifederalists in their critique of the scheme of national representation embodied in the Constitution. See, in particular, "Brutus's" letter to the *New York Journal*

there is no guarantee that in a regime of equal prospects of *electoral* success voters will have equal chances of seeing their policy preferences satisfied (that is, equal prospects of *political* success). All that is promised is that the composition of the legislature will reflect the distribution of political preferences as the voters themselves identify them. Popular minorities will be represented; but their representatives will constitute legislative minorities, unable except through compromise to effect their constituents' will. Accordingly, it cannot be assumed a priori that proportional representation will enhance the prospects of minorities in comparison to what might be anticipated under some alternative system satisfying equal power but not equal prospects of success (such as a district system designed to encourage two-party competition). Indeed, under social circumstances making for the proliferation of parties, proportional representation might actually have an adverse long-run effect on the equitable treatment of interests by undermining the stability required for effective implementation of policy.

Another way the interest in equitable treatment might be implicated is suggested by the argument that proportional representation ensures that legislative majorities will represent popular majorities: it eliminates the possibility inherent in district representation that a popular minority could gain a majority of seats.[22] The argument rests on the view that decisions reached by a majority vote in the legislature are legitimate only if the legislative majority was elected by an affirmative vote of a majority of the electorate, and this in turn is apparently regarded as a derivation from the simple majority principle normally thought to apply in a small committee or a system of direct democracy.[23] Now as I argued earlier (chapter 3), the

---

of 15 November 1787, in *The Complete Anti-Federalist*, ed. Herbert J. Storing (Chicago: University of Chicago Press, 1981), vol. 2, pp. 380–81.

[22] As Hoag and Hallett write, PR "is by all odds the most reliable means of making majorities in the legislative body reflect majorities at the polls." *Proportional Representation*, p. 93. See also Hare, *The Election of Representatives*, pp. 2–3; Sterne, *On Representative Government and Personal Representation*, pp. 58–59; and Lakeman, *Power to Elect*, p. 164.

[23] The latter is explicit in Sterne, who describes representative government as "not an original organic form" but rather as an attempt to realize in large societies the ideal of "government by the people for the people" reflected, as he thought, in the model of Athenian democracy. *On Representative Government and Personal Representation*, pp. 23–25.

simple majority principle is not to be taken as a controlling or foundational requirement of political morality but rather as one element of a set of conditions of fair participation appropriate to committees and the like. The reasons that explain its appropriateness in those circumstances do not obviously require it to be applied in the very different circumstances characteristic of representative institutions in large and possibly diverse societies. Such institutions, which are typically embedded in a context of party competition and interest group activity, are likely to behave according to different principles and to some extent to serve different ends. Moreover, the pressure of party and group competition, combined with possibilities for adjustments in the institutional structure to minimize the threat of permanent minority rule, creates opportunities in representation systems for the equitable balancing of conflicting interests that simply have no analogs in committees or popular assemblies. (I consider some of these in subsequent chapters.) Therefore, without more, straightforward application of the majority principle does not lend much support to the case for proportional representation.

Against this, it might be maintained that the significance of proportional systems is to be found in their more accurate representation of opinion (rather than in their bearing on people's leverage over legislative outcomes). Opinion in the legislature will "mirror" opinion in the population.[24] There are several reasons why this might seem desirable. First, representatives of all significant population groups could participate in the public forum; even if they were excluded from the direct exercise of influence over the conduct of government, they would be able to present their views and demand a public justification when their interests were threatened by legislation or policy.[25] Beyond this, as Cohen and Rogers suggest, the more accurate representation of opinion would serve the goal of

[24] The distinction between the "right of decision" and the "right of representation" appears in many arguments for PR. For an early example deriving from Hare, see Sterne, *On Representative Government and Personal Representation*, p. 50. Sterne quotes Mirabeau as saying to the Constituent Assembly that "the representative body should at all times present a reduced picture of the people . . . and that presentation should bear the relative proportion to the original. . . ." Pages 50–51.

[25] The argument is suggested in William Nelson's remarks on Mill's conception of "open government." *On Justifying Democracy* (London: Routledge & Kegan Paul, 1980), pp. 115–16.

"manifestness" by rendering it more clearly to the electorate at large that minority positions are accorded a hearing.[26] The system might therefore be more stable because fringe groups, having won a place in the legislative arena, would gain incentives to adhere to norms of democratic practice.[27] Finally, by creating incentives for those with views far from the center to make their voices heard, proportional representation would enforce a broad scope for public debate and would encourage the development of judgmental competence among the electorate.[28]

All of these points appeal to the values represented by the interest in deliberative responsibility. One might grant the premise that proportional representation serves this interest better by affording a legislative voice to representatives of a wider range of views but object that the gain is not worth the disadvantages of such systems. Such an objection would draw strength from the observation that a system with wider access and a broader range of public debate would not necessarily give any greater weight to fringe positions that would be excluded in alternative systems; those positions would be the first to be excluded at the legislative stage in the search for winning legislative coalitions. So the gains for deliberative responsibility would be of limited importance in the balance with the presumed disadvantages of proportional systems.

Rather than pursue this point, however, I would like to question the premise of the argument. Under many circumstances it is not true that the positions represented in public debate within a proportional system would not also be represented in a system of district representation. The real differences between these systems involve the stage within the process of election and representation at which the positions are articulated and the framework within which divergent positions are compromised to form workable political coalitions. In proportional representation, these functions take place largely within the legislature itself under the aegis of parties or groups of legislators representing various constellations of interest;

[26] Cohen and Rogers, *On Democracy*, pp. 156–57.

[27] As G. Bingham Powell argues. *Contemporary Democracies* (Cambridge: Harvard University Press, 1982), p. 223. For a similar argument, see Hoag and Hallett, *Proportional Representation*, pp. 97–98.

[28] Joshua Cohen, "An Epistemic Conception of Democracy," *Ethics* 97 (1986), p. 36.

in district representation, they normally occur at an earlier stage—for example, in the selection of party candidates and in the formation of party platforms—where there may be substantial competitive incentives to take account of minority interests. In the latter case, much obviously depends on the way in which the process of candidate selection and the internal governance of the parties are regulated, and it seems plausible (as I argue below) that the interest in deliberative responsibility imposes conditions in both regards. If these kinds of regulation are feasible, then proportional representation will not necessarily promote a broader scope for public debate. (In fact, it seems likely that the main determinants of the scope of public political debate involve other aspects of the political culture, such as the tolerance of diversity and the vitality of the public media.)

These comments do not speak to the claim that when the legislature "mirrors" the population, it will be made manifest that the political process is open to all shades of opinion. However, it is not clear why the goal of "manifestness," taken by itself, should be accorded much weight. Perhaps the thought is that a manifestly open system will be more stable, in the sense of being more widely supported by its citizens; but this is an empirical claim that needs support, and in view of the other potential sources of instability in proportional systems, it does not seem plausible.[29] Or it might be thought that a manifestly open system would be publicly perceived as more fully respecting the equal rights of all to participate; but it is not clear why as much could not be said for alternative systems satisfying equal power but not equal prospects of success. Or the concern about manifestness may simply restate the claim that proportional systems tend to produce outcomes that treat people more equitably; but, as we have seen, this is not necessarily the case. So the fact, if it is a fact, that proportional systems more accurately mirror divisions of opinion in the population does not by itself provide a good reason to reject other kinds of systems.

Finally, a comment on one familiar source of the concern for "mirroring." It has been observed that representative democracy is

[29] Again, this applies in the general case. In special circumstances—e.g., in some plural societies—things may be different. Arend Lijphart, *Democracy in Plural Societies* (New Haven: Yale University Press, 1977), pp. 38–41, 64f.

"at best a working model of direct democracy."[30] The legislature should reproduce the array of views held in the population at large so that debates and decisions will be as close as possible to those that would take place if, *per impossible*, the entire population were able to meet together to conduct its business as an assembly. But the idea of a "working model" conceals the complexity of the transition from small, working assemblies to legislatures representing large, diverse populations.[31] It is easy to lose sight of the wide variety of conditions that need to be satisfied in order for assembly democracy to be a feasible method of social decision making. Rousseau was clear about this: a wide range of economic, social, and (Rousseau thought) even climatic conditions are necessary to ensure that assembly democracy will produce substantively acceptable outcomes. According to Rousseau, these conditions operate in two ways: first, they ensure that there will not be excessive conflicts of interest in society at large; second, they increase the chances that citizens meeting in the assembly will concern themselves with the public good rather than with narrow individual goods.[32] In abstracting from these conditions, the idea of representative democracy as a "working model" distorts the circumstances in which modern political institutions must operate. Differences in interest, wealth, and political competence, as well as information and bargaining costs deriving from the size of the polity, combine to make the setting of modern representative institutions significantly different from that of the small assemblies that are often idealized as the definitive form of democratic government. Moreover, the machinery of representation (whatever its structure) introduces further difficulties for the analogy. Indeed, in view of these differences, it is not clear what "a working model" can be a model *of*: certainly not assembly democracy in its classical form. As a matter of democratic theory, it is simpler, and surely less prone to error, to treat the question of the nature of fair representation in

[30] John R. Chamberlin and Paul N. Courant, "Representative Deliberations and Representative Decisions: Proportional Representation and the Borda Rule," *American Political Science Review* 77 (1983), p. 718.

[31] For an elegant discussion of many of these factors, see George Kateb, "The Moral Distinctiveness of Representative Democracy," *Ethics* 91 (1981), pp. 357–74.

[32] There is a further discussion of Rousseau's view in chapter 3, above, where the appropriate references can be found.

large, modern societies as an issue of first impression rather than as one to be settled by analogy with forms of democratic government conceived for societies vastly different from our own.

To conclude, although it is true that proportional representation achieves one kind of equality that will not normally obtain in district systems, it is a kind of equality in which there is no general reason to take an interest. Hence there is no general reason to reject a system of representation simply because it does not adhere to the proportionality principle. Of course, it does not follow that district systems are always to be preferred. In many cases, the most that can be said may be that either type of system could be fair, at least provided that the structure of constituencies and the rules governing access to the ballot were acceptably arranged. And it bears repeating that in some cases proportional representation might enjoy a theoretical advantage owing to the social and demographic features of the polity in question. We have established only the negative conclusion that considerations of fairness do not always favor proportional systems. The choice of representation systems is not usefully seen as a problem that can be resolved in abstraction from the historical circumstances of particular societies.

CHAPTER SEVEN

Fair Representation

and Legislative Districting

Proportional representation recommends itself mainly because it guarantees the representation of groups roughly in proportion to their share of the electorate. I have argued that this is not a requirement of fairness. This is not to say, however, that there is *no* reason for concern about how a representation system affects the political prospects of various population groups. In this chapter, I explore the ways that such a concern might enter into judgments about the fairness of a system of representation employing district rather than proportional representation.

The problem arises in American constitutional litigation as a consequence of the distinction between the "quantitative" and "qualitative" dimensions of fair representation.[1] Speaking roughly, the first of these involves the allocation of voting power among those eligible to vote for members of the legislature. Since the Supreme Court's early reapportionment decisions, the meaning of quantitative fairness has become a settled matter: it requires adherence to the precept "one person, one vote."[2] However, some important problems concerning the fair representation of groups can occur even when voting power is equal. Perhaps the clearest cases involve dilution of the votes of racial groups: gerrymandering techniques are employed to reduce the legislative representation of ra-

---

[1] These terms are used in Laurence H. Tribe, *American Constitutional Law* (Mineola, N.Y.: Foundation Press, 1978), p. 749. Henceforth, I dispense with the quotation marks; but it should be understood that these are terms of art.

[2] *Reynolds v. Sims*, 377 U.S. 533 (1964), at 577. I leave aside the question of how far an apportionment scheme can deviate from the standard of mathematical equality without running afoul of this precept.

cial minorities without denying anyone an equally weighted vote. "Qualitative fairness" pertains to issues of this kind, which are both more complex and more obscure than the issues of quantitative fairness that have dominated judicial and scholarly attention.

Theorists have long understood that issues concerning the representation of groups pose a different problem than the quantitative irregularities in the more familiar reapportionment cases.[3] What is not obvious is how (if at all) considerations of fairness bear on the design of representation systems beyond the minimal requirement of equal voting weights. What is "qualitative fairness" in representation, and what (if anything) is *unfair* about it?[4]

To answer these questions, I shall proceed in three steps. First, more needs to be said about the character of the issue at stake in controversies about qualitatively fair representation. We shall see that these controversies derive from an ambiguity in the concept of power discussed earlier; once this is recognized, it will become clear why quantitative and qualitative fairness are distinct ideas that raise different problems of political morality. Second, I shall examine critically several common diagnoses of the distinctive unfairness of the phenomena conventionally thought to be "qualitatively" deficient. Although none of these diagnoses is adequate, they suggest some criteria that a better account of qualitative unfairness should satisfy. Finally, I shall explain how complex proceduralism accommodates what appears to be the truth in these common views.

---

[3] See, for example, Robert Dixon, *Democratic Representation* (New York: Oxford University Press, 1968), pp. 582–83; J. Roland Pennock, *Democratic Political Theory* (Princeton: Princeton University Press, 1979), pp. 8–9; Ronald W. Rogowski, "Representation in Political Theory and in Law," *Ethics* 91 (1981), pp. 395–430. In *Reynolds v. Sims*, the Supreme Court recognized that there was more to fair representation than "one person, one vote." 377 U.S. 533, at 565–66. However, the Court has noted the general significance of the point only recently. *Davis v. Bandemer*, 106 S. Ct. 2797 (1986), at 2806.

[4] Related questions have been especially vexing in connection with judicial interpretation and legislative revision of section 2 of the Voting Rights Act of 1965 (as amended most recently in 1982), which forbids election laws and regulations that "deny or abridge" the right to vote. See generally Abigail M. Thernstrom, *Whose Votes Count?* (Cambridge: Harvard University Press, 1987).

THE NATURE OF "QUALITATIVE UNFAIRNESS"

Problems about qualitative unfairness can occur in a variety of settings, including both partisan and racial gerrymandering, multi-member districting, and at-large election systems. Although we shall be concerned with qualitative fairness as a basic problem in democratic theory, it is convenient to choose illustrations from constitutional law. Thus, in *Gaffney v. Cummings*, the Supreme Court was urged to strike down a system of state legislative districts in which constituency boundaries had been manipulated in an effort to ensure approximate proportionality between the electoral strength and the legislative representation of the major parties.[5] In *United Jewish Organizations v. Carey* (the "Williamsburg" case), the Court faced a complaint of unequal treatment in connection with "compensatory" or "racial" gerrymandering aimed at increasing the legislative representation of racial minorities.[6] In *Rogers v. Lodge*, vote dilution was alleged in a one person, one vote, at-large system of election for county commissioners under which a large racial minority had been consistently unable to elect any of its members.[7]

The systems challenged in all of these cases provided equal voting power to all voters.[8] Nevertheless, some sort of unfairness was alleged to have occurred in violation of the Equal Protection Clause. We need not agree that there is anything substantial behind these

[5] *Gaffney v. Cummings*, 412 U.S. 735 (1973).

[6] *United Jewish Organizations v. Carey*, 430 U.S. 144 (1977).

[7] *Rogers v. Lodge*, 458 U.S. 613 (1982). In addition to those cited above, the leading cases concerning qualitative fairness include *White v. Regester*, 412 U.S. 755 (1973) (multimember districting), *Mobile v. Bolden*, 446 U.S. 55 (1980) (at-large elections), and *Davis v. Bandemer*, 106 S. Ct. 2797 (1986) (partisan gerrymandering).

[8] Or could have been altered so that equal power would be realized without curing the "qualitative" defect. For example, in *Gaffney*, one of the issues was the degree of permissible deviation from precise mathematical equality in district size that could be justified by the aims of maintaining the integrity of local boundaries and of producing proportional legislative representation for parties. But in considering the constitutionality of the second of these aims, the Court clearly assumed that, taken on its own, proportional representation for parties would not necessarily require *any* variation from precise mathematical equality. 412 U.S., at 751–54.

allegations to inquire about the nature of the problem to which they apply.

One way to characterize controversies about qualitatively fair representation employs the distinction between power and prospects of electoral success.[9] The fact that a system is "quantitatively" fair (that is, it adheres to "one person, one vote") means that the distribution of procedural opportunities provides everyone with the capacity to overcome the same amount of resistance. The system satisfies equal power. However, this provides no assurance that it also satisfies equal prospects of success. In the cases of interest here, this is precisely the problem: owing to the distribution of preferences across territorial constituencies, some may expect to encounter more resistance than others, so that chances of electoral success are unequal. This explains why controversies about qualitative fairness only appear when the likely political preferences of voters are taken into account. Thus, a districting plan can be seen to present problems of partisan gerrymandering only when the plan itself is considered together with information about the geographical distribution of party strength, which provides a basis for predicting how voters will vote. Similarly, at-large election schemes will display problems of racial vote dilution only when the racial composition of the population is taken as indicative of the likely division of electoral preferences and it appears on that basis that the interests of racial minorities are unlikely to be adequately represented.

It is common to regard qualitative unfairness as an imbalance in voting power among *groups*, just as quantitative unfairness is an imbalance among individuals.[10] However, framing the contrast in this way can give rise to confusion. If power is conceived as the capacity to get the outcome one wants, then in a regime in which individuals have equal voting power, the voting power of a group simply reflects its proportionate share of the electorate. Supposing

---

[9] On the distinction between power and prospects, see chapter 1.

[10] For example, as Tribe formulates the Supreme Court's rule regarding qualitative fairness, "an apportionment scheme is unconstitutional, despite its compliance with the one person, one vote mandate, if it cancels or minimizes the voting power of cognizable population groups." *American Constitutional Law*, p. 750. Compare Owen M. Fiss, "Groups and the Equal Protection Clause," *Philosophy & Public Affairs* 5 (1976), esp. pp. 151–54.

that the requirements of quantitative fairness were already settled, there would be no independent question about qualitative fairness: the distribution of power among groups would be fixed by the distribution of power among individuals. On such a view, qualitative fairness poses no distinguishable problem of political morality at all. But it is clear from the cases that substantial issues of qualitative unfairness can arise even when quantitative fairness is assured. This fact can be made comprehensible only by recognizing that the contrast between two kinds of fairness is not a contrast between the distribution of voting power among individuals, in one case, and among groups, in the other. In both cases the ultimate concern is the political status of individuals; however, different dimensions of political status are involved—power, in the first case, and prospects of success, in the second. This is not to deny that reference to group membership is required to identify qualitative unfairness. To assess someone's prospects of success, it is necessary to know something about the likely political preferences of other voters so that the person's relative chances of success can be estimated. When people are seen as members of "cognizable groups," their group membership serves as a basis for inferring their (and others') political interests, hence their likely political preferences, hence their prospects of success. Thus, for example, in racial vote dilution cases what is really being claimed is that under the existing districting system members of the group are less likely to be successful than they would be under another possible system.[11] To say this is not to say that qualitative fairness involves the question of how power should be distributed among groups in the same sense in which quantitative fairness involves its distribution among individuals. Qualitative fairness presents a different issue altogether.[12]

[11] See, for example, *Wright v. Rockefeller*, 376 U.S. 52 (1964).

[12] Recently it has been observed that "[t]he standard of 'one person, one vote' is . . . best understood as a rule to combat gross political gerrymandering. . . ." Leaving aside the question of historical accuracy, the remarks in the text above show that, as a theoretical matter, this is misleading. It is true that enforcement of "one person, one vote" may help indirectly to frustrate crude efforts at gerrymandering; but even if it did not, it would still ensure equality of voting power. As I argue below, this has independent importance for political fairness. For the passage quoted, see Dean Alfange, Jr., "Gerrymandering and the Constitution: Into the Thorns of the Thicket at Last," *Supreme Court Review* (1986), p. 192.

GERRYMANDERING AND IMPARTIALITY

It is one thing to identify the issue that qualitative fairness presents and another to say whether, and if so why, it should matter to us that districting arrangements might be qualitatively unfair. Thus far, our concern has been purely analytical: we have been considering what is common in the varied phenomena that are the subject of complaints about qualitative unfairness. I turn now to the normative question of whether such complaints are well founded.

If there is anything objectionable about what is called qualitative unfairness, it cannot be that it involves an unequal or otherwise unacceptable distribution of voting power among individuals. I will consider three other possibilities. First, qualitative unfairness might reflect some type of formal inequality or violation of impartiality in the method by which districting systems are devised. Alternatively, it might be objectionable simply because it violates equal prospects of success, which might be seen as an independent requirement of political fairness. Finally, it might reflect some distributive infirmity that does not directly involve *political* inequality at all (for example, that it promotes an unequal distribution of interest satisfaction). I shall argue for a version of the last of these, mainly by arguing against the first two. Of course, it might also be that there is *nothing* unfair about what is called "qualitative unfairness"— perhaps any districting scheme satisfying equality of power is equally fair. I shall not consider this possibility explicitly, but it will be clear, *inter alia*, why it seems implausible.

Consider first the idea that qualitative unfairness consists in a violation of impartial treatment in the design of districting systems. This is a generalization of a common complaint about gerrymandering, and I shall discuss it in that connection.[13] Traditionally, gerrymandering has been criticized for what may be called its formal features: unusual or complex district shapes, district boundaries that depart from those of established political subdivisions, and so forth. These criticisms, in turn, have elicited a range of formal norms for acceptable districting practices, such as the precept that

[13] Such a view is briefly suggested in John Rawls, *A Theory of Justice* (Cambridge: Harvard University Press, 1971), p. 223. It is given ambiguous but more extended expression in the Common Cause report, *Toward a System of "Fair and Effective Representation"* (Washington: Common Cause, 1977), esp. pp. 12–30.

districts should be compact and contiguous.[14] What might appear to recommend these norms is a pretension to impartiality; because they exclude the known political characteristics of the population from consideration in the composition of a districting system, they are at least facially neutral between parties and other aggregations of interest.

The question is why this should be counted as a virtue. A common reply is that impartial criteria are intrinsically fair. But it is difficult to see how this can be made plausible. Two premises are needed: first, that the composition of constituencies involves the kind of allocation decision to which interest-blind criteria are appropriate; second, that impartial criteria are interest-blind in the required sense.[15] Neither premise is correct. Recalling that the goods in question are prospects of electoral success, I believe it is clear, on reflection, that none of the conditions in which blind criteria are appropriate describes the districting decision.[16] However, I shall not argue this in detail. For even if the first premise were granted, the defense of impartial criteria would fail. The reason is that a system of territorial constituencies constructed according to facially impartial criteria will produce political outcomes that reflect the existing spatial distribution of interests. For example, geographically concentrated minorities will typically be more successful in electing representatives than dispersed minorities of the same size.[17] Because the spatial distribution of interests is not usually random—it

[14] See, for example, William Vickery, "On the Prevention of Gerrymandering," *Political Science Quarterly* 76 (1961), pp. 105–10.

[15] An argument resting on both premises is given in Diana T. Meyers, "In Defense of Blind Apportionment Criteria" (Comment presented to the Conference on Equal Opportunity, University of Delaware, May 1985), pp. 5–8.

[16] The main categories of cases in which blind criteria appear to be appropriate are the following: (a) when the good to be allocated is relatively unimportant and the use of outcome-sensitive criteria would be excessively time consuming; (b) when no outcome-sensitive criterion applies at all (so that the allocation of the good is morally a matter of indifference); or (c) when the applicable outcome-sensitive criteria cannot be implemented without substantial risk of injustice.

[17] For a brief discussion, see Bernard Grofman, "For Equal Member Districts Random Is Not Equal," in Grofman et al., eds., *Representation and Redistricting Issues* (Lexington, Mass.: Lexington Books, 1982), pp. 55–58. More generally, see Edward Tufte, "The Relationship Between Seats and Votes in Two-Party Systems," *American Political Science Review* 67 (1973), pp. 540–54.

may be a function, for example, of factors such as income class, ethnicity, or race—facially "impartial" districting criteria will not normally be interest-blind in the sense required for genuine impartiality.

In response, someone might think that the territorial basis of constituencies should itself be given up.[18] Perhaps districts should be composed in an entirely random way, without any of the traditional spatial constraints, so that, for example, residents of the same locality (even of the same apartment house) might be members of different constituencies. Such a view is the natural consequence of carrying the idea of impartial criteria to the limit. This is not only a theoretically interesting alternative; a random district system might also serve as a benchmark for the assessment of actual systems employing territorial constituencies. (Thus, deviations from a hypothetical random system that systematically disadvantaged members of identifiable interest groups might be said to be objectionable.) Of course, random districting would have a variety of undesirable results for the conduct of electoral politics; but, these points aside, it is worth asking whether considerations of fairness lend any weight to it at all. I do not believe they do. For example, if it turned out that the interests of particular minorities were unrepresented, or if as a consequence of the composition of constituencies these interests were ill served, that would be a reason to reconsider the pattern of apportionment. The fact that it had been generated through a random process would not provide a warrant for these outcomes that would not have existed if the districting system had been composed in some other way.

As Robert Dixon wrote, "all districting is gerrymandering" in the sense that "whether or not there is a gerrymander in *design*, there normally will be some gerrymander in *result* as a concomitant of all district systems of legislative election."[19] Whatever criteria are used to construct a district system, some interests will be advantaged and others disadvantaged in comparison to what their prospects would have been in a system constructed according to different criteria. If there is any point of view from which outcomes matter—as obviously there is—and if the political circumstances warrant any

[18] I am grateful to David Hoekema for pointing out this possibility.
[19] Dixon, *Democratic Representation*, p. 462 (emphasis in original).

definite predictions about the relationship between districting arrangements and outcomes, then this is not something to which we should be indifferent.

Of course, there are other ways to defend impartial or neutral districting criteria than to hold that they are intrinsically fair. One might think that the use of impartial criteria, perhaps in conjunction with some nonpartisan (or bipartisan) scheme for making apportionment decisions, would be the best way to avoid the substantive evils associated with gerrymandering. For example, impartial methods might be minimally vulnerable to self-serving manipulation by the party in power.[20] As a practical matter, there is doubtless much to recommend this idea. But we must note that on this view, there is no claim that neutral criteria are intrinsically fairer than others; it simply happens that the use of politically neutral criteria helps to avoid outcomes that we have independent reasons to want to avoid. The theoretically interesting question is what kinds of reasons these might be; but any answer to this question must invoke result-oriented considerations (for example, concerns about the inequitable character of the outcomes likely to be produced when the dominant party manipulates the structure of representation in order to insulate itself from competitive electoral pressures). This invites the further question why these considerations rather than others should determine judgments about fair representation. The idea of procedural impartiality simply cannot answer this question; a more substantive conception of the aims of representation is needed.

I will not pause to generalize these remarks about partisan gerrymandering to the idea that qualitative fairness in representation involves some sort of formal neutrality or impartiality in the construction of districting systems. It is enough to point out that there is no plausible alternative, in analyzing qualitative unfairness, to a consideration of the political results anticipated from the districting arrangements in question. Thus, if there is a general principle of qualitative fairness, it must specify the kinds of outcomes that fairness forbids. And if qualitative fairness is to be brought within a

[20] Such a view was held by Robert Dixon. See his prepared statement in U.S. Senate, Committee on Governmental Affairs, *Congressional Anti-Gerrymandering Act of 1979 [S. 596]: Hearings* (Washington: Government Printing Office, 1979), pp. 218–44.

theory of political equality, it must be shown how equality bears on this requirement.

EQUAL PROSPECTS AND PROPORTIONALITY

The most obvious outcome-oriented view regards qualitative unfairness as a deviation from equality of prospects of success, just as quantitative unfairness is a deviation from equality of voting power. This thought gains plausibility from the analogy with proportional representation, whose claim to embody a special kind of fairness stems precisely from the fact that it confers on nearly every voter an equal chance of voting for a winning candidate. I have already explained why, considered apart from other concerns, this seems to me to be a matter of little moral importance. I shall not repeat the argument here, except to recall that the prospects in question are chances of casting a winning vote for a candidate for the legislature, not chances of getting the legislation one wants. There is no guarantee that in a regime of equal prospects of electoral success, voters will have equal chances of seeing their policy preferences satisfied, or even that they will have better chances than they would have under some schemes in which their prospects of *electoral* success were highly unequal.

Even if equal prospects of success were thought to be a goal worth pursuing, a special problem arises when it is sought within a system of district, rather than proportional, representation. The difficulty derives from the different ways in which constituencies are composed in these systems. In proportional representation, constituencies define themselves through the voting process; it is up to individual voters to decide how to rank their political interests and which candidates are most likely to serve those interests effectively. By contrast, in district representation, constituencies are established by the politicians and judges who apportion the population among districts. If their aim is some sort of proportionality between the electorate and the membership of the legislature, they must first adopt a criterion of proportionality—for example, party affiliation, race, religion, and so forth. Then, taking demographic information into account, they must draw district lines accordingly—which is to say, they must engage in gerrymandering calculated to maximize the probability that each group identified by the criterion will be represented in proportion to its size.

It follows from this contrast that whereas proportional representation can almost completely equalize chances of electoral success, district representation, no matter how subtly gerrymandered, usually cannot. In proportional representation, because each winning candidate has a unanimous constituency, nearly every voter is represented by a legislator for whom he voted. But the same cannot be said of the kind of gerrymandering efforts in question here; given geographical constituencies, there will virtually always be voters who voted for losers. To seek equality of success within a system of district representation is to seek a goal that cannot normally be attained. So the egalitarian argument for proportional representation, whatever its strength in that case, is much weaker when applied to efforts to manipulate districting systems to secure proportional representation for groups identified independently of the voters' own expressed preferences. As I suggest below, in some cases there may be other reasons to undertake such efforts, but their force does not derive from egalitarian considerations of the kind that might be thought to make proportional representation a desirable ideal.

There is a further point about the contrast between proportional representation and district representation that has been gerrymandered to achieve some sort of proportionality. In addition to its association with equal prospects of electoral success, proportional representation might seem attractive because it reproduces in the legislature the same balance of political interests that exists in the electorate at large. As a result, legislative compromise and accommodation will generate coalitions (and corresponding legislative outcomes) that replicate those that would arise if the entire electorate were somehow able to meet as a legislative assembly. Let us call this "interest proportionality." Its linchpin is that the system allows voters to vote for the candidate whose program most closely reflects their interests as they themselves rank order them. Now, whatever the significance of this aspect of proportional representation, gerrymandered district representation yields what is at best a pale imitation. The reason is that the proportionality achieved in the legislature under such a system will not necessarily reflect the voters' own identification and ranking of their interests but rather that presumed by the designers of the district system. The degree of fit between the latter and the former is an empirical question, but it will be approximate at best. Consider, for example, district systems designed to produce legislative representation proportional to party strength.[21] Party-strength proportionality will have the same legislative effects as interest proportionality only if it mimics it; but it will mimic it only if the rank-ordered political interests of a party's voters are accurately reflected in the party's program (and if every voter is a member of a party). This, of course, is highly unlikely. Large parties necessarily formulate their programs in ways intended to attract the support of coalitions of voters with differing interests and differing views about their relative importance. This coalition-building activity will yield a legislative party whose program may not be accepted by any individual voter as her most-preferred legislative agenda; accordingly, the process of legislative compromise and accommodation will begin from a different balance of interests than that found in the electorate at large and may have correspondingly different outcomes. Again, there may be reasons to strive for party-strength proportionality in the design of representation systems, but those reasons must be different from those that make interest proportionality seem to be a desirable objective. (Much the same could be said about other kinds of proportionality that might be sought in districting, such as race proportionality.)

EQUAL SATISFACTION

I observed earlier that equal prospects of electoral success, even if they could be attained, will not necessarily produce equal prospects of political satisfaction. I meant to discredit the idea that qualitative fairness should be conceived as requiring equal prospects of

[21] That this should be the aim of fair districting is an increasingly widely held view among political scientists. More precisely, the view is that the system of districts should have a "neutral" electoral effect in the sense that the ratio of votes to seats should be the same for both parties. Each party would then be represented roughly in proportion to the aggregate partisan division of the vote. Richard G. Niemi and John Deegan, Jr., "Competition, Responsiveness and the Swing Ratio," *American Political Science Review* 72 (1978), pp. 1304–23. In its first effort to formulate a criterion for identifying impermissible partisan gerrymanders, the Supreme Court rejected this view. *Davis v. Bandemer*, 106 S. Ct. 2729 (1986), at 2806.

electoral success. Perhaps a more plausible analysis of qualitative fairness could be framed in terms of prospects of political satisfaction. We might say that a system is qualitatively fair to the extent that it yields political decisions that satisfy everyone's political preferences equally often. Qualitative unfairness, then, would arise when there was a structural bias that tended systematically to produce inequalities in the distribution of preference satisfaction. This is the third view of qualitative fairness that we shall examine. As stated, it suffers from serious defects, but I believe that it points in the right direction.

The view derives from a familiar theory of the justification of democracy and from the conception of political equality associated with it. The conception holds that everyone has an equal right to have their political preferences satisfied; but since it will normally be impossible to satisfy all political preferences simultaneously, some compromise is necessary, and the only compromise consistent with equality is that political decisions should satisfy the preferences of each member of the population an equal proportion of the time.[22]

The analysis of qualitative fairness as equal prospects of political satisfaction arises from the fact that a representation system satisfying equal power will yield equal preference satisfaction only if various empirical conditions are met in society. For example, there must be neither intense nor permanent minorities.[23] Obviously, however, these conditions need not hold. When they do not, preference satisfaction will likely be distributed unequally; minorities may be disproportionately disadvantaged and in the extreme case may be excluded altogether. Moreover, even when the conditions are satisfied, cleverly constructed districting arrangements could lead to distortions in the distribution of preference satisfaction. To maximize the probability that political outcomes will yield equal

[22] Something like this idea seems to be suggested by Brian Barry in "Is Democracy Special?" *Philosophy, Politics, and Society*, 5th series, ed. Peter Laslett and James Fishkin (New Haven: Yale University Press, 1979), pp. 176ff. The version of the view presented in the text is suggested by Peter Singer's discussion of procedural fairness in *Democracy and Disobedience* (New York: Oxford University Press, 1973), pp. 30–41, discussed above in chapter 4.

[23] For a helpful discussion of these conditions, see Barry, "Is Democracy Special?" pp. 176–77.

satisfaction over time, equal power must therefore be supplemented by a further procedural requirement. Such a requirement would correspond to a principle of qualitative fairness and would mandate manipulation of the districting system to compensate for the predictable inequalities in preference satisfaction that would otherwise be produced.

This interpretation of qualitative fairness seems initially to meet the desiderata that have emerged in the foregoing discussion: it is outcome-oriented, and it clearly embodies an egalitarian principle. It has particular appeal because it provides a rationale for objecting to districting irregularities involving dilution of the votes of blacks and other minorities, which are among those most frequently challenged in recent constitutional litigation.[24]

Nevertheless, the interpretation is flawed as it stands. The critical defect lies in the premise that people have equal rights to have their political preferences satisfied, so that it could be reasonable for someone to object to a districting system on the grounds that his chances of satisfaction would be less than someone else's. This principle is not very plausible. Like its cousin in the welfare economic injunction to move toward the Pareto frontier, this principle will appeal only if the prior distribution of preference satisfaction has some independent justification. If not—if the economic system tends to produce unwarranted inequalities in the overall distribution of goods, for example—then a representation system that was egalitarian in the present sense might succeed only in perpetuating unwarranted distributive inequalities. Since there is no reason in the general case to assume that the status quo distribution has any special warrant, the principle cannot stand.[25]

I will not say more here about the defects of the conception of political fairness associated with the principle of equal satisfaction. The important point is that the resulting doctrine of qualitative fairness is defective in its conception of equality but not necessarily in its structure. The question we should explore is whether a more satisfactory doctrine of qualitative fairness can be constructed by

[24] A summary may be found in Stephen L. Wasby, *Vote Dilution, Minority Voting Rights, and the Courts* (Washington, D.C.: Joint Center for Political Studies, 1982).

[25] Even if the prior distribution were acceptable, the possibility that political decisions could give rise to external benefits and costs means that the desirable features of the prior distribution might not be preserved through subsequent reallocations of relative satisfaction.

accepting the instrumentalism of the view I have been criticizing, while substituting a more discriminating conception of the equality to which democratic systems should aspire. The result is an application of complex proceduralism to the design of a system of representation.

QUALITATIVE FAIRNESS AND
THE INTERESTS OF CITIZENSHIP

It is primarily the first two regulative interests—in recognition and equitable treatment—that are implicated in issues involving representation. Citizens must be treated equally as participants in politics; but they must also be treated equitably as the subjects of public policy. How do these interests bear on the design of a system of representation?

The answer I shall suggest interprets the distinction between quantitative and qualitative fairness as defining, so to speak, a division of moral labor within the system of representation, with the first corresponding to the interest in recognition and the second, to that in equitable treatment. Thus, the concern for equal recognition is satisfied within systems of district representation when everyone has equal power to affect the outcomes of the legislative process. A necessary condition is that each person be entitled to cast an equally weighted vote for a representative who will be entitled, in turn, to cast an equally weighted vote in the legislature. I have already noted that equal power, even if fully realized, may not guarantee very much about the likely distribution of prospects of electoral success or of political preference satisfaction; but because it requires that each citizen be given procedural opportunities to overcome the same amount of resistance, there is a clear sense in which equal power gives public expression to the equal status of democratic citizens as participants in political decision making. For this reason, equal power is an important requirement independent of its effects on electoral and legislative outcomes.[26]

[26] Thus, Bagehot argued for extension of the suffrage to the working class (regardless of its effects on the content of legislation, about which he was apprehensive) on the ground that it would provide public recognition that the members of the class have interests and views deserving to be heard in the public forum. Walter Bagehot,

Whereas the aim of quantitative fairness is to give public recognition to the equal political status of democratic citizens, the aim of qualitative fairness is the promotion of equitable treatment of interests. The function of equality of power is primarily (although, of course, not exclusively) expressive, while that of efforts to influence the distribution of prospects of success is more instrumental. Now, as I warned earlier, it would be a mistake to overstate the degree to which variations in procedural arrangements can be systematically associated with variations in the contents of political decisions; the direction of legislation is determined jointly by a great variety of factors, among which the structural features of the system of representation play what is at best a subordinate role. But we need not conclude that an instrumentalist approach to qualitative fairness is either a hopeless or a pointless venture. Although it may be too much to expect that by manipulating the structure of representation equitable legislation can be systematically promoted, it may at least be possible to minimize some of the familiar dangers to which representation schemes have historically been prone. These include in particular the danger of majority tyranny—that is, the danger that the majority in the legislature will be insufficiently attentive to the interests and rights of popular minorities in its substantive policy choices, or worse, that it will enact procedural contrivances aimed at containing or frustrating the capacity of minorities to participate more effectively in public deliberation and political bargaining.

A variety of strategies might be employed to give the interests of minorities some degree of protection in the structure of representation. By way of illustration, I mention two that might be implemented in systems based on single-member districts.[27] First, the system can be organized so as to promote party competition. This requires increasing the proportion of districts in which the normal or expected partisan voting strength is relatively evenly divided. The assumption is that the more competitive the districts, the greater the incentives for parties and candidates to orient their pro-

---

The English Constitution, 2d ed. [1871] (London: Oxford University Press, 1928), pp. 152–55.

[27] Alternatives involving multimember districts are discussed in Daniel R. Ortiz, "Alternative Voting Systems as Remedies for Unlawful At-Large Systems" [Note], Yale Law Journal 92 (1982), pp. 144–60.

grams to attract the support of disaffected minorities.[28] Second, when minorities are geographically concentrated and politically isolated, and when it is unlikely that their interests would be taken into account by the established parties even under the pressures of normal party competition, the system can be adjusted to increase the chance that these minorities will at least have a legislative voice.[29] (Measures that enable the interests of disadvantaged minorities to be articulated in the public realm may also serve the interest in recognition: not only through the direct effects on self-esteem, but also through the less direct consequences of the processes of group political activity likely to be set in motion.)

Both strategies for protecting minority interests may require the use of gerrymandering techniques to achieve their objectives. Operationally, both strategies may seek some sort of proportionality between a party or group's share of the electorate and the portion of the constituencies it controls. But in neither case is the underlying aim to promote proportional representation overall. Rather, it is to promote equitable treatment by creating conditions in which the chances of predictable injustice are minimized. The choice among quantitatively fair procedures depends on the goal of securing a desirable pattern of substantive legislative results.

This conception of fair representation reflects a theoretical compromise between concerns about recognition and about equitable treatment. It is reasonable to wonder why the compromise should be struck in the way I have suggested rather than in some other way. For example, suppose that the interests of some minority group are unlikely to be treated fairly under a system of equal votes within the prevailing system of districts: why would it be inappropriate to enact a compensatory system of plural voting favoring members of that group? That is, why not give multiple votes to members of the minority and one vote to everyone else?[30] Under

[28] For an exploration of the difficulties in implementing this proposal, see Niemi and Deegan, "Competition, Responsiveness, and the Swing Ratio."

[29] A similar result would be reached by applying to districting questions the theory of equal protection for "specially disadvantaged groups" set forth by Owen Fiss in "Groups and the Equal Protection Clause." An application of such a theory to the issue of racial vote dilution may be found in Howard M. Shapiro, "Geometry and Geography: Racial Gerrymandering and the Voting Rights Act" [Note], *Yale Law Journal* 94 (1984), pp. 189–208.

[30] Note that this appears to be precisely what would be implied by an application

the specified conditions, this would be a more direct means of improving the minority's political prospects, and so of advancing the
interest in equitable treatment, than the forms of district manipulation I have endorsed. What would be wrong with it?

It is true that a compensatory plural voting scheme might offend
the interest in recognition of those whom it disadvantages, but in
complex proceduralism this would not, in itself, be sufficient to
rule out such schemes. The reason is that the appropriate balance
among the regulative interests is something to be worked out in the
context of application, taking account of relevant historical circumstances; it is not specified by the terms of the theory itself. Accordingly, what must be argued is that under the circumstances the sacrifice of the values associated with recognition would be an
unreasonable price to pay for the improvement in the prospects of
the endangered minority. Whether this will be the case depends on
various contingent matters, including the severity of the likely impact of the compensatory scheme on public perceptions of the political status of those disadvantaged by it, the gravity of the threat to
the minority in the absence of such a scheme, and the availability
of less drastic alternatives. In the circumstances of contemporary
American politics, any such argument for compensatory plural voting seems unlikely to be persuasive, in part because the alternative
set forth earlier is readily available, and in part because the formal
equality of the vote has come to play such an important role in expressing the equal status of citizenship. But complex proceduralism
plainly affords no basis for ruling out all such schemes from the
start. The stability of the theoretical compromise reflected in our
conception of qualitative fairness depends on a series of plausible,
but hardly invariable, assumptions about society's historical situation.

OBJECTIONS TO OUTCOME-CONSCIOUS
DISTRICTING PRACTICES

The criterion of fair representation I have suggested includes an
outcome-oriented component applicable to qualitative issues be-

of Rawls's "general conception of justice" to problems of procedural design. *A Theory of Justice*, p. 62.

yond the weight of the vote. Consistent with equal voting weights, procedures should be shaped so as to minimize the chances of predictable kinds of injustice. This aspect of the view gives rise to two objections.

The first arises as follows. The assumption in connection with both of the strategies I have suggested for protecting minority interests is that otherwise the minorities in question would fail to be treated justly—for example, by being denied their just distributive share or by having their rights infringed by an indifferent or hostile majority. As I have emphasized, this is a historical assumption, whose validity in any particular case depends on the facts of that case. It is a further assumption that manipulation of the districting system will, in fact, avoid or help remedy the injustices at which they are aimed, and the validity of this assumption also depends on empirical judgments about particular historical situations. But someone might object that the application of fundamental principles of democratic theory should not be so dependent on the contingencies of social and political life. For it means that questions of institutional design will turn on empirical judgments that are both subject to significant error and (perhaps for that reason) inherently controversial, and this might undermine the perceived legitimacy of democratic legislation.[31]

This is not an idle concern. It is not implausible that the popular legitimacy of a representation system might be undermined by the widespread perception that its structure was open to frequent revision aimed at conferring procedural advantages on identifiable population groups. There is special cause for concern when the structural revisions come about as a result of judicial intervention rather than by legislation. However, the force of this concern must be kept in perspective. There are two points. First, it is easy to overestimate the possibilities for popular disaffection. A general belief that the system yields legislation that is acceptable on the whole is a powerful antidote to disaffection flowing from countermajoritarian procedural arrangements or from particular instances of unpopular legislation. (For example, the popular legitimacy of the U.S. Congress is not perceptibly influenced by its various antiegalitarian internal procedures.) Second, the kinds of manipulation that I have

---

[31] Justice Brennan expressed this fear in his opinion concurring in part in *United Jewish Organizations v. Carey*, 430 U.S. 144 (1977), at 174.

suggested have a limited potential for producing legislation at odds with the desires of the majority. There is no threat to majoritarianism in efforts to insure proportional representation for parties; indeed, the opposite will more often be the case. And gerrymandering to give a legislative voice to disadvantaged minorities will accomplish only that—it will enable those minorities, through their representatives, to put their case to the legislative majority and to play a part in the process of legislative compromise, but it can hardly guarantee them the legislation they want regardless of the desires of others.

The other objection is this. The doctrine of qualitative fairness that I have outlined allows choices about procedures to be conditioned on the probability that some procedures more than others will encourage patterns of legislative results that can be recognized as desirable from the point of view of a substantive theory of justice. But result-oriented considerations of this kind may seem to have no place in matters of procedural choice. Democracy is rule by the people, and this implies that the people may be—indeed, have a right to be—wrong on the merits. The manipulation of procedures to avoid or minimize this possibility may therefore appear to be an unwarranted interference in the process of self-government.[32]

For reasons set forth earlier, I believe that this objection rests on an implausible view of the moral basis of democracy. But a more specific reply is possible here. The idea of "rule by the people" is ambiguous and vague. Surely its minimal content is that there should be some institutional connection between the expressed political preferences of the people and the choice of policy; but beyond this, the idea is simply too general to provide much guidance in matters of procedural design. It is an illusion fostered by the undiscerning rhetoric of popular sovereignty that this protean idea will by itself settle controversy about fair representation. Similar observations apply to the simple view of political fairness as equal power over outcomes; this idea, too, is too formal to resolve those questions about the structure of representation that go beyond quantitative equality. Inasmuch as *no* system of legislative districting can

---

[32] This objection was suggested to me by Michael Walzer's remarks in "Philosophy and Democracy," *Political Theory* 9 (1981), pp. 379–99. But I am not sure that Walzer would endorse the objection as formulated in the text.

be neutral in its results, some further basis is needed for choosing among those alternative feasible arrangements that are consistent with the requirement of equal power.[33] The suggestion that the choice should be guided by the aim of protecting minorities against predictable injustice therefore cannot be disposed of merely by observing that it involves appeal to substantive principles.

This is a point about democratic theory, not constitutional law. However, it has an implication for recent controversy in the courts concerning the need for proof of discriminatory intent in challenges to districting arrangements that adversely affect the electoral prospects of minorities. In a 1980 case, the Supreme Court held that a showing of "discriminatory purpose" is necessary to sustain an allegation of constitutionally impermissible vote dilution. The Court said that evidence regarding the adverse *effects* of the arrangements in question is relevant only to the extent that it supports inferences of discriminatory intent.[34] Many commentators, including some who believe the Court has been insufficiently attentive to problems of vote dilution, share this view.[35] However, the position is counterintuitive, as consideration of an extreme possibility illustrates: a districting system that excluded a racial minority of substantial size from any legislative representation whatsoever over an extended period of time would not seem more acceptable if it arose from historical accident rather than from conscious design.[36] The illustration confirms what our theory of qualitative fairness implies: racial ger-

[33] A similar point is made by Justice White in *Wells v. Rockefeller*, 394 U.S. 542 (1969), at 554–55 (dissenting).

[34] *Mobile v. Bolden*, 446 U.S. 55 (1980). The Court's holding represents a narrowing of its earlier position. In dicta in a 1965 case, it held that allegations of vote dilution must show that a plan "designedly *or otherwise*" would "operate to minimize or cancel out the voting strength" of racial or political groups. *Fortson v. Dorsey*, 379 U.S. 433 (1965), at 439 (emphasis added). Similar language can be found in *White v. Regester*, 412 U.S. 755 (1973), at 766–67, 769–70. The plaintiffs in *Mobile* brought their case under the Fourteenth and Fifteenth Amendments as well as section 2 of the Voting Rights Act of 1965. Partly in reaction to the *Mobile* decision, the Congress in 1982 amended the Act to make clear that proof of discriminatory intent was not necessary to make good claims of vote dilution. So the question of the relevance of intent to discriminate may be moot as a matter of statutory construction, though not of constitutional interpretation.

[35] See, e.g., John Hart Ely, *Democracy and Distrust* (Cambridge: Harvard University Press, 1980), pp. 139–40.

[36] Tribe, *American Constitutional Law*, p. 754.

rymandering and other forms of vote dilution are mainly objectionable (when they are objectionable at all) because they subject minorities to the predictable threat that their rights and urgent interests will be insufficiently attended to in the legislature. This is not to say that considerations about intent are irrelevant. For one thing, if districting provisions were clearly motivated by a prejudiced intention to deny fair consideration to minorities, the interest in recognition would be offended even if the provisions failed to accomplish their purpose and there was, in fact, no discriminatory effect. And of course—to reverse the common view—proof of discriminatory intent may provide reason to infer, or at least to inquire into, possible discriminatory effect. The thought that qualitatively unfair treatment can exist only when there is discriminatory intent is a vestige of the idea that qualitative fairness is a process-oriented rather than an outcome-oriented conception; but as we have seen, this position lacks a persuasive defense.

The objection can take a second and less abstract form. It holds that the deliberate manipulation of districting arrangements in order to secure particular patterns of results violates the political rights of those who are disadvantaged by the manipulation. Consider the racial gerrymandering case of *United Jewish Organizations v. Carey* (the "Williamsburg" case).[37] This case concerned a state legislative district in Brooklyn with a large Hasidic majority. In order to increase the number of districts likely to return black and Puerto Rican members, a redistricting plan divided the Hasidim into two districts, in neither of which they commanded a majority. They complained that their rights to equal protection had been offended. Some commentators have seen in this case an illustration of the general proposition that deliberate, outcome-conscious districting policies will inevitably offend the rights of those disadvantaged by the policies; and they have claimed that only interest-neutral districting criteria can respect these rights equally for all.[38] If the analysis set forth earlier is accepted, then this claim can-

[37] 430 U.S. 144 (1977).

[38] See, for example, David Wells, "Against Affirmative Gerrymandering," in *Representation and Redistricting Issues*, ed. Bernard Grofman et al. (Lexington, Mass.: Lexington Books, 1982), pp. 83–85. In cases decided subsequent to the Williamsburg case, the Court has embraced a similar view. See, e.g., *Karcher v. Daggett*, 462 U.S. 725 (1983), esp. 744–65 (Justice Stevens, concurring) and 765–83 (Justice White, dissenting). For a discussion, see Alan Howard and Bruce Howard, "The Dilemma of

not stand. Outcome-conscious districting policies like that at issue in the Williamsburg case do not violate the right to equal power; instead, they alter the distribution of prospects of electoral success implied by the existing spatial distribution of political interests. They seek to achieve by design a distribution likely to yield more equitable outcomes than the distribution that prevails by historical accident. The appropriate question in any particular case is whether the adjustment contemplated in that case will accomplish this goal at less cost in other important values than the other means available.[39] There is room for dispute about the right answer to this question in connection with the Williamsburg case. But this is a different issue than that raised by the plaintiffs, which was whether the use of *any* outcome-conscious districting criterion offends the rights to political equality of some of those affected.

A final comment about the status of this argument. I have not claimed that principles of democratic theory *require* courts and legislatures to adopt outcome-conscious districting strategies of the kind I have been discussing. The principles of democratic theory do not have so direct an application. Instead, they identify goals to be sought in the political system as a whole and constraints within which it is permissible to seek these goals. Within these constraints, historical and contextual considerations play an important role, both in identifying those strategies most likely to achieve the goals at acceptable cost and in determining the likelihood that in the absence of affirmative efforts in institutional design these goals will fail to be met. The argument set forth earlier identifies some particular hazards that might arise in a system of representation employing single-member territorial constituencies under contemporary conditions and exhibits certain sorts of constrained manipulation of district structure as permissible strategies for avoiding these hazards. To reiterate, it does not follow that the hazards cannot be avoided otherwise or that under different historical circumstances they would be sufficiently grave to compel similar forms of remedial action.

---

the Voting Rights Act—Recognizing the Emerging Political Equality Norm," *Columbia Law Review* 83 (1983), pp. 1615–63.

[39] Thus, for example, Howard and Howard argue that the aims of affirmative racial gerrymandering might be accomplished through the use of different means. "The Dilemma of the Voting Rights Act," pp. 1656–63.

CHAPTER EIGHT

The Formation of

the Political Agenda

Restrictions on the composition of the ballot could make a mockery of efforts to ensure fair representation. So it is noteworthy that access to the general election ballot is limited in virtually all U.S. jurisdictions. Being a willing candidate who satisfies the qualifications for office is seldom sufficient to attain a position on the ballot; further requirements usually apply as well, such as the filing of nominating petitions, payment of filing fees, and endorsement by a political party.

These barriers can seem unfair in several respects. They introduce inequalities in the distribution among willing candidates of opportunities to contend for office. They affect the capacities of actual or potential political groups to present their views to the electorate at large and to participate in the working out of political coalitions. Like patents and franchises in goods markets, they restrain competition and create opportunities for collusion, which could compromise whatever socially desirable properties the competitive political process might possess. Most importantly, provisions regulating access to the ballot affect the character and quality of public political deliberation. These provisions are among the chief institutional means for managing the content and diversity of the alternatives presented for public consideration. So it would not be an overstatement to say that the terms of access govern the constitution of the political agenda itself.

Matters are complicated by a recognition of the pivotal role of the major political parties. Frequently (as in most American jurisdictions), this role is reinforced by ballot access regulations giving preferential treatment to the candidates of the major party organizations. But even where major parties are not accorded any such treatment, structural elements in the political system, such as the use of single-member districts with a plurality rule, may have the effect of granting a small number of established parties something like a natural oligopoly.[1] Either way, major parties are likely to dominate the selection of candidates for office and to define the boundaries of popular political debate. Groups without the resources and the legal recognition of established party organizations will have considerably less opportunity to influence the political agenda or to field candidates with realistic chances of winning. In view of this, it would be a mistake to conceive the scope of a doctrine of fair access to the political arena too narrowly. Its subject matter extends beyond the legal regulation of access to the general election ballot itself and also includes those aspects of party structure and procedure that govern the selection of candidates and the formulation of policy platforms.[2] Thus, recent debate about the candidate selection procedures of the major national parties should not be seen as raising only internal issues for party organizations; these issues are matters of general public concern.[3]

[1] On the relationship between political structure and party system, see especially Maurice Duverger, *Political Parties*, trans. Barbara and Robert North (London: Methuen, 1954), pp. 245–55, 328–37. For a contemporary discussion of the issue as it arises in the U.S., see Samuel J. Eldersveld, *Political Parties in American Society* (New York: Basic Books, 1982), pp. 68–71.

[2] In fact, it is difficult to separate the questions of ballot access regulation and regulation of procedures of party governance, even for analytical purposes, since the overall aims of fair access to the political agenda might be served by complex combinations of rules restricting direct access to the ballot and rules governing the candidate selection and platform formation procedures of the major parties. Several possibilities are discussed in John H. Barton, "The General-Election Ballot: More Nominees or More Representative Nominees?" *Stanford Law Review* 22 (1970), pp. 165–95.

[3] The reform effort in the Democratic party was considerably more ambitious than that of the Republicans. Its focus was the party's Commission on Party Structure and Delegate Selection (the "McGovern-Fraser" Commission). See its report, *Mandate for Change* (Washington: Democratic National Committee, 1970); and, for an illuminating discussion by one of the participants, Austin Ranney, *Curing the Mischiefs of Faction* (Berkeley: University of California Press, 1975). The most detailed study of the reform process is Byron E. Shafer, *The Quiet Revolution* (New York: Russell Sage Foundation, 1983). Among the many provocative studies of the results, see especially Scott Keeter and Cliff Zukin, *Uninformed Choice: The Failure of the New Presidential Nominating System* (New York: Praeger, 1983); and Howard L. Reiter, "The Limitations of Reform: Changes in the Nominating Process," *British Journal of Political Science* 15 (1985), pp. 399–417. For a discussion that places these

Although its importance is clear enough, the subject of fair access is exceedingly difficult to conceive abstractly. (Perhaps this is why less theoretical attention has been given to it than to any of the other leading institutional questions involving political equality.)[4] One is tempted to treat particular issues in isolation and to assume that they can be resolved without reference to general considerations of political fairness. I shall argue that this is incorrect. I begin by examining three reasons for objecting to (at least some kinds of) institutional constraints on the political agenda. The reasons derive from concerns about the impact of access constraints on the fruitfulness of public deliberation, the accuracy of preference aggregation, and the availability of opportunities to contend for public office. Critical consideration of these objections helps to identify a set of aims that fair agenda-structuring institutions should seek to achieve, which I illustrate briefly with reference to the system of party competition. As we shall see, this conception of fair access might license legal regulation of certain aspects of party governance that are regarded in contemporary constitutional law as protected against state interference by the doctrine of freedom of association. I consider at the end whether this special protection can be justified as a matter of political theory.

Access Constraints
and Fruitful Deliberation

There is of course no necessity for an election system to employ restrictive devices at all. At the limit, one can imagine a single-stage election system (perhaps employing some scheme of prefer-

---

reforms in historical perspective, see James W. Ceaser, *Presidential Selection* (Princeton: Princeton University Press, 1979).

   [4] It may also explain the considerable doctrinal confusion to be found in constitutional law concerning the implications of egalitarian principle for ballot access provisions. The leading cases are *Williams v. Rhodes*, 393 U.S. 23 (1968), *Jenness v. Fortson*, 403 U.S. 431 (1968), *Storer v. Brown*, 415 U.S. 724 (1974), *American Party v. White*, 415 U.S. 767 (1974), and *Anderson v. Celebreeze*, 460 U.S. 780 (1983). For commentary, see "Developments in the Law—Elections," *Harvard Law Review* 88 (1975), pp. 1121–50 (ballot access) and 1151–1216 (party nominating procedures); and Laurence H. Tribe, *American Constitutional Law* (Mineola, N.Y.: Foundation Press, 1978), pp. 774–98.

ential voting) in which access to the general election ballot is open on equal terms to all candidates who satisfy whatever qualifications attach to the office itself. Today, few people advocate such an unstructured system of election, at least for offices above the local level; indeed, many take it as obvious for a variety of reasons that the range of alternatives should be rather severely constrained. But this has not seemed obvious to everyone.

Consider, for example, the Hare scheme of personal representation, which employs a single-stage election system in which any voter can record a preference for any qualified candidate. The chief aim, of course, is to facilitate the proportional representation of opinion in the legislature. However, by itself this does not require the use of an unconstrained, single-stage election system; multi-stage systems that limit access to the final ballot might accomplish the same aim. Hare's choice of a single-stage system was influenced by a further consideration: providing voters with "the most enlarged field of choice, and the most unfettered means of exercising it" would "give to individuality that free agency which is the mother of responsibility."[5] The argument is not altogether clear, but a plausible reconstruction is this. When the range of alternatives is at its widest, the proportion of voters able to find candidates with whose positions they can identify would be at a maximum. More people would be motivated to devote their energetic attention to politics and therefore to develop and exercise the capacities of understanding and judgment. Being better informed and more acutely attentive, voters would deliberate and vote more effectively, and the quality of representation (and hence of legislation) would be enhanced.[6]

But the idea that more choice necessarily leads to better judgment is naive. It does not attend to the scarcities—of time, information, and cognitive ability itself—that inevitably constrain political deliberation. These constraints make it unlikely that most voters will be able to take seriously more than a relatively limited number of candidates or range of factors relevant to choosing among them. When the field is too large, the quality of judgment might be re-

[5] Thomas Hare, *The Election of Representatives, Parliamentary and Municipal,* 4th ed. (London: Longmans, Green, Reader, and Dyer, 1873), pp. 94–95.

[6] Ibid., pp. 95–100.

duced. Indeed, the multiplication of alternatives may even decrease the incentive to participate at all: the investment in acquiring enough information to decide responsibly among a wide range of alternatives could appear excessive in relation to the chance that one's vote will affect the outcome.

In the context of large organizations, better decisions are sometimes reached when deliberative capacities are concentrated on an appropriately limited range of alternatives than when the range of choice consists of all feasible possibilities. In the latter case, time and resource scarcities usually have a more adventitious impact on the process of deliberation, the outcomes of which are therefore likely to be less reliable.[7] In the political context, citizens will often be even more limited in the time and resources available for investigation, analysis, and choice; and the chances of bad decisions being taken when the agenda is relatively unstructured may therefore be even greater. Better decisions might be reached when the range of alternatives is restricted—even, perhaps, if the abstractly best alternative is among those excluded from the agenda.

The idea of an unconstrained agenda also faces a problem of equity. The problem has two aspects, one arising from differences in the capacities and resources of individual voters and the other from differences in the resources of candidates and their supporters. First, consider that the distribution among voters of the capacity to acquire and appraise information about the alternatives will inevitably be uneven, as will be the opportunity costs of devoting a given level of resources to politics rather than to other pursuits. In election systems with relatively larger numbers of alternatives, one might therefore expect that outcomes will tend to favor those who are advantaged with respect to information resources, time, or intellectual capacity. Those who are less advantaged in these ways might be better served where institutions are designed to narrow the choice to a smaller number of alternatives, at least where there

---

[7] The *locus classicus* is Herbert A. Simon, "A Behavioral Model of Rational Choice," *Quarterly Journal of Economics* 69 (1955), pp. 99–118. Also, see Simon, "Rationality as Process and as Product of Thought," *American Economic Review* 68 (May 1978), pp. 1–16; James G. March, "Bounded Rationality, Ambiguity, and the Engineering of Preferences," *Bell Journal of Economics* 9 (Autumn 1978), pp. 587–608; and Jon Elster, *Ulysses and the Sirens* (Cambridge: Cambridge University Press, 1979), pp. 133–37.

is reason to believe that the narrowing mechanism would not exclude representatives of their interests.[8]

The other aspect of the equity problem concerns differences in the resources of candidates and their supporters. Consider again Hare's system. He assumed that when legal, financial, and logistical barriers to candidacy were held at a minimum, the balance of public attention paid to the various alternatives would be largely determined by the actual distribution of opinion and preference.[9] However, even if barriers to access were minimized, the focus of public consideration would be affected by forces that do not necessarily reflect the distribution of opinion in the electorate as a whole, such as the news media and the various concentrations of wealth and influence capable of commanding public attention. Where the agenda is officially unconstrained, these unofficial constraints are likely to be more rather than less effective in determining which alternatives actually dominate the main arenas of public deliberation.[10]

These considerations suggest that both individual deliberation and social choice may be more successful in multistage systems in which the range of alternatives is narrowed and its composition adjusted before the final choice is made than in systems of the kind that Hare advocated. Of course, narrowing mechanisms might be preferred for other reasons as well. For example, they might be seen as a response to the fear that the confusion likely to occur when there are large numbers of alternatives would compromise the legitimacy of the system as a whole in the eyes of its constituents. And it may be that multistage systems would have various extrinsic benefits; they might, for example, promote stable government by encouraging the formation of coalitions at an earlier stage and by

[8] Reasoning of this kind is the basis of a venerable tradition of argument regarding the egalitarian consequences of political organization and party systems. Inclusion in a coalition party with a common program enables groups that would otherwise be politically impotent to press their claims. The main source is E. E. Schattschneider, *Party Government* (New York: Rinehart, 1942). See also Sidney Verba, Norman H. Nie, and Jae-on Kim, *Participation and Political Equality: A Seven-Nation Study* (New York: Cambridge University Press, 1978), esp. pp. 14–15.

[9] Hare, *The Election of Representatives*, p. 100.

[10] Compare the discussion of "the information problem" in Joshua Cohen and Joel Rogers, *On Democracy* (Harmondsworth, Middlesex: Penguin Books, 1983), pp. 62–64.

increasing the chance that one of the alternatives considered at the final stage would gain the support of a large plurality or of a majority of the voters. One might accept such views but believe that they represent considerations to be balanced against the costs to effective deliberation brought about by preelection narrowing mechanisms. The foregoing remarks illustrate that this is incorrect. There is no necessary conflict between the interests in conditions of effective deliberation and in procedural simplicity, legitimacy, or governmental stability. The real theoretical difficulties associated with the deliberative interests arise from the impact of agenda-structuring arrangements on the character (rather than the size) of the public agenda. We consider these difficulties below.

AGENDA STRUCTURE AS
PREFERENCE AGGREGATION

Hare's conception of the requisites of fruitful deliberation led him to reject all institutional mechanisms that exclude willing candidates from the election ballot. I turn now to a different critique of agenda constraints, which operates in a more selective way. According to this view, narrowing procedures constitute the early stages of a continuous process of preference aggregation terminating in the identification of a social choice. They are unacceptable when they distort this process by contributing to the selection of an outcome different from that which would be specified by the appropriate social choice function.

To illustrate, suppose that there are two parties, each of which nominates one candidate to contend in the general election. Minorparty and independent candidacies are effectively prohibited; thus, in the general election, the winner is selected by majority vote. Suppose also that there are only two candidates for each party's nomination, in each case a centrist and an extremist. Owing to the intraparty distributions of opinion, each extremist is nominated. Now there is no general reason to believe that whichever candidate were to win a majority in the general election against the other party's extremist would have won against the other party's moderate; indeed, in a four-way race, one of the moderates might even have been the first choice of a majority of the whole electorate (that is, a Condorcet candidate). According to the view we are considering, the candidate selection system in this example is unfair because it makes possible the election of a candidate who stands lower in the voters' preferences than some other candidate who was excluded at an earlier stage.

Unlike the Hare view, this position does not oppose the use of all multistage selection procedures. However, it holds that the design of such procedures should be assessed with reference to criteria applicable in the first instance to the election process as a whole. Although the design of narrowing mechanisms poses a separate issue of institutional design, it does not pose a separable issue of democratic theory in the sense that different or special criteria apply to it. Instead, it is seen as part of the larger problem of implementing the social choice function.[11]

On such a view, the process of agenda formation should be, so to speak, voluntary; ideally, at least, decisions resulting in a reduction in the range of choice facing the people would be made by the people themselves and, moreover, would be made consistently with the ultimate aim of identifying the one alternative (or set of alternatives) more strongly favored by them than any other. If this were the case, there would be no sense in which the range of alternatives could be seen as arbitrarily fixed or as imposed by structural aspects of institutions that do not reflect the actual distribution of preferences.

As we noted earlier, the Arrow result and related considerations show that in the general case the possibility of arbitrary institutional effects cannot be ruled out. The ideal set forth in this view of fair access could be realized only when various background conditions concerning the structure of individual preferences were somehow known to be satisfied. Even then, however, the conception of agenda formation as preference aggregation would be suspect, for it reflects an unrealistic and misleading understanding of the nature of the political activity that is stimulated and organized by agenda-

---

[11] This is how the agenda problem is conceived by those writers in the theory of voting who take it up at all. See, for example, Michael Dummett, *Voting Procedures* (Oxford: Clarendon Press, 1984), pp. 50, 243–93. Most writers in this tradition, however, take the agenda as given. Michael Taylor, "The Theory of Collective Choice," *Handbook of Political Science*, vol. 3, ed. Fred I. Greenstein and Nelson W. Polsby (Reading, Mass.: Addison-Wesley, 1975), p. 469.

structuring institutions in modern democratic politics. In this conception, preferences are assumed to be determined exogenously to
the process of preference revelation and aggregation. But the assumption is false. The process through which the range of alternatives is narrowed is also, inevitably, a process of learning, deliberation, and debate. As the process runs its course, some will revise
their prior preferences, and others, who began with no clear preferences at all, will form them. The formation of preferences is at least
partially endogenous to the narrowing process itself.[12]

An analogous difficulty has often been noticed by welfare economists in connection with the assessment of policies that affect people's tastes.[13] In both cases, policies are evaluated according to some
function of the preferences of those affected. However, when the
policies themselves have the capacity to influence the relevant
class of preferences, the fact that one policy is more successful than
any other in satisfying those preferences will not necessarily justify
the selection of that policy. For it can always be asked why those
affected should want to have *these* preferences rather than those
that would have been produced if some other alternative had been
chosen. In some cases it might be possible to answer this question
by showing that this rather than that array of *ex post* preferences
would be rational for anyone who had the preferences that actually
existed *ex ante*.[14] But this reply is not promising in connection with
the selection of institutions governing the structure of the political
agenda, since one of the aims of these institutions is to engender
favorable conditions for the evaluation of preferences. The fact that
any such institutions produce *ex post* preferences that appear to be
rational in view of the participants' preferences *ex ante* clearly does

---

[12] For a discussion of endogeneity of voter preference in connection with theories
of party competition, see Patrick Dunleavy and Hugh Ward, "Exogenous Voter Preferences and Parties with State Power: Some Internal Problems of Economic Theories
of Party Competition," *British Journal of Political Science* 11 (1981), pp. 351–80.

[13] For the seminal discussion, see John Kenneth Galbraith, *The Affluent Society*,
4th ed. (Boston: Houghton Mifflin, 1984), pp. 126–33. See also Herbert Gintis, "Welfare Criteria With Endogenous Preferences: The Economics of Education," *International Economic Review* 15 (1974), pp. 415–30.

[14] Such an approach has been advanced in consumer theory. See, e.g., C. C. von
Weiszacker, "Notes on Endogenous Change of Tastes," *Journal of Economic Theory*
3 (1971), pp. 345–72. There is a brief discussion in Elster, *Ulysses and the Sirens*, pp.
77–86.

not imply that the institutions embody desirable conditions of deliberation; as the *ex ante* preferences themselves may have been insufficiently reflective or informed, they are ill suited to serve as the baseline for evaluating the outcomes produced by the institutions that guide their assessment and revision.

The larger point is this. The guiding normative idea underlying the conception of agenda structuring as preference aggregation is a concern that the participants' (preexisting) preferences be accurately represented in the outcome. Fair procedures are those that treat voters equitably in the sense of being maximally faithful to their preferences. However, the agenda-structuring process is more complex than this conception allows, and the concern about the fairness of the process cannot be interpreted simply in terms of the faithfulness of its outcomes to preexisting preferences. To the extent that the interest in equitable treatment plays any role in evaluating this process, it needs a more objective interpretation. But this is not the only, and perhaps not the most important, interest involved. Because the process defines a framework of individual deliberation and choice, participants should also be concerned that it embody conditions in which they have reason for confidence in their judgments. For example, a sufficiently wide range of alternatives should be presented so that people would be enabled to assess how their political aims could best be achieved in view of the constraints imposed by the competing aims of others. Moreover, the process should embody conditions of fair debate analogous to a committee's rules of order. Both points reflect the influence of the regulative interest in deliberative responsibility, which operates independently of the interest in equitable treatment. Neither of these interests is accorded its appropriate weight when agenda-structuring institutions are assessed solely in terms of their preference-aggregating properties.

AGENDA CONSTRAINTS
AND POLITICAL LIBERTY

Finally, I turn to the thought that agenda-structuring provisions may be unfair because they restrict opportunities to contend for public office, both by denying such an opportunity absolutely to some willing candidates and by introducing inequalities in the prospects of those to whom the opportunity is made formally available.

Rawls apparently holds such a view. He characterizes the opportunity to run for office as a "basic liberty" that may be burdened only when necessary to secure the other basic liberties, and then only in a manner that imposes the burden equally on all.[15] Now if one accepts that responsible deliberation requires some constraint on the size of the ballot, then it might be said that restrictions on the opportunity to contend for office are necessary to secure the other basic liberties. Accordingly, the operative element of the view is the requirement that any such restrictions should apply equally to all. Thus, perhaps, ballot access provisions according preferential treatment to the candidates of established political parties would be unacceptable. Similarly, if less clearly, party nominating procedures (or laws allowing them) that disadvantage candidates with substantial popular support but without the support of party officials might also be forbidden.

Why should the opportunity to contend for office be seen as a basic liberty at all? Rawls associates it with the other political liberties such as the right to vote and the right to participate in public political deliberation.[16] These other rights are normally exercised by everyone, or nearly everyone, in circumstances of political choice; they are the means by which citizens are enabled to influence outcomes. This strategic role in the popular determination of policy explains why they count as "basic." However, the right to run for office is not basic in this way. Arguably, voters may have an interest in being able to vote for positions close to their own, and citizens may have an interest in the representation of their concerns in public deliberation and in the legislative process; but neither of these concerns implies that every willing candidate should have equal access to the competitive political process. The right to have one's position represented or taken into account is not the same as the right to represent one's own position.

The latter is more properly conceived as an opportunity for service and self-development, analogous, perhaps, to the right to

---

[15] John Rawls, *A Theory of Justice* (Cambridge: Harvard University Press, 1971), pp. 61, 223–24.
[16] Ibid.

choose a career. As such it might be a means of realizing important elements of one's personal good. However, this does not distinguish public office from many other social positions. Moreover, if the arguments set forth earlier are correct, then whatever interest the prospective candidate has in access to the political arena must be compared with the competing interests of voters and citizens in the ends served by constraining the agenda. Suppose, for example, that a structure containing inducements for the formation of coalitions at the preelection stage would make for more stable government and greater continuity of policy; and suppose that such a structure requires preferential treatment for the candidates of the major political parties. Under these assumptions, the interest of the prospective independent candidate could only be realized if the interests of citizens generally were compromised; and in view of the importance of the latter, it does not seem plausible that the interests of prospective candidates should win out. Accordingly, it does not appear that agenda-structuring arrangements are unfair *simply* because they establish inequalities in the distribution and value of opportunities to contend for public office.[17] Everything depends on the purposes and effects of the exclusionary provisions, viewed within the context of the system as a whole.

AIMS OF AGENDA-STRUCTURING INSTITUTIONS

These considerations suggest several elements that a more satisfactory conception of fair access to the political arena should embody. I begin by considering at the most general level the goals that anyone motivated by the regulative interests would wish agenda-structuring institutions to advance. Then, I discuss the dimensions on which these institutions can vary and indicate how the goals bear on each dimension. In the following section, I will illustrate briefly how the view applies to a system of election based on competition between two major political parties.

The main consequence of the discussion thus far is to emphasize the importance of the role of agenda-setting institutions in organ-

[17] Of course, as with access to other social positions, considerations of a more general kind apply, such as those associated with the concept of equality of opportunity.

izing and stimulating political deliberation. The formation of the agenda is not accurately perceived as a process of identifying alternatives that are ranked highly in some function of the citizens' preexisting preferences or judgments; instead, it is an educative and deliberative process in which judgments can be arrived at and revised on the basis of the information and arguments supplied in the course of public debate. Without a favorable background of public political debate, the judgments expressed at the general election are likely to be ill informed and inadequately reflective and, consequently, of diminished significance as the foundation of democratic choice; citizens could not regard their judgments as responsible in the sense of resting on informed comparisons among the alternatives presented. The provision of a framework that facilitates well-informed and adequately reflective judgment is therefore among the most important general aims of a system of agenda formation.

It is not, however, the only aim. Access provisions have another significance as well: they affect the chances of various positions to gain adherents and ultimately to influence the outcomes of electoral competition. Thus, the interest in equitable treatment also bears on the design of agenda-structuring mechanisms. The main point is that, to the extent feasible, these mechanisms should ensure public presentation of positions responsive to the needs and interests of all significant portions of the citizenry. Otherwise, the chances that democratic choice will produce equitable outcomes would be diminished. (This is what remains of the concern about the fidelity of outcomes to popular preferences once the difficulties arising from their endogenous character has been appreciated.) In addition, access provisions should encourage accountability in government, in order to increase the incentives for public officials to carry out the policy commitments that led to their election.

In view of this, what properties would it be desirable for the framework to possess? An answer should address both the quantity and the quality of the alternatives that fair agenda-structuring institutions should seek to elicit. The meaning of the first of these is clear enough; but more needs to be said about the dimensions on which the quality of the alternatives can be characterized. Three qualitative dimensions seem particularly important. These are the completeness, coherence, and range of the alternatives. The dimensions of completeness and coherence arise from the fact that the components of the political agenda are not usually single-purpose policies but positions consisting of combinations of policies, each with a different domain; or, more accurately, they are candidates or parties representing such positions. The *completeness* of a position is a question of the number of distinguishable issues that compose it; for example, the position represented by a "single-issue candidate" is relatively incomplete, while that represented by the candidate of a programmatic party is very likely much less so. The *coherence* of a position is the degree to which the policies that make it up could be jointly carried out without undermining any of their purposes; thus, prima facie, a position advocating both increased government expenditures and reductions in government revenues is less coherent than one advocating increased expenditures together with a tax increase. Finally, the dimension of *range* refers to the set of alternatives as a whole: it is a question of its breadth or compass relative to the distribution of interests in society at large.

Turning now to the properties of fair agenda-structuring institutions, the question of the number of alternatives is the most straightforward. The number should be small enough, given prevailing scarcities of time and resources, so that informed comparative judgments are reasonably possible. Otherwise, individual preferences would lack secure foundations, and those holding them could not regard themselves as fully responsible participants in public life.

In addition, alternatives that are relatively more complete are preferable to those that are less so. This is largely for reasons of accountability. Citizens will wish to regard their votes as determining the course of public affairs, and this aim is best served when the positions among which they choose bear on a relatively broad set of public issues. Candidates whose platforms address only a single issue or a small number of issues do not offer such programs, even though (we assume) the offices for which they contend require that they take decisions on the full range of public issues. In the case of single-issue candidates, this means that beyond the boundaries of that issue, successful candidates will not be constrained by prior commitments, and there will be no clear sense in which their performance in office could be said to represent the wishes of those who elected them.

Someone might object that provisions disadvantaging positions that embrace only a small number of issues would be unfair to those voters for whom these issues are all that matter. In considering this objection, we must distinguish between two kinds of voters who might be thought to be treated unfairly: we might call them reflective voters and bullet voters. Reflective voters, after considering a wide range of public issues, come to regard one or a few of these as so important that the others seem trivial in comparison. Their support for a single-issue candidate reflects a judgment about political priorities. In this case the problem of accountability would not arise in the form discussed above. The problem arises only in connection with bullet voters, who fix on a single issue without making any similar judgment; it is not that other issues do not matter but that the question whether they matter has not been considered. Now, the difficulty about single-issue candidacies is that they are more likely to encourage bullet voting than reflective voting; by concentrating public attention on a single issue, they discourage deliberation about others and about their overall coherence and interrelationships. Thus, perhaps oddly, the single-issue *candidate* may be the enemy of reflective single-issue *voting*.[18]

The question of range is the most difficult. The interest in responsible deliberation argues for some significant degree of difference among the alternative positions. Otherwise there would be little to provoke dispute or even to engage one's attention; institutions that tended routinely to elicit broadly similar alternatives would more likely discourage involvement in public deliberative activity.[19] But it is plainly not enough that the alternatives be diverse; their range could be sufficiently broad to engage attention and provoke reflection yet still be unacceptable. For example, there is little to recommend institutions that elicit the most attentive and well-considered of choices if positions responsive to the vital

[18] It does not follow from the remarks in the text that prospective candidacies should be individually assessed with regard to the completeness of the positions they represent and allowed or excluded on that basis. We are concerned here with the broader question of what kinds of candidacies the agenda-structuring *system* should encourage.

[19] In a more general form, the argument can be found in Mill. *On Liberty* [1859], chap. 2, in *Collected Works*, vol. 18, ed. J. M. Robson (Toronto: University of Toronto Press, 1977).

interests of a disadvantaged group are systematically excluded at the outset.

One way to formulate the underlying idea is to say that institutions should not exclude *salient* positions from the political agenda.[20] But what is a salient position? It would be a mistake to identify salience with positions that, in fact, enjoy some quantum of public support. Because the formation of political judgment is at least partly endogenous to the narrowing process, an account based on actual preferences would be suspect; the presence or absence of support for a position might result from its inclusion or exclusion from public deliberation in its earlier phases. (Thus, for example, it is sometimes said that the absence of an articulate socialist presence in electoral politics in the United States is a consequence of structural factors such as the tendency of the system to favor moderate parties, rather than a reflection of the distribution of actual political interest in the population.) The authority of existing preferences, as criteria of salience, is tainted by their causal history. Alternatively, a counterfactual preference-based account might seem attractive: salient positions might be those that *would* attain the required quantum of support if they were sufficiently represented in public deliberation. However, in addition to formidable problems of application, this interpretation is question begging. Estimating the capacity of a position to attain support requires a comparative, not an absolute, judgment; but this depends on the other positions represented on the political agenda, and there is no way of specifying these without referring to preferences whose authority is tainted in the same way as on the view rejected earlier.

These considerations suggest that a satisfactory conception of salience cannot be derived from considerations about the range of preferences that actually exist in society. Nor will an appeal to deliberative considerations solve the problem; the interest in deliberative responsibility requires that there be a significant range of alternatives available for public discussion, but it does not resolve the question how this range should be composed. In seeking a better account, it helps to return to the example of the systematic exclu-

---

[20] I adopt the term from Donald E. Stokes, "Spatial Models of Party Competition," *American Political Science Review* 57 (1963), reprinted in Angus Campbell, Philip E. Converse, Warren E. Miller, and Donald E. Stokes, *Elections and the Political Order* (New York: John Wiley, 1966), p. 168.

sion of positions responsive to the urgent needs of a disadvantaged group. Why is this a troubling possibility? The most straightforward explanation is simply that it would be a bad thing for the urgent needs of *any* group to be left out of political account, and all the more so if the group were already disadvantaged and therefore comparatively ill equipped to obtain satisfaction through private means. This suggests that we would do better to abandon appeals to preferences altogether and regard salience as a substantive criterion from the start. Thus, one might say that a salient position is one whose representation in electoral competition would increase the chances that the urgent interests of some significant portion of the population would be adequately attended to.

Fair Access and Party Competition

Schattschneider described modern democracy as "a competitive political system in which competing leaders and organizations define the alternatives of public policy in such a way that the public can participate in the decision-making process."[21] These organizations are the major political parties ("the orphans of political philosophy," as Schattschneider accurately observed).[22] Any conception of fair access with pretensions to practical relevance should take account of the impact of access provisions on the structure and dynamics of party competition; for this is normally among the most important determinants of the character of the political agenda and so of the extent to which the aims we have identified are likely to be realized.

The central issue can be clarified by considering two leading traditions of thought about party competition in the United States. We may think of these as the doctrines of *elite* and of *programmatic* competition.

The first derives from Schumpeter. It is best understood as an alternative to what he called the "classical" model of democracy, which was apparently intended as a summary description of the

[21] E. E. Schattschneider, *The Semi-Sovereign People* (1960; reprint, Hinsdale, Ill.: Dryden Press, 1975), p. 138; the emphasis in the original has been removed.

[22] Schattschneider, *Party Government*, p. 10. The phrase dates from 1942 but is, unfortunately, still applicable.

views of Rousseau and the early utilitarians, particularly James Mill.[23] According to this model, democratic politics consists of a process of public deliberation that eventuates in the formation of a "popular will," and elections "are the transmission belt whereby the people's will is communicated to the smaller number of persons who actually make law."[24] Schumpeter criticized the model as both incoherent and unrealistic. Its incoherence derived from a reification of the idea of a popular will. In this respect Schumpeter plainly misread the texts to which he was apparently referring, and I shall pass over the point without further comment. The argument of unrealism is more important. Schumpeter argued that the "classical" view rests on premises concerning the political capacities and behavior of citizens that do not apply under modern conditions of mass politics. In contrast to these premises, he held that voters are for the most part ill informed about the content and context of the policy alternatives facing political leaders, that their voting behavior reflects retrospective rather than prospective judgments, and that their policy preferences (to the extent that they have any) do not normally cohere with their preferences about candidates and parties.[25] Even if the idea of a popular will could be given a coherent formulation, there would be no reason to suppose that democratic politics would succeed in identifying it. According to the doctrine of elite competition, a more realistic understanding of the political capacities of ordinary citizens requires a different conception of the goals that democratic institutions could reasonably be expected to serve and a correspondingly different conception of how such institutions ought to be framed.

These goals are stability of succession and protection of widely shared vital interests, among which Schumpeter took the interest in personal liberty to be the most essential. He argued that both

[23] Joseph Schumpeter, *Capitalism, Socialism, and Democracy*, 5th ed. (London: Allen and Unwin, 1976), p. 282. As Plamenatz suggests, perhaps "popular" would have been a more accurate term than "classical." He is certainly right that neither Rousseau nor the English utilitarians held the view that Schumpeter describes. John Plamenatz, *Democracy and Illusion* (London: Longman, 1973), p. 39.

[24] David Miller, "The Competitive Model of Democracy," in *Democratic Theory and Practice*, ed. Graeme Duncan (Cambridge: Cambridge University Press, 1983), p. 133.

[25] Schumpeter, *Capitalism, Socialism, and Democracy*, pp. 256–64.

goals could be achieved by a system of regular electoral competition
between two elite-led political parties regarded as constituting alternative governments. Such a system can serve its goals only if the
parties themselves adhere to certain self-denying ordinances in
their "competitive struggle for the people's vote."[26] Thus, they
should not compete ideologically or in ways that draw into question
the legitimacy of the system of competition itself. Indeed, parties
should not compete by offering rival platforms or policies at all but
instead by offering rival expertise in the conduct of government.
The democratic character of party competition consists primarily in
the capacity of the electoral process to function as a self-protective
mechanism for the population; it enables a limited degree of popular control to be brought peacefully to bear by offering the people a
chance to turn out of office any government whose conduct (particularly with regard to respect for individual liberties) is widely believed to be unacceptable.[27]

The doctrine of programmatic competition, which is associated
with Schattschneider, stands in contrast to this.[28] According to this

[26] Ibid., p. 269.

[27] Spatial theories of party competition, such as that of Anthony Downs, are frequently regarded as heirs of Schumpeter (e.g., by Downs himself: *An Economic Theory of Democracy* [New York: Harper & Row, 1957], p. 29). But this is misleading, at
least with respect to the democratic character claimed for the competitive process.
In a two-party system, assuming (roughly) that voter preferences can be located along
a single dimension, and that there is a normal distribution of preferences along this
dimension, Downs argues that at the equilibrium reached as the parties compete for
votes, the average distance between the winning party's position and that of each
voter will be minimized (p. 118). In this sense, party competition maximizes the
satisfaction of voter preferences. He represents the model as analytical rather than
normative (p. 31), but the ethical inference to be drawn from this analytical conclusion is unmistakable. Because their concern is the extent to which party competition
satisfies voter preferences, spatial models are more accurately seen as expressions of
the popular will theory; and because they assume these preferences to be determined
exogenously to the competitive process, their application to normative issues is open
to the same criticisms as those set forth above. See also Brian Barry, *Sociologists,
Economists and Democracy* (London: Collier-Macmillan, 1970), p. 108; and William
H. Riker and Peter C. Ordeshook, *An Introduction to Positive Political Theory* (Englewood Cliffs, N.J.: Prentice-Hall, 1973), pp. 370–75.

[28] The view can be found in Schattschneider, *Party Government*. Its most influential formulation is in the Report of the Committee on Political Parties of the American Political Science Association, *Toward a More Responsible Two-Party System*
(New York: Rinehart, 1950; originally published in *American Political Science Review* 44 [September 1950 supplement]). Schattschneider chaired the committee. For

view, elite competition, in practice, tends to foster a process of legislation based on temporary coalitions of pressure groups, which operates without the discipline of a coherent conception of the public interest and is shielded from public scrutiny by a dynamic of party competition from which programmatic dispute is effectively excluded. Party platforms, where they exist, are widely understood to have little relevance to the performance of the party once in office. Thus, the democratic character claimed for elite competition is spurious.[29] By contrast, the doctrine of programmatic competition holds that parties should set forth programs consisting of substantive commitments regarding public policy and reflecting a coherent conception of the public interest; these would constitute the "work program" of the party in office and a foundation for criticism by the party in opposition. Electoral competition would not so much present a choice among rival elites as among rival programs. The democratic character of programmatic competition rests on two points. First, voters can reasonably regard their votes as an indication of a judgment about policy: "When there are two parties identifiable by the kinds of action they propose, the voters have an actual choice."[30] Second, because it requires parties to announce their programs in advance of elections, programmatic competition enables voters to hold parties responsible for the policies they undertake once in office. Neither point applies to elite competition.

These contending doctrines have different implications regarding access to the political arena. As Schumpeter's analysis makes clear, elite competition is a form of political oligopoly. It requires two relatively stable organizational structures operating in an environment that discourages programmatic or ideological conflict. There is no need for minor parties or independent candidacies (indeed, either might upset the dynamic of elite competition by invoking programmatic appeals), which would be destabilizing in any case. Moreover, mechanisms that enable party members to participate in party governance should be resisted, because they would only serve to constrain the leadership. Indeed, were it not for the need for personnel to carry out the normal activities of electioneering, there

a discussion, see Frank J. Sorauf, *Party Politics in America*, 5th ed. (Boston: Little, Brown, 1984), pp. 388–414; and Eldersveld, *Political Parties in American Society*, pp. 428–33.

[29] *Toward a More Responsible Two-Party System*, p. 19.

[30] Ibid., pp. 18–19.

would be no obvious reason to conceive of parties as membership organizations at all.

On the other hand, in programmatic competition minor parties and independent candidacies need not be regarded as a threat to the competitive dynamic (though they might be seen as ineffectual).[31] More importantly, the participation of the rank and file in the determination of the party program is an indispensible element of party responsibility, both because it encourages party loyalty and because it constrains party leaders to conduct electoral activity on programmatic grounds.

It seems clear that programmatic competition offers the better hope of satisfying the aims that a system of agenda structure should puruse. Parties that face incentives to compete on the basis of substantive programmatic commitments will obviously contribute more to a fruitful process of public political deliberation than parties that hold themselves aloof from such commitments; in the latter case, public deliberation would concentrate on substantive issues of dispute, if at all, only accidentally. Similarly, the public nature of a party's programmatic commitments enables voters to hold the party and its elected officials accountable for their performance in office. And programmatic competition among organized parties increases the chances (though it hardly guarantees) that voters will face relatively complete and coherent alternatives.

These straightforward arguments for programmatic competition might be questioned for reasons similar to those that animated Schumpeter's critique of the "classical" model. Thus, the doctrine of programmatic competition might be thought to depend on unrealistic assumptions about political behavior. For example, as contemporary partisans of elite competition point out, survey research demonstrates that voters are normally ill informed about the platforms actually set forth by the parties as well as the background facts required for assessing them.[32] Therefore, it might be said, programmatic competition, even if it succeeds in accomplishing its de-

---

[31] As they were, for example, by the authors of the APSA report, *Toward a More Responsible Two-Party System*, p. 18.

[32] For the standard criticisms of responsible party doctrine, see Evron M. Kirkpatrick, "Toward a More Responsible Party System: Political Science, Policy Science, or Pseudo-Science?" *American Political Science Review* 65 (1971), esp. pp. 971–74. See also Samuel Brittan, "The Economic Contradictions of Democracy," *British Journal of Political Science* 5 (1975), pp. 133–35.

liberative aims, is not likely to produce equitable outcomes; programmatic constraints are more likely to induce leaders to adopt bad policies than to enable them to implement good ones.

Although there is room for dispute about the findings relied on in this critique, I shall not pursue this question here.[33] For even if their accuracy is granted, they do not show that citizens lack the capacity for the kind of informed participation required by programmatic party competition. The dominant features of political behavior in a population are not independent of the structure of its electoral institutions. Just as different systems of party competition might either elicit or submerge ideological or programmatic dispute, so these (and other) institutions might either encourage or discourage popular participation in substantive disagreement about the course of state policy. It is a mistake to conceive the forms of political behavior observed in any given setting as fixed by general facts of psychology and sociology. Obviously, such general facts play a constraining role, and no plausible normative theory could posit forms of behavior inconsistent with them. But there is likely to be room for variation left open, and within this space institutions may play an important role in determining which capacities will develop and thus which behavioral traits will predominate.[34] Accordingly, the fact (if it is a fact) that voters in systems of elite competition are typically ill informed about party positions does not by itself show that they would be equally ill informed in a system in which programmatic competition was the norm. The key question is whether the political behavior of the ordinary voter would be much better informed or more discriminating, assuming the most favorable institutional background, than it is under existing institutions. Although this is obviously an open question, there does not appear to be persuasive evidence that more informed and responsible participation would be impossible to achieve.

If, as these observations suggest, the normative aims of a system of agenda structure would be better served by programmatic than by elite competition among the major parties, then practical issues about access to the political agenda should be resolved in ways that

[33] For a discussion, see David Robertson, *A Theory of Party Competition* (London: John Wiley, 1976), pp. 44–49.

[34] Such a view has, of course, been held by many writers, in particular the "citizenship theorists" of the early twentieth century. Dennis F. Thompson, *The Democratic Citizen* (Cambridge: Cambridge University Press, 1970), pp. 86–119.

encourage parties to compete on the basis of program. In particular, procedures of party governance, including those concerning candidate selection and platform formation, should be open to participation by party members. The reason is not that the rank and file have rights to participate resting on considerations independent of the dynamics of party competition itself (as some advocates of party reform have maintained); rather, it is that in the absence of participation, the main incentives governing the selection of candidates and the formation of platforms will be those of the market for votes, which (as Schumpeter clearly understood) are more likely to produce a convergence of positions in a system of insubstantial elite competition than to elicit alternatives affording voters a choice of program or principle. Accordingly, though opportunities for participation should afford members significant leverage over decisions regarding candidates and platforms, considerations of fair access do not imply that these opportunities need be equal.

However, even a well-ordered regime of programmatic competition may not satisfy the aim of placing before the voters a sufficiently broad range of alternatives. In spite of competitive incentives, organizational inertia and historical practice might leave salient positions unrepresented by any established party. There is no general reason to suppose that openness of party governance to participation by the rank and file would change this.[35] Thus, additional measures might be required. One traditional remedy has been to grant access to the ballot to the candidates of minor parties and to independent candidates. These are often seen as ineffectual; but even if minor parties have no real chance of victory, their appearance can supply incentives for established parties to modify their programs to avoid attrition or to gain an electoral advantage by mobilizing the support of new voting groups.[36] Although the deliberative interests impose some limit on the size of the ballot, it is hardly obvious that this requires the alternatives to be restricted to

[35] Accordingly, it seems shortsighted to suggest that party democracy and open access to the general election ballot are simply different devices for affording representation to divergent viewpoints. The suggestion is found in Barton, "The General Election Ballot," pp. 166–67.

[36] Thus, for example, Martin Van Buren, who was perhaps the founder of the doctrine of two-party competition in the United States, advocated the creation of third parties when consensus between the established parties led to rigidities of program. Ceaser, *Presidential Selection*, pp. 142–43.

two, particularly where there is evidence that a minor party or independent candidate enjoys a significant amount of popular support.

There are more radical remedies as well. For example, some people have thought that a sufficiently broad range of public debate could only be ensured with a proportional scheme of legislative representation (usually based on party lists), perhaps together with a parliamentary rather than a presidential system of executive authority. Indeed, I believe that the most persuasive arguments for proportional systems are those that appeal to the deliberative interests. Without exploring these views in detail, the point to note is that their force in reasoning about institutional reform is a contingent matter; everything depends on whether the remedies suggested would actually encourage representation of salient positions in the public arena in comparison with what might be expected under the feasible alternative arrangements. Where this is the case, then, assuming that they would not produce countervailing harms of other kinds, these remedies would have considerable merit.

Finally, it bears recalling that institutional opportunities such as access to the election ballot are only as valuable as the resources available for taking advantage of them. Minor parties lacking the resources needed to bring their programs to public attention pose no real threat to the established parties and so provide them with little incentive to recast existing programs so as to broaden their constituencies. Similarly, representatives of differing interests within a party who are unable to compete effectively for intraparty influence may not be capable of affecting the definition of the party program. The aims of fair access to the political agenda are only incompletely realized by making available appropriate opportunities to participate. A fair distribution of the means to compete effectively is essential. We turn to this subject in the following chapter.

FREEDOM OF ASSOCIATION AND REGULATION OF PARTY PROCESSES

United States courts have held that the internal decision-making processes of the political parties are protected against state interference by the First Amendment doctrine of freedom of association.

Regulation of party affairs is said to be acceptable, if at all, only when required by a "compelling state interest" that cannot be advanced in any less intrusive way.[37]

According to the criteria of fair access we have discussed, parties might legitimately use a wide range of procedures in formulating policy platforms and choosing candidates. Nevertheless, these criteria do impose constraints: for example, a party is not free to choose its candidates by lot or to devise its platform in a way that is indifferent to the interests and concerns of its members. The theory might afford some justification for state interference in internal party affairs, most likely in the form of regulations requiring provisions for regular participation by the membership in selecting candidates and formulating platforms. This raises the prospect of objections based on considerations of freedom of association. While I do not wish to enter the dispute about constitutional doctrine, the underlying moral issue requires a brief concluding comment.

The task is made difficult by the (surprising) absence of any very clear understanding of freedom of association in contemporary political theory. A few brief, general remarks will have to suffice.

Appeals to freedom of association characteristically occur when the state proposes to interfere in the activities of groups on the grounds that those activities would otherwise yield harmful or undesirable consequences. Like freedom of expression, it operates as a constraint on the state's authority to prevent harm. Beyond this purely formal fact, however, freedom of association does not appear to name a single, distinct value; both the degree and the explanation of its significance seem to vary by context. Thus, in one type of case (familiar from Mill) it serves, so to speak, as the group form of the principle that forbids paternalistic interference by the state

---

[37] The leading case is *Cousins v. Wigoda*, 419 U.S. 477 (1975). In fact, Justice Brennan's opinion for the Court is ambiguous about the status of First Amendment interests; as Justice Rehnquist notes, the Court seems to rest its holding as much on the importance of the "pervasive national interest" served by the parties in nominating candidates as on considerations of freedom of association. *Cousins v. Wigoda*, at 495 (concurring). See also *Ripon Society v. National Republican Party*, 525 F.2nd 567 (1975) (D.C. Circuit); *Democratic Party of the United States v. LaFollette*, 450 U.S. 107 (1981). For comment, see Tribe, *American Constitutional Law*, pp. 785–90; Julia E. Guttman, "Primary Elections and the Collective Right of Freedom of Association" [Note], *Yale Law Journal* 94 (1984), pp. 117–37.

in individual choices whose harmful consequences, if any, are confined to the chooser (provided that the choices satisfy appropriate conditions of voluntariness—e.g., that they are uncoerced and suitably informed).[38] It is this sense of freedom of association that might be invoked, for example, if the state threatened to interfere with a religious association's practice of a doctrine whose tenets required adherents to forego ordinary forms of medical care. We are prepared to regard such interference as illegitimate, even though we recognize that it would alleviate the prospect of harm, because the harm can be seen as voluntarily chosen by those who suffer it. A different type of case arises when the risk of harm that might arise from a group's activity is not confined to its members, but we judge that the imposition of risk is justified by the other values that would be brought about if the activity were allowed to proceed. For example, perhaps an organization seeks to advance the political views of its members by means of public demonstrations that others regard as deeply offensive. Because the interests of nonparticipants are involved, this is a more complicated kind of case, requiring a comparison of the values advanced by permitting the activity in question to take place with the magnitude of harm that is involuntarily imposed on others.[39] Consequently, it seems unlikely that freedom of association in this sense can be regarded as an absolute value.[40]

An example of the first kind of appeal to freedom of association can be found in the opinion of a federal appellate court in *Ripon Society v. National Republican Party*, a leading case concerning the apportionment of delegates to a party nominating convention. Emphasizing the voluntariness of party membership, the court held that considerations of freedom of association justify the members

[38] Gerald Dworkin, "Paternalism," in *Morality and the Law*, ed. Richard Wasserstrom (Belmont, Calif.: Wadsworth Publishing, 1971), pp. 491–506.

[39] The example may seem inapt, because it refers to the public activities of an association rather than to its internal practices. But a moment's reflection shows that this difference is irrelevant. It is the presence of harmful external effects—that is, effects imposed on nonparticipants without their consent—rather than locus of the activity itself that characterizes cases of this kind.

[40] A reflection of this can be found in the White Primary Cases, involving racial discrimination in procedures governing participation in party primaries and caucuses. *Nixon v. Herndon*, 273 U.S. 536 (1927), *Nixon v. Condon*, 286 U.S. 73 (1932), *Smith v. Allwright*, 321 U.S. 649 (1944), and *Terry v. Adams*, 345 U.S. 641 (1953).

of a party in employing "representational schemes of their own choosing" in order to advance the individual interests of its members that the party exists to serve.[41] But the court's reasoning is doubly flawed. One problem is that the delegate selection procedures of the major American parties are not chosen by the members themselves; in the Republican party, they are chosen by the officials of the state party organizations (who may or may not be representative of their memberships in any significant sense), and in the Democratic party, they are chosen (or, more precisely, approved) by officials responsible to the national party convention, whose membership is, of course, chosen through the very procedures its officials are authorized to approve.[42] It is inaccurate to characterize regulation of internal party affairs as interference in procedures that *the members themselves* have accepted; the force of objections to interference that emphasize the voluntary character of membership is therefore severely attenuated.[43] The second, and more basic, problem is that party activities have consequences that extend far beyond the membership. The framing of issues for public deliberation, the mobilization of excluded groups, and the selection of candidates for office are all vital public functions, as important to the success of democratic government as any that can be imagined. If it is true, as I suggested earlier, that the performance of these functions might be frustrated if parties adopted exclusionary or discriminatory internal processes, then the autonomy of the party cannot be defended by appeal to antipaternalist considerations of the kind that ground the first form of appeal to freedom of association.

The second form of appeal is not likely to be more successful in defending the procedures of party governance against the kinds of regulation that our theory recommends. On the one hand, there is no denying the importance of the public functions that the parties

[41] 525 F.2d 567 (1975), at 581, 584–85.

[42] William Crotty and John S. Jackson III, *Presidential Primaries and Nominations* (Washington: Congressional Quarterly, 1985), pp. 60–61.

[43] The *Ripon* court remarked that those who are dissatisfied with the internal procedures of an established party are free to withdraw: they can "gain access to the ballot by means other than a major party nomination." 525 F.2d 567 (1975), at 586. Having been denied effective voice, party members retain the possibility of exit. But this is not much comfort where the political structure and positive law confer substantial competitive advantages on the two major parties.

serve in framing the political agenda. On the other, it is not obvious that the activities that only autonomous parties could coordinate promote countervailing values of even greater urgency. The most plausible argument to the contrary is that the regulation of party affairs constitutes interference in the individual rights of party members to advance their political concerns in the electoral process.[44] However, as I have argued, there is no basic right to participate that exists independently of the institutional framework; entitlements to participate in electoral competition are creatures of this framework, in the sense that their contours depend on how the general aims of the system are most likely to be achieved. The urgency of each individual's interest in being able to advance her concerns in the political process has already been taken into account in the formulation of criteria of fair access. There is no *further*, separate value to which an appeal to freedom of association can be attached. (This applies *a fortiori* to the values connected with freedom of expression, which are discussed further in chapter 9, below.)

It follows that considerations of freedom of association ought not to operate as a bar to state regulation of internal party processes when this regulation is necessary to ensure that party competition satisfies the aims of fair access to the political arena. The major parties enjoy an oligopoly status arising from both structural and legal elements of the political system; they are no more entitled to protection against regulation to advance the public interests served by the competitive process than are business enterprises with an analogous status in the economic system.

[44] Thus, the *Ripon* court held that "a party is after all more than a forum for all its adherents' views. It is an organized attempt to see the most important of those views put into practice through control of the levers of government." 525 F.2d 567 (1975), at 585.

CHAPTER NINE

Political Finance

The historical movement toward democratic forms in industrial societies is plausibly understood as a series of efforts to offset the political effects of inequalities in wealth, class, and status. But the achievement of democratic forms—even those satisfying requirements of the kinds discussed thus far—is obviously no guarantee that the course of public life will not be affected by inequalities in the social and economic background. Substantial background inequalities will be reflected in the outcomes of the political process however that process is organized.

This historical observation has a counterpart in democratic theory. The forms of fairness that might be achieved in the systems of voting, representation, and agenda formation are, by themselves, an insufficient basis for fair democratic politics. Institutions that are open to distortion due to excessive inequalities in social and economic background conditions will be objectionable for reasons associated with all three of the regulative interests. One could hardly take seriously one's status as an equal citizen, for example, if owing to a lack of resources one was precluded from advancing one's views effectively in the public forum. One could not regard oneself as a responsible participant in political deliberation if the range of positions available for public consideration was arbitrarily constrained. Most importantly, one could have little reason for confidence that the outcomes of democratic decision making would treat one's prospects equitably if the distribution of political resources favored those with vested interests in the defense of prevailing patterns of social advantage.[1]

---

[1] Although this chapter is devoted primarily to political finance in the United States, it is worth noting as a theoretical matter that nothing in the foregoing observations turns on any assumptions about the source of distorting background inequalities, in particular whether they arise within capitalist or socialist regimes. Forms of state socialism with formally competitive parties, but in which the domi-

These problems might be addressed at either (or both) of two levels, that of political procedures and that of the social structure. Thus, some have argued that the political process should be regulated so as to insulate it from the influence of background inequalities, for example, by restricting the political uses of private wealth or by providing public subsidies for political activity.[2] Others have held that an egalitarian political process requires more or less direct constraints on those elements of the background that might otherwise distort the process, such as the distribution of income or the distribution of control over the means of production.[3] In this chapter I shall concentrate on the first possibility, even though it is plain that no strategy of insulation can, by itself, succeed in eliminating the political influence of material inequality. The main reason is that the issues of recent practical controversy in the United States that bear on the political influence of material inequality are virtually all concerned with procedural rather than structural reform. But there is another reason as well: analogs of most of these procedural issues will likely arise even when objectionable structural inequality, however that is conceived, is eliminated. Neither point forecloses the larger argument, which I leave for another occasion.

The two possible components of an insulation strategy are restrictions on the political uses of private means ("ceilings") and public measures to subsidize political activity ("floors"). Both elements can be found in the United States in the system of campaign finance for federal office resulting from recent reform legislation.[4]

---

nant party monopolizes the public media to the disadvantage of other political interests, would be objectionable for some of the same reasons as forms of capitalism in which the political influence of private wealth is unregulated.

[2] For example, see the remarks on the "fair value" of political liberty in John Rawls, *A Theory of Justice* (Cambridge: Harvard University Press, 1971), pp. 224–27, and Rawls, "The Basic Liberties and Their Priority," in *The Tanner Lectures on Human Values*, vol. 3, ed. Sterling McMurrin (Salt Lake City: University of Utah Press; Cambridge: Cambridge University Press, 1982), pp. 39–49.

[3] This is in the tradition of Rousseau. *The Social Contract* [1762], in *The Social Contract and Discourses*, trans. G.D.H. Cole (London: J. M. Dent, 1973), bk. 2, chap. 11, p. 204. Compare Joshua Cohen and Joel Rogers, *On Democracy* (Harmondsworth, Middlesex: Penguin Books, 1983), chap. 6; Norman Daniels, "Equal Liberty and Unequal Worth of Liberty," in *Reading Rawls*, ed. Norman Daniels (New York: Basic Books, 1975), pp. 253–81.

[4] The principal legislative instrument is the Federal Election Campaign Act (FECA) of 1971, as substantially amended in 1974. The main portions are codified at 2 U.S. Code, secs. 431–55; and 26 U.S. Code, secs. 9001–42. For a review of the develop-

Public funds are available for both primary and general election campaigns for the presidency (though not for congressional office), and individuals are limited in the amounts they may contribute to candidates for any federal office and to multicandidate election campaign committees. However, more ambitious provisions regulating the overall campaign expenditures of candidates who do not receive public funds, and provisions limiting "independent expenditures" made by individuals or groups on behalf of a candidate but without his approval or cooperation, were struck down as violations of the First Amendment guarantee of freedom of expression. (Provisions regulating expenditures by groups such as political action committees were also held to violate the guarantee of freedom of association.)[5] The elimination of restrictions on campaign expenditures by candidates and campaign committees, and on independent expenditures by individuals, yielded a campaign finance system fundamentally different—and of more uncertain consequence— than that which was envisioned by the authors of the reforms.[6]

As these summary remarks suggest, recent controversy about the regulation of campaign finance has focused on the supposed conflict between political equality and freedom of expression. Less attention has been paid to the prior question of the requirements of political equality itself. Yet it is hardly clear how and why egalitarian concerns bear on the organization of the system of campaign finance. In what follows I concentrate on this central normative issue. The role of considerations of freedom of expression is a subsidiary (though not an unimportant) matter, which I take up briefly at the end.

---

ment of campaign finance legislation in the United States, see Herbert E. Alexander, *Financing Politics*, 3d ed. (Washington, D. C.: Congressional Quarterly Press, 1984).

[5] *Buckley v. Valeo*, 424 U.S. 1 (1976). Overall expenditure limitations continue to apply to candidates for the presidency who accept public subsidies.

[6] Many commentators hold that the new system shares the main defects of the old. See, for example, Elizabeth Drew, *Politics and Money: The New Road to Corruption* (New York: Macmillan, 1983); and J. Skelly Wright, "Money and the Pollution of Politics: Is the First Amendment an Obstacle to Political Equality?" *Columbia Law Review* 82 (1982), pp. 609–45. For a critical assessment of this analysis, see Joel Fleishman and Pope McCorkle, "Level-Up Rather Than Level-Down: Toward a New Theory of Campaign Finance Reform," *Journal of Law and Politics* 1 (1984), esp. pp. 213–22.

RECEIVED VIEWS

What does political equality have to do with campaign finance? More generally, what would a fair system of campaign finance be like? Both advocates and students of campaign finance reform have presupposed answers to these questions. Although I do not believe that any of the prevailing positions withstands philosophical scrutiny, an exploration of the defects of these positions helps to orient the search for a more satisfactory view.

Inasmuch as philosophical conceptions of political equality tend not to be made explicit in discussions of political finance, one must reconstruct them from the approaches to reform advocated by various writers. These can be divided into three groups, each representing a different conception of equality. The first position is distinguished by its focus on inequalities of political influence among voters that are thought to arise from differences in the ability to contribute. In a seminal work on campaign finance, Alexander Heard wrote:

> A deeply cherished slogan of American democracy is "one man—one vote." . . . Concern over the private financing of political campaigns stems in significant measure from the belief that a gift is an especially important kind of vote. It is grounded in the thought that persons who give in larger sums or to more candidates than their fellow citizens are in effect voting more than once.[7]

The core of this idea is that contributions of private resources, like votes, are means of exercising power over electoral outcomes and ought to be regulated according to similar principles. The aim is to prevent material inequalities from generating inequalities in the

---

[7] Alexander Heard, *The Costs of Democracy* (Chapel Hill: University of North Carolina Press, 1960), pp. 48–49. Similar sentiments have been expressed by many other writers; e.g., David W. Adamany, *Financing Politics: Recent Wisconsin Elections* (Madison: University of Wisconsin Press, 1969), p. 12; Marlene A. Nicholson, "Campaign Financing and Equal Protection," *Stanford Law Review* 26 (1974), pp. 815–54; Joel Fleishman, "Private Money and Public Elections: Another American Dilemma," in *Changing Campaign Techniques*, ed. Louis Maisel, Sage Election Studies Yearbook, vol. 2 (Beverly Hills, Calif.: Sage Publications, 1976), pp. 19–20; Alexander, *Financing Politics*, 3d ed., pp. 1–4.

value of formally equal political liberties.[8] When conjoined with empirical premises to be considered below, this conception of the bearing of political equality on campaign resources yields what we may call the principle of proportional finance: "Since all citizens have an equal right to political participation . . . all interests and points of view [should] receive financial support and expression in proportion to the numbers of their adherents."[9] Perhaps the simplest way to conceive of how such a principle might be implemented is to imagine a voucher system entitling each voter to designate one candidate in each race to receive an equal contribution from public funds, while prohibiting campaign expenditures from any other source.[10]

A second view is suggested by the current provisions for the financing of general election campaigns for the presidency, which provide equal public subsidies to the (major party) candidates while prohibiting those who accept these subsidies from expending any private funds.[11] Many regard these provisions as a model for reform of congressional election finance as well.[12] In contrast to the first position, this view identifies fairness in the allocation of campaign resources with equal treatment of *candidates* rather than of *voters*. Obviously, these forms of equality are likely to conflict: if each voter contributes an equal amount to her preferred candidate, then unless each candidate enjoys an equal share of public support, the resulting intercandidate distribution of financial resources will be

[8] This appears to be the position taken in Rawls, "The Basic Liberties and Their Priority," p. 78.

[9] David W. Adamany and George E. Agree, *Political Money: A Strategy for Campaign Financing in America* (Baltimore: Johns Hopkins University Press, 1975), p. 2.

[10] Adamany and Agree propose a voucher system as part of a scheme of partial public subsidies, but since they would permit some private contributions as well, their proposed scheme taken as a whole would not appear to conform to the principle of proportional finance set forth in the quotation in the text above. *Political Money*, pp. 196–201.

[11] In fact, interpretations of the statute by the federal election authorities, together with exceptions provided in the statute itself, have vitiated the effects of this prohibition by allowing unreported private funds to be expended by the local and state party committees for certain purposes related to presidential campaigns. Herbert E. Alexander, "Making Sense About Dollars in the 1980 Presidential Campaigns," in *Money and Politics in the United States*, ed. Michael J. Malbin (Washington: American Enterprise Institute, 1984), pp. 19–29.

[12] See, e.g., Wright, "Money and the Pollution of Politics," p. 611.

unequal. The motivation of the second view must therefore be both different from, and more complex than, that of the first. Equality for candidates reflects a desire to establish an equilibrium within the campaign process regarded as a competitive struggle, while the reliance on public subsidies, and the prohibition of private contributions, is an effort to remove incentives for corruption and the purchase of influence.

The third view is associated less with any particular scheme of campaign finance than with a criterion for evaluating the political consequences of the various alternatives. The criterion is electoral competitiveness. The degree of competitiveness of an election is understood, roughly, as a function of the closeness of the proportions of the vote won by the winner and by the runner-up. The closer the vote, the more competitive the election.[13] The third view holds that campaign finance arrangements should be organized so as to maximize the average level of competitiveness of the elections to which the arrangements apply.[14] The apparent motivation is a concern to maximize the responsiveness of the election system to intertemporal changes in the party preferences of voters; in relatively competitive systems, correspondingly smaller shifts in the electoral strength of the parties would be required to bring about a shift in the division of partisan control over public offices. Why this should matter and, in particular, how it might be relevant to a principled concern about equality are difficult questions to which we shall return.

In considering these positions, one should take care not to employ unrealistic or naive empirical premises concerning the relationship between the supply of campaign resources and electoral success.[15] There is obviously *some* relationship; but it matters pre-

[13] While I think this is a faithful report of the usage of "competitiveness" in the finance literature (see, e.g., Gary C. Jacobson, *Money in Congressional Elections* [New Haven: Yale University Press, 1980], pp. 163–64), the term has a more precise technical meaning in statistical election studies. There, competitiveness is inversely proportional to the degree of confidence with which the outcome of an election can be predicted on the basis of known characteristics of the constituency. See David J. Elkins, "The Measurement of Party Competition," *American Political Science Review* 68 (1974), esp. pp. 683–86.

[14] See, e.g., Jacobson, *Money in Congressional Elections*, pp. 211ff.

[15] There is a more extensive survey of these empirical matters in my article, "Po-

cisely how the relationship is understood, since this will shape the criteria of reform. To illustrate, consider the plausible sounding (and common) hypothesis that each candidate's chances of victory are proportional to his share of the total resources expended in the campaign. The marginal value of financial resources is the same for everyone. A priori, the difficulty is this. While it may be true, other things equal, that it is better for a candidate to have more campaign resources than less, the amount by which a candidate's chances of winning are increased by a given increase in resources might depend on such other factors as the political characteristics of the district, the candidate's ideological position, and whether the candidate is an incumbent. Recent research confirms this suspicion, at least with regard to campaigns for congressional office. Incumbency is clearly the most important factor in predicting electoral success. Moreover, it is significant in determining the value of the financial resources devoted to a campaign. A given level of resources will make a substantially greater contribution to the chances of victory for challengers and other nonincumbents than for incumbents.[16] Of course, this is hardly surprising; challengers need money to purchase public attention that incumbents either already enjoy or can attract through the adroit use of the perquisites of incumbency. What may be surprising is that the returns to increasing campaign expenditures diminish much more rapidly for incumbents than for nonincumbents.[17]

These findings refer to the relationship between candidates'

litical Finance in the United States: A Survey of Research," *Ethics* 95 (1984), pp. 129–48.

[16] Jacobson, *Money in Congressional Elections*, pp. 136–57; for more recent data that support this hypothesis, see Jacobson, "Money and Votes Revisited: Congressional Elections, 1972–1986," *Public Choice* 47 (1985), pp. 13–28. See also Stanton A. Glantz, Alan I. Abramowitz, and Michael P. Burkart, "Election Outcomes: Whose Money Matters?" *Journal of Politics* 38 (1976), pp. 1033–38. In view of these findings, the *Buckley* court was almost certainly wrong in holding that the FECA's low contribution limitations did not disproportionately favor incumbents. *Buckley v. Valeo*, 424 U.S. 1 (1976), at 31–33.

[17] Jacobson, *Money in Congressional Elections*, p. 157. It is not clear that this point can be generalized to all elections. One study of campaign spending in gubernatorial elections found no significant difference in the impact of spending by incumbents and challengers. See Samuel C. Patterson, "Campaign Spending in Contests for Governor," *Western Political Quarterly* 35 (1982), pp. 457–77.

shares of campaign resources and their chances of *electoral* success. As one might expect, nonelectoral mechanisms such as the party caucuses employed in some states to choose delegates to national nominating conventions display somewhat different characteristics. In particular, the importance of financial relative to other kinds of resources (such as incumbency and public recognition) is apparently much greater.[18]

The main point illustrated here is that financial support is only one of several types of campaign resource that combine to determine a candidate's chances of victory. Incumbency with its various perquisites is another. A third may be the organizational strength of the candidate's political party.[19] No doubt there are others as well. Among other things, these findings show the need for caution about too straightforward an application of "one person, one vote" to campaign spending. Because money is only one of several kinds of campaign resources, each of which affects a candidate's chances of winning, this precept should be applied, if at all, to campaign resources as a whole (including the perquisites of incumbency) rather than only to campaign funds. Only then would the application of the principle be faithful to the underlying concern to ensure that a candidate's chances of winning be proportional to the level of popular support.[20]

[18] For example, in the 1984 Democratic Party caucuses, campaign spending was among the two most significant variables affecting vote shares. T. Wayne Parent, Calvin C. Jillson, and Ronald E. Weber, "Voting Outcomes in the 1984 Democratic Party Primaries and Caucuses," *American Political Science Review* 81 (1987), p. 80.

[19] In "Campaign Spending in Contests for Governor," Patterson reports that in the 1978 gubernatorial elections Democratic but not Republican spending was subject to the law of diminishing returns. With incumbency and party registration controlled for, the effect of Democratic spending dropped off rapidly beyond a certain point; but for Republicans, each additional dollar spent was associated with an increase in votes in more or less direct proportion. The explanation plausibly suggested was that because of the greater strength of their party organization Democrats can mobilize more people to provide free help in campaign and election activities than Republicans, who typically pay for the same kinds of assistance.

[20] Various devices can be imagined to accomplish this, although with uncertain prospects of success. The perquisites of incumbency might be reduced. Or, compensating advantages could be provided for challengers. Thus, as Sen. James Buckley suggested in the Senate debate on the FECA amendments of 1974, "some sort of equity as between incumbents and challengers" in congressional campaigns could be achieved by permitting challengers to spend 30 percent more than incumbents in

The complexity of the relationship between campaign spending and electoral success also complicates the case for intercandidate equality. Virtually all studies of the effects of campaign spending have shown that the marginal value of spending declines as total expenditures increase (although, as noted earlier, the *rate* of decline varies with incumbency status and other factors). Thus, if the concern for intercandidate resource equality is motivated by a desire to eliminate distortions in relative chances of success flowing from differential access to campaign resources, it may be that resource equality is an inappropriate or at least an unnecessary goal; the distorting effects of unequal campaign resources could be minimized by ensuring adequate funds for all candidates—that is, by establishing floors rather than ceilings.[21]

Let us consider the three received views in reverse order. Beginning with the interpretation of equality as electoral competitiveness, the first point is that this is not the same as, and cannot be reduced to, either of the other two interpretations. From the fact that elections tend to be more rather than less competitive, it does not necessarily follow either that the influence of voters over outcomes is relatively equal or that candidates have been afforded equal terms of competition. These are entirely contingent matters. If the preferences of the electorate were evenly divided between two

---

election campaigns. *Congressional Record*, 8 October 1974, p. S18537. The proposal was, of course, defeated; but even if it had been successful, incumbents would have had little to fear. The financial advantage of incumbency is greater than Buckley supposed. The market value of the perquisites of incumbency (use of the frank, office space, staff allowances, data processing, printing and mailing services, use of television and radio facilities, etc.) used in a typical congressional campaign in the mid-1970s was estimated at $567,191 in 1977 dollars. By contrast, the *total* raised and spent by the average challenger was about $75,000 (Herbert E. Alexander, "Election Reform and National Politics," Smithsonian Institution Lecture, 23 April 1980, p. 146).

[21] Interestingly, whereas reformers have usually placed priority on setting contribution and expenditure ceilings, academic writers on campaign finance have long stressed the greater importance of ensuring that all candidates would have access to an adequate minimum. See, e.g., Louise Overacker, *Money in Elections* (New York: Macmillan, 1932), pp. 380–82; Heard, *The Costs of Democracy*, pp. 430–31, 470; Herbert E. Alexander, *Financing Politics*, 2d ed. (Washington, D.C.: Congressional Quarterly Press, 1980), pp. 17ff; Adamany, *Financing Politics*, pp. 256–72. At the same time, these writers have typically been skeptical about the wisdom and efficacy of ceilings.

candidates, for example, low competitiveness would indicate an absence of equality in some part of the electoral structure; if preferences were significantly skewed in one or the other direction, *high* competitiveness might indicate an absence of equality. If competitiveness is not necessarily a mark of equality of voter influence or of equal treatment for candidates, one may wonder in what *other* sense it can be understood as an egalitarian conception. The answer must be that, under high competitiveness, candidates have relatively equal chances of winning. But why should *that* matter? That candidates should have equal chances of winning regardless of the distribution of voter preferences is surely not implied by *any* plausible conception of political equality. Of course, it may be that for contingent reasons competitiveness would be an appropriate target for egalitarian reform; for example, as I suggested earlier, it may encourage parties to compete for the votes of disaffected minorities or provide an incentive for accountability in office. But in either case competitiveness would have no special status as an element of fairness in its own right; instead, it would be a derivative condition reflecting requirements of a quite different nature.

The interpretation of political equality as equal treatment for candidates in the system of political finance is, at least, not vulnerable to the charge that it may not be an interpretation of equality at all. However, as in the previous case, one might wonder why equality in this sense should be accorded any special weight. Certainly a straightforward application of the principle of equal participation will not make this plausible. That principle defines the rights of citizens as equal participants in political decision making; equality for candidates would follow only on the hypothesis that opposing candidates were likely to be supported by roughly equal portions of the electorate, and there is no reason to believe this in the general case. Alternatively, someone might think that intercandidate equality would promote the goal of competitiveness; but in view of the empirical findings noted earlier, this is implausible as well. And in any case, there would be the further problem of explaining how competitiveness and equality are related. Equality for candidates requires a different kind of argument, but no such argument presents itself that could plausibly be described as deriving from a conception of political equality.

The remaining position holds that the campaign resources devoted to a candidacy should be proportional to that candidate's share of public support; in this way it may be thought that the equal influence of the vote itself can be protected against distortion by inequalities of private means. For the reasons already given this is likely to seem the most plausible of the received views. It is characteristic of this view that it regards campaign finance—or overall campaign resources—as morally on a par with votes. Votes and campaign resources are treated as so many different causal factors that determine a candidate's probability of success, and elections are seen as mechanisms where these factors come together and identify the winners. Because no distinctions are made among the various causal factors, one is tempted to apply the same regulative principle to resources as to votes. But there is this important distinction: unlike votes, resources exercise their causal influence on electoral outcomes by way of the effects of campaign activities over time on the beliefs and attitudes of voters. The influence of financial contributions on election outcomes is mediated by the campaign activities that the contributions make possible. The causal influence of votes, on the other hand, is not mediated in any analogous way.

The main public purpose of campaign activities is communicative. We do not take an interest in them only because, like voting, they are elements in a causal chain linking the preferences of citizens with the formal mechanism for identifying winners and losers. Campaign activities have a different kind of value, which has at least two aspects. First, citizens have an interest in campaign activities as channels of communication of information and argument about candidates and issues. Any regulatory scheme should establish conditions in which the contending positions are adequately represented in the public arena and citizens are enabled to form their judgments under favorable circumstances of deliberation. Second, citizens have an interest in campaign activities as parts of a process of representation through which legislators are made accountable to their constituents. The public commitments made in the course of political campaigns supply the basis for judgments of the efficacy and fidelity of the victors after they take office. These points are distinct. The first refers to an interest that citizens have as participants in a public deliberative process who need a background of information and argument as a condition of intelligent

choice. The second refers to an interest that citizens have as subjects of government (whether they vote or not) whose welfare will
be affected by legislation and public policy and who need assurance
of the accountability of public officials.

Neither of these interests pertains to the distribution of voting
power. That question is settled by other considerations: if the view
set forth earlier is correct, these derive mainly from the regulative
interests in recognition and in equitable treatment. Since campaigning, unlike voting itself, involves the deliberative interests as
well, we should not expect the considerations that establish an appropriate distribution of voting power to be sufficient to resolve
controversies about the structure of the system of campaign finance. These raise a distinct normative problem that requires a solution in its own right.

AIMS OF THE SYSTEM
OF POLITICAL FINANCE

These remarks suggest that the system of political finance should
be governed by two types of aims. First, it should protect the integrity of the system of representation; second, it should ensure fair
access to the public arena at each stage of political competition for
those candidates entitled to participate at that stage. Each point requires elaboration.

Protection of the integrity of representation is largely a matter of
regulating the extent to which the need for election campaign resources is permitted to influence the incentives facing elected officials in the conduct of their public responsibilities. Historically,
this has been viewed as the prevention of corruption, construed as
the quasi-contractual exchange of financial support for favorable
treatment (or, as the buying of influence). But the concern to prevent corruption need not be interpreted this narrowly. Whether a
contribution was made as part of an explicit or implicit bargain, or
was in this respect benign, does not affect the structure of incentives facing an official after a contribution has been made. The probability that contributors will receive favorable treatment would be
the same in either case. Corruption in the traditional sense is objectionable because it skews legislative judgment and helps to produce

outcomes that disproportionately favor the interests of contributors, and this difficulty will arise equally for corrupt and for benign contributions.

The difficulty is not only a matter of the distribution of influence among members of an elected official's constituency. Whereas the system of constituency representation confines the direct political influence of voters to those officials for whom they are entitled to vote, the influence of contributors under a system of unregulated private finance need not respect constituency boundaries at all. Thus, it has frequently been noted that the growth of organized political fund-raising in the United States has produced a national system of campaign finance in which financial support in large amounts is routinely channeled across constituencies.[22] When financial incentives encourage legislators to subordinate the interests of their constituents to those of others elsewhere, an additional form of distortion in the system of representation is introduced.

Whether regulatory measures are necessary to prevent corruption in either the traditional or the enlarged sense depends on whether the receipt of private contributions in fact corrupts legislative performance. Some writers are skeptical, perhaps because the exchange of legislative action for financial support seems too crude and unprincipled to be likely to take place with significant regularity.[23] A common view is that if contributions purchase anything, it is "access," not influence.[24] Now, of course, the fact that contributions

[22] The trend is chiefly the result of the recent increase in the size and number of political action committees (PACs). See Alexander, *Financing Politics*, 3d ed., pp. 97–99. There is some danger of overstating this concern, since many PACs have local or regional memberships and confine their attention to local issues. See Theodore J. Eismeier and Philip J. Pollock, "Political Action Committees: Varieties of Organization and Strategy," in *Money and Politics in the United States*, ed. Michael J. Malbin (Washington: American Enterprise Institute, 1984), pp. 122–41.

[23] Or perhaps because it is hard to believe that the expected utility of legislative vote-buying is greater than the expected costs, taking into account the dangers of discovery and prosecution. See James F. Herndon, "Access, Record, and Competition as Influences on Interest Group Contributions to Congressional Campaigns," *Journal of Politics* 44 (1982), pp. 999–1000.

[24] Ralph K. Winter, *Campaign Finance and Political Freedom*. Domestic Affairs Study 19 (Washington, D.C.: American Enterprise Institute, 1973), pp. 52ff; Michael J. Malbin, "Of Mountains and Molehills: PACs, Campaigns, and Public Policy," in *Parties, Interest Groups, and Campaign Finance Laws*, ed. Michael J. Malbin (Washington, D.C.: American Enterprise Institute, 1980), pp. 152–84.

may purchase access is damaging enough.[25] Beyond this, however, there is a considerable amount of systematic, if circumstantial, evidence that interest-group financial support is related to legislative performance on behalf of the group's interests.[26] In response, some have suggested that contributors merely give to those whose positions they find congenial, so that contributed funds reflect rather than influence the policy positions of their recipients.[27] But recent studies suggest that this is incorrect in a significant range of cases.[28]

It is true that financial support is not the primary determinant of legislative performance. Contributions apparently affect legislative performance, if at all, only at the margin where other influences are ineffective or balance each other; thus, the danger of corruption may seem to be easily overstated.[29] However, this is too sanguine. Legislative deliberation relies particularly on those who are relatively detached from direct concern with an issue to assess the issue on its merits in relation to broader conceptions of the public interest. The threat of corruption resulting from dependence on private contributions is precisely the threat that performance of this important representative function will be compromised. The fact (if it is a fact) that contributions affect legislative voting only at the margin therefore is hardly reason for complacency.

The other governing aim is that the system of campaign finance

[25] See Laurence H. Tribe, *American Constitutional Law* (Mineola, N.Y.: Foundation Press, 1978), p. 802, n. 7.

[26] For case studies of the influence of interest-group contributions on the behavior of members of the U.S. Congress, see, for example, W. P. Welch, "Campaign Contributions and Legislative Voting: Milk Money and Dairy Price Supports," *Western Political Quarterly* 35 (1982), pp. 478–95; John P. Frendreis and Richard W. Waterman, "PAC Contributions and Legislative Behavior: Senate Voting on Trucking Deregulation," prepared for presentation at the Annual Meeting of the Midwest Political Science Association, Chicago, 20–23 April 1983; Henry W. Chappell, Jr., "Campaign Contributions and Voting on the Cargo Preference Bill: A Comparison of Simultaneous Models," *Public Choice* 36 (1981), pp. 301–12.

[27] Winter, *Campaign Finance and Political Freedom*, p. 5.

[28] In all three of the cases cited in footnote 26, the relationship between contributor interests and legislative performance persisted even when other factors likely to influence legislative behavior, such as constituency characteristics, party affiliation, and ideology, were controlled for.

[29] Frendreis and Waterman, "PAC Contributions and Legislative Behavior," pp. 28–30; Robert J. Samuelson, "The Campaign Reform Failure," *The New Republic*, 5 September 1983, p. 33.

should ensure effective access to the public arena at each stage of political competition for those candidates formally entitled to participate at that stage. In this respect, a doctrine of fairness in the allocation of campaign resources is parasitic on a view about fair agenda-structuring institutions. Candidates do not have, so to speak, base-level rights of fair access to the public forum. Rather, the provision of the means to contend effectively in the public forum is an institutional strategy for serving the essential voter interest in conditions of informed deliberation and intelligent judgment over the full range of positions represented on the political agenda. The idea is to engender a rich public debate whose structure elicits presentation of the contending positions in sufficient detail to be reasonably grasped and assessed and in a manner enabling voters to take due account of all of them.[30]

Now the period of political competition preceding the general election is best conceived for present purposes as divided into two stages, the agenda-formation stage and the election campaign stage. Both stages are elements of a public process of political deliberation, and in both stages the requirements of fairness derive from the interests of citizens conceived as participants in such a process. In both stages there is a concern to secure conditions that will facilitate informed and intelligent judgment. However, in the earlier stage there is the additional concern to identify the alternatives most likely to attain substantial support later on in view of the salience of the interests to which they respond. Accordingly the requirements of fairness with respect to the supply of campaign resources may differ.

At the earlier stage, the alternatives are likely to be more numerous, and it will be more difficult to predict which ones are likely to attract a substantial following. For purposes of facilitating informed judgment, those candidates who are able to demonstrate the capacity to attract substantial support should be provided with sufficient resources to place their positions and qualifications before the relevant publics. However, considerations of cost together with the need to encourage compromise and coalition formation may justify

[30] The idea of a "rich public debate" is the legacy of Alexander Meiklejohn. See *Political Freedom* (New York: Harper & Brothers, 1960); and, for a discussion, Owen M. Fiss, "Free Speech and Social Structure," *Iowa Law Review* 71 (1986), pp. 1405–25.

measures to deny further resources to those who fail, during the agenda formation process, to gain many adherents. There does not appear to be any simple basis for reconciling these potentially conflicting considerations, and in practice the design of financing devices will inevitably be somewhat ad hoc; but it is clear that the range of alternatives need not be kept too narrow.

At the election campaign stage, matters appear simpler, at least at the level of principle. Now there is no concern to encourage pre-election compromise, and cost constraints are likely to be less pressing. A main aim of any system of campaign finance at this stage must be to ensure that candidates who survive the narrowing process not be denied adequate access to the public forum for lack of the necessary material resources.

This is not necessarily an egalitarian maxim. If the possession of a sufficient *minimum* were ensured, for example by public subsidy, further measures to enforce equality of aggregate resources (such as constraints on expenditures by candidates of privately provided funds) might not be warranted by the interest in engendering conditions of informed deliberation and choice.[31] Some have argued that equal overall expenditure constraints, like rules of order allocating time in a town meeting, are required to avoid distortion of the deliberative process.[32] ("Distortion" might be conceived in either quantitative or qualitative terms; thus, it might be thought that unequal resources enable some candidates to purchase greater exposure than others ["drowning out" their voices], or that unrestricted expenditures encourage the use of forms of communication, such as some kinds of mass media advertising, lacking in substantive content.) But this is a contingent matter requiring a three-step judgment: first, that material inequalities would distort the deliberative process in some significant sense even if a sufficient minimum were ensured for all candidates; second, that this form of distortion could be avoided with expenditure constraints of the sort envisioned; third, that the benefits of reducing distortion

[31] Recall that the interest in protecting the integrity of the system of representation is a separate concern, which might provide an independent justification of some kinds of constraints (particularly on the size of individual contributions and of "independent expenditures," as opposed to aggregate expenditures by candidates).

[32] Wright, "Money and the Pollution of Politics," p. 641. The analogy of the town meeting is due to Meiklejohn, *Political Freedom*, pp. 24–28.

outweigh whatever costs would be imposed on the election system as a whole by expenditure constraints. Each step raises empirical questions we cannot explore here. However, in view of the widespread belief that the contingencies are unproblematic, it bears repeating that there is substantial reason to doubt that equal expenditure constraints would always prove beneficial as a strategy for promoting a rich public debate. Consider as an illustration the proposal that candidates in congressional election campaigns be provided with equal public subsidies and that expenditures from privately provided funds be severely restricted.[33] Earlier I noted empirical findings suggesting that the marginal value of financial support is greater for congressional challengers than for incumbents. If this is true, then the measures proposed would most likely contribute further to the advantage of incumbency, thereby decreasing the competitiveness of congressional election campaigns involving incumbents and reducing the capacity of the election system to hold members accountable to their constituencies. Moreover, this result is not extrinsic to the process of deliberation that election campaigns aim to foster; it flows directly from the greater access to the public forum that incumbents are likely to enjoy. On the other hand, providing sufficient resources to all candidates might be enough to ensure that no candidate could substantially increase her chances of winning by gathering additional resources from private sources.[34] If these empirical findings are true, then considerations of fairness supply greater support for floors than for ceilings.

The point of theoretical significance is that whether the interest in favorable conditions of deliberation requires *equality* of resources is a matter of contingent judgment rather than of political principle. Equality may, of course, play a role in regulatory arrangements. For example, the system might allocate equal public subsidies to the contending candidates; or, it might require television and radio broadcasters to provide each candidate with an equal amount of broadcast time for the discussion of political issues. But the explanation would not be that equality of resources has intrin-

[33] Wright, "Money and the Pollution of Politics," p. 643; Drew, *Politics and Money*, p. 147.

[34] In addition to the sources cited earlier, see the discussion of this matter in Fleishman and McCorkle, "Level-Up Rather Than Level-Down," pp. 251–59.

sic or fundamental importance but rather that it serves as a convenient proxy for a more complex criterion that would be excessively difficult to interpret and administer. What a doctrine of political fairness must require is that the system of political finance ensure *adequate* access to the public arena; it is a criterion of sufficiency, not necessarily of equality.

POLITICAL FINANCE AND FREEDOM OF EXPRESSION

As a consequence of the Supreme Court's decision in *Buckley v. Valeo*, controversy about matters of principle involved in the regulation of campaign finance has concentrated on how, if at all, the doctrine of freedom of expression circumscribes the state's right to interfere in the market for financial support. Among other things, the legislation at issue in that case sought to regulate three aspects of campaign finance: contributions by individuals to candidates and multicandidate financing entities, aggregate campaign expenditures by candidates and their campaign committees, and independent expenditures undertaken on behalf of candidates, but without their approval or cooperation. It was argued that all three kinds of regulation unduly restricted the rights of freedom of speech and association of individual contributors and of candidates. The Court sustained the limitations on individual contributions, holding that the public interest in avoiding corruption or its appearance was sufficient to justify what it considered the relatively small offense to individual interests in unfettered expression. However, it struck down limitations on overall campaign expenditures and on independent expenditures, finding that they were not necessary to avoid corruption, whereas they posed a substantial threat to interests in expression and association. In addition, the Court held that the interest in ensuring fair access to the public arena for all qualified candidates was insufficient, by itself, to justify any form of regulation that restrained expression.[35] The last point was the most con-

---

[35] *Buckley v. Valeo*, 424 U.S. 1 (1976), at 23–29 (contributions limits), 39–51 and 54–58 (expenditure limits), 56–57 (insufficiency of the interest in equalizing access as a justification of restraints on speech).

troversial, not only as a matter of constitutional law, but as a matter of democratic theory as well.[36]

If the empirical speculations set forth above are correct, then it may be unnecessary for practical purposes to consider these questions further; for at least one of the main aims of fairness in connection with political finance may be better served by the public provision of adequate resources than by enforcement of constraints on expenditures of privately provided funds. However, further study may prove that those speculations are wrong. Moreover, another of the aims of fairness—protecting the integrity of the system of representation—supplies additional grounds for some kinds of restrictions, including those on independent expenditures. For both reasons, the matter of principle ought not to be left aside.[37]

Since I am not in a position to set forth a comprehensive theory of freedom of expression, it is best to proceed informally. The question to consider is what interests would be set back by legal constraints on either contributions or expenditures, and how these might be balanced against the interests presumably served by those constraints.

Both contribution and expenditure constraints obviously affect one's capacity to participate in public deliberation, so it is not incorrect to say that the interest in "political speech" could be set back by them. It is, however, somewhat misleading. The significance of the interest in political speech flows from two sources. One is the directly political concern to influence the outcome of the election by making one's voice heard; the other is the less directly political concern to contribute to a more general public process of political argument, even if there is no realistic prospect of affecting the outcome of the present campaign.

Now let us assume arguendo that unconstrained private campaign spending would distort public political deliberation and that some feasible policy involving constraints on private spending would be more desirable. On these facts, the analogy of spending

---

[36] See, e.g., Wright, "Money and the Pollution of Politics."

[37] The issue is considered here as a question in political theory rather than in constitutional law; I shall not take up the question of how First Amendment doctrine ought to be construed in the campaign finance context. For illuminating remarks about the capacity of established First Amendment doctrine to accommodate concerns like those referred to in the text, see Fiss, "Free Speech and Social Structure."

constraints and time limitations in a town meeting would hold; for it would be true that constraints on spending would be both necessary and effective in ensuring that voters would be presented with sufficient information about all of the alternatives to reach informed and balanced judgments. The policy of constraints would advance the interests of citizens in favorable conditions of public deliberation. (There might also be other reasons to support a policy of constraints. For example, it might be thought necessary to limit individual contributions, and for that matter independent expenditures, in order to minimize incentives for corruption or to control the effects of cross-constituency giving. I omit consideration of these reasons here because their weight, as justifications for a policy of constraints, is not in dispute.)[38]

How should these "voter interests" be reconciled with the "speaker interests" of those who would be barred by a policy of constraints from devoting private resources to political speech? Considering first the speaker interest in influencing election outcomes, there is a strong case to be made that voter interests should take priority. The considerations that govern the distribution of access to the public forum are, so to speak, internal to the conception of a public deliberative process. The success of the election system as a whole depends on the integrity of the conditions of public deliberation. These conditions chiefly require that citizens be provided with reasonably adequate opportunities to learn the positions of the candidates and parties among which they must choose. Assuming that constraints on private spending in fact enable these conditions to be met—as in a town meeting or deliberative body whose time limits allow representatives of the major positions fair opportunities to speak—each position will be assured its fair share of public attention. If those with greater private wealth assert a claim to a larger share, it can be replied that their fair share of this particular means of influencing outcomes has already been provided; granting them a larger share would diminish rather than enhance the integrity of the public deliberative scheme. Any other argument in favor of the claim to a larger share would appear to be a form of special

[38] Thus, in *Buckley*, the Court accepted prevention of corruption as a warrant for the FECA's contributions limits, while acknowledging that these limits would, in fact, restrict political expression. 424 U.S. 1 (1976), at 26–27.

pleading. It is only by invoking an abstract right to speak that such claims can be made to appear plausible; but the appearance dissolves once the basis of the abstract right is brought into question. This reasoning applies as much to limitations of independent expenditures made by individuals on behalf of a candidate, but without his endorsement, as to limitations on contributions made by individuals to the candidate's official campaign organization. As a matter of democratic theory, the *Buckley* court's distinction between these two forms of campaign contribution is insupportable.

A consequence of conceiving the question in this way is that both elements of the underlying conflict are revealed to involve aspects of individual liberty. The speaker interest in uninhibited expression is counterpoised against voter interests in conditions of effective and responsible citizenship. Both categories of interest should play a role in any plausible theory of freedom of (political) expression. Traditionally, they have been thought to operate in tandem. What is novel about the campaign finance case, under the empirical hypothesis we have accepted arguendo, is that it illustrates how these categories of interest can come apart; one can be enforced to the limit only at the expense of the other. More generally, it shows that the issue of principle underlying dispute about freedom of expression and the regulation of campaign finance is wrongly conceived as expressing an abstract conflict between individual liberty and social equality; instead, it expresses a conflict between two aspects of liberty, or more accurately, between two distinct liberties. It is a conflict *within* the theory of freedom of expression.

The other speaker interest—that in affecting the longer-term and more general process of public political debate—cannot be disposed of by considerations internal to the concept of election campaign deliberation. It has been suggested that this interest is particularly implicated in efforts to restrict the independent expenditures of groups not formally affiliated with any particular candidate.[39] But in fact the interest is potentially implicated in any policy of constraint, since virtually any form of political speech, including speech limited in terms to advocacy of one rather than another election outcome, may be motivated by an interest in influencing the

[39] T. M. Scanlon, "Freedom of Expression and Categories of Expression," *University of Pittsburgh Law Review* 40 (1979), p. 540.

longer-term course of political thought. (Consider, for example, the motivations of those who support minor-party candidates with no realistic chance of winning.) In this case there is no alternative to acknowledging the conflict of speaker and voter interests and considering how they ought to be balanced in view of the weights it is appropriate to assign to each. Offhand, the weight to be assigned to speaker interests seems to be reduced by a recognition that public political debate can be carried on in other fora than that of the election campaign and that access to these fora is not normally foreclosed by restrictions on campaign finance. In contrast, the weight to be assigned to voter interests seems to be increased by a recognition that the system of elections occupies such a strategic position in determining the course of public life and that in the nature of the case there is no alternative forum to that of the campaign itself in which deliberation and judgment about its possible outcomes can take place. Accordingly, I believe that when these interests come into conflict in connection with policies of constraint, the conflict should be resolved in favor of the interests of voters. The setback to speaker interests is hardly irremediable.

To conclude, considerations of freedom of expression do not appear to be decisive against campaign finance measures that would restrict the capacity of individuals to devote private means to political campaigns. Whether such measures are desirable is another matter; it depends on complex judgments about whether they are necessary to establish conditions of rich public debate. In the foregoing discussion of freedom of expression, I have assumed for the sake of argument that these judgments would come out in favor of a policy of restrictions; but this assumption may be incorrect. The difficult issue about campaign finance is not how to resolve a supposed conflict of political liberty and social equality or even how freedom of expression should be compromised with a broader conception of political liberty. It is what combination of regulation and subsidy is most likely to yield an environment of public political deliberation in which all of the contending positions can receive a fair hearing and in which citizens can judge among them responsibly.

Conclusion

CHAPTER TEN

Substance and Method

Political equality is the central organizing idea of modern democratic belief. Theorists and reformers often speak and write as if they think its meaning is obvious: it is simply that citizens should be equally entitled to participate in the decision-making process or that they should have equal power over its outcomes. But these formulas are easily seen to be ambiguous and vague, and it is uncertain how clarity would best be attained. In the face of this, there is a tendency either to represent the choice among the possible interpretations as essentially arbitrary (perhaps as a matter of philosophical intuition or taste) or to infer from their variety that the egalitarian ideal has no determinate political content at all.

In this book I have proposed a different approach, one that I believe has less skeptical consequences and that better illuminates the richness of the egalitarian ideal we inherit from the democratic revolutions of the seventeenth and eighteenth centuries. This approach seeks to explain what political equality means and why, so understood, it should matter to us, in terms of a deeper and more general perspective on political morality. Taking up this deeper perspective helps to make clear what values are served by the ideal of equality, in what ways they should be reflected in the structure of our institutions, and how we ought to reconcile conflicts among these values when they arise.[1]

The essentials of the view I have set forth might be summarized as three related theses.

The first involves the *subject matter* of a theory of political equality: Its central concern is the fairness of the terms of participation embodied in the institutions of democratic choice, not the sense in which these institutions might be said to be formally or

[1] I am grateful to William N. Nelson for suggesting this formulation.

procedurally egalitarian. Equality enters at the more abstract level
of reasoning about the basis or foundations of the institutional requirements of political fairness; it is a condition on the justification
of these requirements, not on the structure of institutions themselves. If there is some reason to care about equality at the level of
institutional structure and process, this should be seen as the conclusion of a theory, not as its premise. Indeed, as I remarked earlier,
were it not for a desire to respect the traditional usage, we should
dispense with the phrase *political equality* altogether and refer instead to the more fundamental value of political fairness.

The second thesis concerns the *justification* of requirements of
political fairness: Fair terms of participation are those upon which
democratic citizens may reasonably expect each other to enter into
the cooperative political activity required for self-government. They
are terms it would be unreasonable for anyone in society to refuse
to accept, given that each desires to come to agreement with others
on a mechanism that enables everyone to participate in making political decisions. The egalitarianism of the view lies in this idea that
the terms of participation should be reasonably acceptable to all citizens. A corollary is that political fairness is not a matter of maximizing some value for society at large or of arranging institutions
so that the decisions reached are in any sense best overall. Instead,
it requires avoiding certain forms of harm, so far as this is possible
by means of institutional reform and can be accomplished without
producing consequences that would be even more objectionable. In
this sense, the practical force of political fairness is primarily negative—though, obviously, avoiding harm can dictate affirmative as
well as negative requirements for institutions.

Finally, about the *content* of political fairness: Citizens might
reasonably bring several kinds of interests to bear in evaluating the
terms of participation their institutions make available. Chief
among these regulative interests of citizenship are interests in public acknowledgement of one's status as an equal member of the polity, protection against political outcomes that would place one's
prospects in serious jeopardy, and conditions of public deliberation
conducive to responsible judgment about public affairs. Taking the
second and third points together, complex proceduralism holds that
fair terms of participation are those that no one who had these in-

terests, and who was motivated to reach agreement with others on this basis, could reasonably refuse to accept.

As these summary comments show, complex proceduralism is an unorthodox view in several respects. For example, it is pluralistic: in relying on the regulative interests as the substantive bases of judgments about procedural fairness, the theory portrays these judgments as resting on a set of irreducibly distinct values that reflect the complexity of the role of democratic citizenship. There is no univocal criterion, relating either to the intrinsic properties of decision procedures or to their outcomes, to which appeal can be made to resolve controversy about fairness in procedural design. Relatedly, the theory idealizes the regulative interests: the criteria of fairness are seen as having a normative significance that does not depend directly on the particular desires or interests that the individual members of society may happen to have. As I have remarked, complex proceduralism is an attempt to represent an ideal of democratic citizenship in a way that enables the weight of this ideal to be brought to bear on the design and reform of the institutions of self-government.

To avoid misunderstanding, it is perhaps worth repeating that the theory is not intended as an analysis of the meaning of phrases such as *political equality* or *political fairness* as they occur in ordinary political argument. Indeed, this would be impossible: these phrases have no canonical meaning, and in any case they are commonly used in so many ways that any account of their ordinary usage would be so vague as to be without either theoretical or practical interest. Instead, I have aimed for what might be called a reforming definition. We identified the subject of political equality by examining the role the concept plays in practical reasoning and formulated a theory that would fulfil this role more successfully than other familiar views. Nothing turns on whether the theory can be regarded as an accurate report of the meanings of words, and so nothing would be lost by conceding that, as some people use the term, *political fairness* has a narrower scope or a different content than on the view taken here.

For the most part I have avoided speculation about metatheoretical or methodological issues associated with complex proceduralism in order to concentrate on more substantive questions involving its content and application. However, particularly in view of its unorthodox aspects, doubts may arise concerning the character of the theory and the kind of defense I have given for it. The main problems involve the nature of the justification of the theory, especially the regulative interests; the sense in which the view might be seen as relativistic; and the residual indeterminacy of the view with respect to matters of institutional design. I would like to offer a brief comment about each of these matters.

JUSTIFICATION

I have not provided a systematic justification for complex proceduralism. I have not claimed that it can be derived from any more basic principle, or set of principles, of equality or (generic) fairness; that we are compelled to accept it by any general moral conception that is held to be relatively uncontroversial; or that its normative aspects can be seen as independent requirements of practical reason. I have said that the theory is intended to represent an ideal of democratic citizenship. If a priori moral considerations of a more abstract or general nature do not dictate the content of this ideal, what other reasons might motivate someone to accept it?

One reason is that the ideal is an attractive one; like other perfectionist conceptions, the conception of citizenship this ideal describes, once it is appreciated, is difficult to reject. But I believe it is possible to say more. The further support that can reasonably be claimed for the theory derives from a combination of several considerations: its philosophical superiority to various rival conceptions, its success as an interpretation of an ideal of citizenship we can recognize as rooted in our own traditions and practices, and its capacity to illuminate and help resolve controversial problems of institutional reform. I have tried to develop each point during the course of this book. Thus, I have shown that several prominent theories of political fairness are philosophically defective and illustrated the respects in which complex proceduralism is an improvement; I have contended that the theory is better able to account for our views about relatively uncontroversial (or "paradigmatic") cases of procedural unfairness; and I have examined in some detail how it might be applied to practical issues of contemporary dispute.

Of course, the view may be capable of some more compelling

kind of proof as well. For example, we might consider whether more can be said about our justification for regarding the regulative interests as determining in questions of procedural design. We might ask, Is it simply a cultural fact that our views about procedural unfairness converge in the paradigmatic cases we have considered, or can this fact be explained in terms of a relationship between the regulative interests, which articulate this convergence, and the deeper and evidently more permanent interests of human beings? If such an explanation could be given, then the contractualist defense of the regulative interests could be carried a step further; the criteria of fairness could be exhibited as elements of each person's individual good, so that it would be irrational, as well as unreasonable, to refuse to accept them.[2] However, I have not attempted to provide the regulative interests with any such foundation; there is no claim that we have established the *truth* of the theory in that (or any other) sense. For practical purposes, it is enough that complex proceduralism can be seen as a hypothesis in democratic theory that seems more plausible than the prevailing alternatives, for the kinds of reasons enumerated earlier, but for which no more rigorous proof has been attempted. If this leaves open the possibility that more satisfactory theoretical conceptions of political equality may emerge with further study (as, no doubt, they will), that is as it should be.

RELATIVISM

Both the contractualist framework of complex proceduralism and the interpretation of the regulative interests arise from reflection about paradigmatic cases of procedural unfairness—that is, cases involving features that are uncontroversially unacceptable. I have claimed on behalf of the theory that these points of agreement define an ideal of citizenship that is prominent in the tradition of democratic thought and implicit in contemporary political belief and that this fact constitutes a reason to accept the theory.

In response, someone might object that complex proceduralism is

[2] The pivot of this view would be an account of *objective interest* of the kind advanced by Peter Railton in "Moral Realism," *Philosophical Review* 95 (1986), pp. 173–78.

not itself a widely accepted view and that it cannot plausibly be seen as an expression of a widely held but inchoate conception of political fairness. As an empirical matter these observations are true; however, the objection misunderstands the appeal to common agreement, or more accurately, the place within the theory's justification where such an appeal occurs. The theory is a construction (or, perhaps, an interpretation) that counts the convergence of many people's pre-theoretical judgments about paradigmatic cases of unfairness among its starting points. The authority of the theory rests, in part, on its capacity to supply a coherent rationale for these points of agreement, taken together; it need not provide a faithful description of the deeper pre-theoretical views about the nature of procedural unfairness from which the convergence derives.

The dependency of the theory's justification on beliefs about procedural unfairness that are accepted in our community may give rise to another kind of worry. Regarded as a consequence of a general view about institutional justification, this dependency could be characterized by the doctrine that institutions should be justifiable according to principles that affirm or express values that are widely held in the society in which the institutions are to operate—or, for short, that institutions (or the principles that justify them) should "fit" their communities.[3] The doctrine of fit is sometimes associated with communitarianism in political theory. What makes it suspect is its relativism: it seems to imply that different institutions would count as unfair in different societies. The problem is not only that the *application* of the concept of fairness can vary; its *meaning* might itself be interculturally variable. But we are likely to think that important moral notions, or at least those that are supposed to play a role in resolving important practical conflicts, should possess a degree of objectivity that is inconsistent with this kind of relativism. These notions are supposed to apply "to the whole world";[4] how could a relativistic conception of fairness do that?

The form of relativism I have described might be alarming for

---

[3] I adopt the term from Michael Walzer, "The Moral Standing of States," *Philosophy & Public Affairs* 9 (1980), p. 212; for a more extended discussion of the view, see *Spheres of Justice* (New York: Basic Books, 1983), esp. chaps. 1 and 13.

[4] Bernard Williams, *Ethics and the Limits of Philosophy* (Cambridge: Harvard University Press, 1985), p. 159.

either of two reasons. The first arises from the fact that considerations of fit could collide with moral requirements at a higher level of generality; there is no guarantee that morality approves what common belief accepts. Consider, for example, the beliefs about procedural fairness that were widely held in the antebellum South. Any view in which considerations of fit determine questions of institutional justification seems to allow that institutions that are justified by considerations of fit could simultaneously be objectionable on more general moral grounds; but this is incoherent. (Incoherence could be avoided if the "justification" supplied by considerations of fit were seen as only prima facie; but then considerations of fit would not actually be determining.) Is the justification of complex proceduralism threatened with incoherence in this way?

The doctrine of fit might take any of three forms within a conception of institutional justification. In order of diminishing normative strength, fit might be seen as a sufficient condition, a necessary condition, or a subordinate condition of the justification of institutions. (By a *subordinate condition*, I mean one that comes into operation only after requirements of higher priority are satisfied.) The plausibility of the doctrine clearly depends on its form: for example, it surely counts against either of the doctrine's stronger forms that considerations of fit could conflict with more general moral requirements.[5] However, when fit is conceived as a subordinate condition, the possibility of conflict does not arise, since considerations of fit play a determining role only when more general ethical requirements have already been met.

Thus, it is significant that the justification of complex proceduralism needs only to rely on the doctrine of fit in its weakest form. As I have tried to show, moral considerations of a more general or objective character are underdetermining with respect to the fairness of democratic procedures. To put it briefly, these considerations establish that democratic procedures should treat people equally, in the sense of being reasonably acceptable from each per-

[5] Elsewhere I have criticized Walzer's appeal to "fit" in the context of argument about the basis of the principle of nonintervention in international affairs. One way to summarize the criticism is to say that Walzer employs the doctrine of fit in an objectionably strong form. See "Nonintervention and Communal Integrity: A Rejoinder to Walzer," *Philosophy & Public Affairs* 9 (1980), pp. 385–91.

son's point of view; but without more this contractualist formula lacks definite content. Content is provided by the regulative interests, whose normative significance, as we have seen, depends to some extent on various features of the political beliefs present in our society. However, because the theory assigns a higher priority to moral requirements of greater generality or objectivity, the relativism reflected in the communitarian foundations of the regulative interests does not intimate any conflict with these requirements.

The other reason why relativism might be alarming involves the possibility of disagreement *within* society about the requirements of fairness. As I have already noted, without more, the prospect of disagreement need not be cause for concern. Everything depends on how the disagreement is explained and, in particular, whether it arises, so to speak, within or outside the prevailing convergence. Disagreement would arise within the convergence, for example, if someone agreed that the paradigms we have considered embody procedural unfairness but disputed the rationale for this agreement supplied by the theory. In this case, dispute centers on whether the rationale takes reasonable account of the relevant normative considerations and whether it combines them in a coherent and illuminating way; this is a normal form of moral dispute, and the fact that it cannot be foreclosed need be no more alarming in connection with political fairness than in any other area of moral argument. However, disagreement arising outside the convergence is more serious. It would occur if someone disputed that the paradigms themselves involve unfairness: for example, perhaps someone denies that there is anything objectionable about restrictions on the franchise by race or class, or about procedural arrangements that have functionally similar exclusionary effects. Since agreement about paradigms of unfairness constitutes a starting point of justification, the fact of agreement would not provide someone whose beliefs fall outside that agreement with a reason to accept the theory. This is not to say that substantive moral arguments of the kinds advanced, for example, in connection with the regulative interests could have no appeal; only that considerations of fit, taken by themselves, would have no independent force. But of course convergence might not be brought about by substantive argument, either: that too must start somewhere, and it is always possible that the outsider could reject its starting points as well.

The possibility of deep disagreement about the foundations of ethical argument raises problems for any conception of justification centering on the idea that principles should be reasonably acceptable (or not reasonably rejectable) from all points of view. I know of no general solution to these problems. However, two points might be noted. First, analogous problems arise with regard to alternative conceptions of justification as well; for utilitarian views, for example, they arise in connection with the definition of utility or with the explanation of why we should value it. The problem is not unique to the conception of justification underlying complex proceduralism. Second, whether the theoretical possibility of deep disagreement constitutes a practical problem that should concern us is an empirical and a political question. To answer it, we must return to the paradigmatic cases at which the justification begins and consider the extent to which disagreement about them is actually likely to occur. If the cases are genuinely paradigmatic—if they exemplify instances of procedural unfairness that are very widely acknowledged as such—then the theoretical possibility of disagreement need be no practical embarrassment for the theory.

INDETERMINACY

Complex proceduralism is informal, in the sense that it leaves a great deal to be worked out through moral reasoning of a more or less ordinary kind. It is pluralistic, in the sense that it allows a variety of considerations to play a role in grounding judgments about political fairness. These two features explain the indeterminacy of the theory in connection with problems of institutional design or reform. As we have seen, any resolution of these problems depends on empirical judgments about the likely behavior of political mechanisms of various kinds under prevailing social conditions—for example, their influence on the content of legislation and its distributive characteristics, social and political stability, the nature and dynamics of political culture, and the self-esteem, political education, and political competence of citizens.

If my criticisms of other views are correct, the need to rely on empirical judgments about these matters should come as no surprise. Political equality is not a simple univocal principle capable of being applied directly in the definition of democratic procedures. It is a complex ideal, bringing together diverse and abstract concerns whose application to problems of institutional design inevitably requires a good deal of interpretation and adaptation to political and historical circumstance. Many of the long-standing disputes among political scientists and constitutional lawyers about alternative structures of democratic decision making involve empirical issues of precisely the kinds mentioned above; and I believe it is merit of the theory presented here, not a defect, that it shows how and why these controversies are important for political ethics and establishes a framework in which their consequences can be assessed.

Our attempts to apply the theory to specific institutional problems underscore another kind of indeterminacy, which cannot be characterized as easily. This kind of indeterminacy is more theoretical. It could not be said of any of the practical problems we have considered that the theory would be sufficient, in the presence of adequate empirical information, to resolve the controversies at hand. In each case, more is required; for example, it might be necessary to elaborate the content of the regulative interests or to introduce apparently ad hoc judgments about their relative importance when they come into conflict. Even assuming complete information, the theory will seldom fully determine complicated questions of institutional reform.

Normative theories are often criticized for manifesting this kind of indeterminacy. The criticism reflects an aspiration for a method of resolving practical controversy in such a precise, mechanical fashion that there is no room left over for judgment, no space for controversy. Perhaps understandably, this aspiration seems to occur more frequently in the social and policy sciences than in political philosophy itself. There is no reason to deny that the theory presented here might be improved in a way that reduces its indeterminacy by endowing its analysis of political fairness with greater structure. Even so, it would be unwise to aspire to mechanical precision; for this could be attained, if at all, only at the cost of a degree of simplicity that would do violence to the texture and complexity of our convictions about democratic equality. We have seen evidence of this, for example, in the defects of the simple view considered in chapter 1 and of the kinds of popular will theories criticized in chapter 3. The aspiration for precision is to be resisted for another reason as well: it reflects a radical misconception of the nature of practical reasoning and of the role that political theories can be expected to play in it. Theoretical reflection can help render our pre-theoretical convictions about political ethics in a more orderly and perspicuous form; it can elaborate and clarify the reasons for accepting (or revising) them; and, on this basis, it can seek to resolve conflicts among them when they arise. A theory that achieves these aims will most likely concentrate the force of our normative commitments on the problems of practical decision that confront us in a way that reveals some alternatives to be unacceptable and others to be more or less desirable than they may previously have appeared. The goal is to arrive at choices that are as well founded in considerations of principle as any we are capable of. Yet it is not the theory but the theorist who is responsible for these choices. Political theory should guide practical judgment, not replace it.

The Virtue of Fairness

Finally, there is the question of the philosophical standing of political fairness and its relationship to other values. What is the virtue of fairness in a democratic regime? It is common to think of the ethical significance of fairness as intrinsic rather than derivative of considerations related to the aims and character of institutions themselves, and of its essential content as invariant across institutional contexts. So understood, fairness is a distinct normative property of institutions and procedures.[6] Some such idea is reflected in the simple view of political equality considered at the beginning of this book. Complex proceduralism conceives of fairness differently. It does not represent the judgment that a political system is fair as one that can be reached independently of various other evaluative judgments about the system—for example, that its terms of participation recognize the equal worth of its members or their equal rights to pursue their ends (within certain limits), or that over

[6] This feature of commonsense moral thought is noted by T. M. Scanlon in "Rights, Goals and Fairness," in *Public and Private Morality*, ed. Stuart Hampshire (Cambridge: Cambridge University Press, 1978), pp. 99-100. Scanlon holds that a philosophical account of fairness should include this feature but does not say how the independent normative force of the idea of fairness might be explained.

time the decisions reached are likely to distribute the benefits and costs of social life more or less equitably, or that the political structure facilitates responsible deliberation about public affairs. Political fairness is not one more normative property that a political system can possess (or not) in addition to all the rest. Instead, a judgment about the fairness of a political system functions as kind of summary of these other judgments. To say that a system is fair just *is* to say that its procedures for participation in politics display certain properties, the presence of which makes the system capable of justification to all of its citizens.

This is very abstract, but it is not without practical consequences. For one thing, it suggests that the many relatively concrete issues about which questions of political fairness might arise (for example, those involving voting weights, legislative districting, and so forth) are not best considered separately. What matters in the end is not how any one of these is resolved in isolation from the others but how the resolution of each individual issue affects the system of participation as a whole. This is especially important in view of the tendency of dispute about practical questions of procedural fairness to become fixed on specific formal features of the procedures in question. Relatedly, our perspective invites skepticism about the association of institutional fairness and formal or facial equality. It is true that fair procedures frequently have egalitarian formal features, but, as we have seen, the significance of equality is seldom intrinsic; most often, it arises from some more substantive value that procedures with egalitarian features are expected to advance. There is no general reason to treat formally egalitarian procedures as enjoying any special privilege and no reason to think that inegalitarian or countermajoritarian procedures (such as judicial review, supermajority requirements, and the like) must necessarily be unfair. Finally, this view discourages the search for an unambiguous criterion that can be invoked to settle disagreement about the overall fairness of any given combination of more concrete procedural arrangements. There is strong pressure to arrive at such a criterion, if only for reasons of simplicity, but the pressure is more likely to distort than to illuminate the problems we face in the criticism and reform of popular institutions. It leads to the theoretical error most frequently made in contemporary thought about democratic politics—a misconception of its public character that results in the deliberative interests being accorded too little weight.

These observations point to another answer to our question about the virtue of fairness. Democratic institutions are not best understood as hydraulic mechanisms designed to move society in the direction of the greater force. Nor as pale imitations of ideal computational devices programmed to connect each possible array of individual preferences with a collective choice. Political democracy is a structure of rules in which competition for influence over policy supplies the occasion and the incentive for participation in a public, collaborative enterprise of deliberation and decision. When things go well and democracy flourishes, deliberation is an exercise in mutual education and debate that allows individual political judgments to be scrutinized, and perhaps revised, in light of the needs and interests of others and the shared commitments of the community. Electoral choice is a means of reaching equitable decisions in a way that recognizes the equal public standing and elicits the willing support of each participant. The system can be seen to be justified from both perspectives of citizenship, those of agent and object, maker and matter.

Of course, things need not go so well. A host of forces threatens to subvert democracy's aspirations. Not all of these forces are open to social control or manipulation. Of those that are, the institutional provisions that govern political participation are among the most important. These are the province of political fairness, and this is its peculiar virtue: when institutions are fair, the flourishing of democracy may be a reasonable hope.

Works Cited

Dates in square brackets indicate the year of original publication of the edition cited.

Ackerman, Bruce. *Social Justice in the Liberal State*. New Haven: Yale University Press, 1980.

Adamany, David W. *Financing Politics: Recent Wisconsin Elections*. Madison: University of Wisconsin Press, 1969.

Adamany, David W., and George E. Agree. *Political Money: A Strategy for Campaign Financing in America*. Baltimore: Johns Hopkins University Press, 1975.

Alexander, Herbert E. "Election Reform and National Politics." Smithsonian Institution Lecture, 23 April 1980. Photocopy.

———. *Financing Politics*. 2d ed. Washington, D.C.: Congressional Quarterly Press, 1980.

———. *Financing Politics*. 3d ed. Washington, D.C.: Congressional Quarterly Press, 1984.

———. "Making Sense About Dollars in the 1980 Presidential Campaigns." In *Money and Politics in the United States*, edited by Michael J. Malbin, 1–37. Washington: American Enterprise Institute, 1984.

Alfange, Dean, Jr. "Gerrymandering and the Constitution: Into the Thorns of the Thicket at Last." *Supreme Court Review* (1986): 175–257.

Almond, Gabriel A. "Introduction." In Gabriel A. Almond and James S. Coleman, *The Politics of the Developing Areas*, 3–64. Princeton: Princeton University Press, 1960.

American Party v. White, 415 U.S. 767 (1974).

American Political Science Association. Committee on Political Parties. *Toward a More Responsible Two-Party System*. New York: Rinehart, 1950. Originally published in *American Political Science Review* 44 (September 1950 supplement).

Anderson v. Celebreeze, 460 U.S. 780 (1983).

Aristotle. *The Politics of Aristotle*. Translated by Ernest Barker. Oxford: Clarendon Press, 1946.

Arrow, Kenneth J. *Social Choice and Individual Values*. 2d ed. New York: John Wiley, 1963.

Aylmer, G. E., ed. *The Levellers in the English Revolution*. Ithaca: Cornell University Press, 1975.

Bagehot, Walter. *The English Constitution*. 2d ed. [1872]. London: Oxford University Press, 1928.

Baier, Kurt. "Welfare and Preference." In *Human Values and Economic Policy*, edited by Sidney Hook, 120–35. New York: New York University Press, 1967.

Barry, Brian. "Is Democracy Special?" In *Philosophy, Politics, and Society*, 5th series, edited by Peter Laslett and James Fishkin, 155–96. New Haven: Yale University Press, 1979.

———. "Is It Better to Be Powerful or Lucky?" Parts 1 and 2. *Political Studies* 28 (1980): 183–94, 338–52.

———. *Political Argument*. London: Routledge & Kegan Paul, 1965.

———. "Power: An Economic Analysis." In *Power and Political Theory: Some European Perspectives*, edited by Brian Barry, 67–101. London: John Wiley, 1976.

———. "The Public Interest." *Proceedings of the Aristotelian Society*, supp. vol. 38 (1964): 1–18.

———. *Sociologists, Economists and Democracy*. London: Collier-Macmillan, 1970.

Barton, John H. "The General-Election Ballot: More Nominees or More Representative Nominees?" *Stanford Law Review* 22 (1970): 165–95.

Baty, Th. "The History of Majority Rule." *Quarterly Review* 216 (1912): 1–28.

Beitz, Charles R. "Democracy in Developing Societies." In *Boundaries: National Autonomy and Its Limits*, edited by Peter Brown and Henry Shue, 177–208. Totowa, N.J.: Rowman and Littlefield, 1981.

———. "Equal Opportunity in Political Representation." In *Equal Opportunity*, edited by Norman Bowie, 155–74. Boulder, Colo.: Westview Press, 1988.

———. "Nonintervention and Communal Integrity: A Rejoinder to Walzer." *Philosophy & Public Affairs* 9 (1980): 385–91.

———. "Political Finance in the United States: A Survey of Research." *Ethics* 95 (1984): 129–48.

———. "Procedural Equality in Democratic Theory: A Preliminary Examination." In *Nomos XXV: Liberal Democracy*, edited by J. Roland Pennock and John W. Chapman, 59–91. New York: New York University Press, 1983.

Berger, Fred R. *Happiness, Justice, and Freedom: The Moral and Political Philosophy of John Stuart Mill*. Berkeley: University of California Press, 1984.

Bergson, A. "On the Concept of Social Welfare." *Quarterly Journal of Economics* 68 (1954): 233–52.

———. "A Reformulation of Certain Aspects of Welfare Economics." *Quarterly Journal of Economics* 52 (1938): 310–14.

Black, Duncan. *The Theory of Committees and Elections*. Cambridge: Cambridge University Press, 1958.

Bogdanor, Vernon. "Conclusion: Electoral Systems and Party Systems." In *Democracy and Elections: Electoral Systems and Their Political Con-*

sequences, edited by Vernon Bogdanor and David Butler, 247–62. Cambridge: Cambridge University Press, 1983.

———. "Introduction." In *Democracy and Elections: Electoral Systems and Their Political Consequences*, edited by Vernon Bogdanor and David Butler, 1–19. Cambridge: Cambridge University Press, 1983.

———. *The People and the Party System*. Cambridge: Cambridge University Press, 1981.

Brams, Steven J., and Peter C. Fishburn. *Approval Voting*. Boston: Birkhauser, 1983.

Brittan, Samuel. "The Economic Contradictions of Democracy." *British Journal of Political Science* 5 (1975): 129–59.

Buchanan, James M. *The Limits of Liberty: Between Anarchy and Leviathan*. Chicago: University of Chicago Press, 1975.

———. "Rules for a Fair Game: Contractarian Notes on Distributive Justice." In *Liberty, Market and State*, 123–39. Brighton, Sussex: Wheatsheaf Books, 1986.

Buchanan, James M., and Gordon Tullock. *The Calculus of Consent*. Ann Arbor: University of Michigan Press, 1962.

Buckley, James. Speech on the floor of the U.S. Senate. *Congressional Record*, 8 October 1974, p. S18537.

Buckley v. Valeo, 424 U.S. 1 (1976).

Ceaser, James W. *Presidential Selection*. Princeton: Princeton University Press, 1979.

Chamberlin, John R., and Paul N. Courant. "Representative Deliberations and Representative Decisions: Proportional Representation and the Borda Rule." *American Political Science Review* 77 (1983): 718–33.

Chandler, J. A. "The Plurality Vote: A Reappraisal." *Political Studies* 30 (1982): 87–94.

Chappell, Henry W., Jr. "Campaign Contributions and Voting on the Cargo Preference Bill: A Comparison of Simultaneous Models." *Public Choice* 36 (1981): 301–12.

Cohen, Joshua. "An Epistemic Conception of Democracy." *Ethics* 97 (1986): 26–38.

———. "Reflections on Rousseau: Autonomy and Democracy." *Philosophy & Public Affairs* 15 (1986): 275–97.

Cohen, Joshua, and Joel Rogers. *On Democracy*. Harmondsworth, Middlesex: Penguin Books, 1983.

Coleman, Jules, and John Ferejohn. "Democracy and Social Choice." *Ethics* 97 (1986): 6–25.

Common Cause. *Toward a System of "Fair and Effective Representation."* Washington: Common Cause, 1977.

Cousins v. Wigoda, 419 U.S. 477 (1975).

Crotty, William, and John S. Jackson III. *Presidential Primaries and Nominations*. Washington: Congressional Quarterly, 1985.

Dahl, Robert A. "The Concept of Power." *Behavioral Science* 2 (1957): 201–15.

Dahl, Robert A. *A Preface to Democratic Theory.* Chicago: University of Chicago Press, 1956.

———. "Procedural Democracy." In *Philosophy, Politics and Society*, 5th series, edited by Peter Laslett and James Fishkin, 97–133. New Haven: Yale University Press, 1979.

Daniels, Norman. "Equal Liberty and Unequal Worth of Liberty." In *Reading Rawls*, edited by Norman Daniels, 253–81. New York: Basic Books, 1975.

Davis, J. C. "The Levellers and Democracy." *Past and Present*, no. 40 (1968): 174–80.

Davis v. Bandemer, 106 S. Ct. 2797 (1986).

Democratic National Committee. Commission on Party Structure and Delegate Selection. *Mandate for Change.* Washington: Democratic National Committee, 1970.

Democratic Party of the United States v. LaFollette, 450 U.S. 107 (1981).

"Developments in the Law—Elections." *Harvard Law Review* 88 (1975): 1114–1339.

Dixon, Robert G. *Democratic Representation.* New York: Oxford University Press, 1968.

———. Prepared testimony. U.S. Senate. Committee on Governmental Affairs. *Congressional Anti-Gerrymandering Act of 1979 [S. 596]: Hearings.* Washington: Government Printing Office, 1979: 218–44.

———. "Representation Values and Reapportionment Practice." In *Nomos X: Representation*, edited by J. Roland Pennock and John W. Chapman, 167–95. New York: Atherton, 1968.

Downs, Anthony. *An Economic Theory of Democracy.* New York: Harper & Row, 1957.

Drew, Elizabeth. *Politics and Money: The New Road to Corruption.* New York: Macmillan, 1983.

Dummett, Michael. *Voting Procedures.* Oxford: Clarendon Press, 1984.

Dummett, Michael, and Robin Farquharson. "Stability in Voting." *Econometrica* 29 (1961): 33–43.

Dunleavy, Patrick, and Hugh Ward. "Exogenous Voter Preferences and Parties with State Power: Some Internal Problems of Economic Theories of Party Competition." *British Journal of Political Science* 11 (1981): 351–80.

Duverger, Maurice. *Political Parties.* Translated by Barbara and Robert North. London: Methuen, 1954.

Dworkin, Gerald. "Paternalism." In *Morality and the Law*, edited by Richard Wasserstrom, 491–506. Belmont, Calif.: Wadsworth Publishing, 1971.

Dworkin, Ronald. *Law's Empire.* Cambridge: Harvard University Press, 1986.

———. "What is Equality? Part I: Equality of Welfare." *Philosophy & Public Affairs* 10 (1981): 185–246.

Eismeier, Theodore J., and Philip J. Pollock. "Political Action Committees:

Varieties of Organization and Strategy." In *Money and Politics in the United States*, edited by Michael J. Malbin, 122–41. Washington: American Enterprise Institute, 1984.

Eldersveld, Samuel J. *Political Parties in American Society*. New York: Basic Books, 1982.

Elkins, David J. "The Measurement of Party Competition." *American Political Science Review* 68 (1974): 682–700.

Elster, Jon. *Ulysses and the Sirens*. Cambridge: Cambridge University Press, 1979.

Ely, John Hart. *Democracy and Distrust*. Cambridge: Harvard University Press, 1980.

Epstein, Leon. *Political Parties in Western Democracies*. New York: Praeger, 1967.

Farquharson, Robin. *Theory of Voting*. New Haven: Yale University Press, 1969.

Feld, Scott L., and Bernard Grofman. "On the Possibility of Faithfully Representative Committees." *American Political Science Review* 80 (1986): 863–79.

Fishburn, Peter C. "Dimensions of Election Procedures: Analyses and Comparisons." *Theory and Decision* 15 (1983): 371–97.

————. "The Irrationality of Transitivity in Social Choice." *Behavioral Science* 15 (1970): 119–23.

————. *The Theory of Social Choice*. Princeton: Princeton University Press, 1973.

Fiss, Owen M. "Free Speech and Social Structure." *Iowa Law Review* 71 (1986): 1405–25.

————. "Groups and the Equal Protection Clause." *Philosophy & Public Affairs* 5 (1976): 107–77.

Fleishman, Joel. "Private Money and Public Elections: Another American Dilemma." In *Changing Campaign Techniques*, edited by Louis Maisel, Sage Election Studies Yearbook, vol. 2, 19–54. Beverly Hills, Calif.: Sage Publications, 1976.

Fleishman, Joel, and Pope McCorkle. "Level-Up Rather Than Level-Down: Toward a New Theory of Campaign Finance Reform." *Journal of Law and Politics* 1 (1984): 211–98.

Fortson v. Dorsey, 379 U.S. 433 (1965).

Frendreis, John P., and Richard W. Waterman. "PAC Contributions and Legislative Behavior: Senate Voting on Trucking Deregulation." Prepared for presentation at the annual meeting of the Midwest Political Science Association, Chicago, 20–23 April 1983. Photocopy.

Gaffney v. Cummings, 412 U.S. 735 (1973).

Galbraith, John Kenneth. *The Affluent Society*. 4th ed. Boston: Houghton Mifflin, 1984.

Gauthier, David. "David Hume, Contractarian." *Philosophical Review* 88 (1979): 3–38.

————. "Justice as Social Choice." In *Morality, Reason and Truth*, edited by David Copp and David Zimmerman, 251–69. Totowa, N.J.: Rowman and Allanheld, 1985.

———. *Morals by Agreement*. Oxford: Clarendon Press, 1986.

Gibbard, Allan. "Manipulation of Voting Schemes: A General Result." *Econometrica* 41 (1973): 587–601.

Gilpin, Thomas. "On the Representation of Minorities of Electors." Philadelphia: American Philosophical Society, 1844. Selections reprinted in C. G. Hoag and G. H. Hallett, Jr., *Proportional Representation*, 457–64. New York: Macmillan, 1926.

Gintis, Herbert. "Welfare Criteria with Endogenous Preferences: The Economics of Education." *International Economic Review* 15 (1974): 415–30.

Glantz, Stanton A., Alan I. Abramowitz, and Michael P. Burkart. "Election Outcomes: Whose Money Matters?" *Journal of Politics* 38 (1976): 1033–38.

Goldman, Alvin. "On the Measurement of Power." *Journal of Philosophy* 71 (1974): 231–52.

———. "Toward a Theory of Social Power." *Philosophical Studies* 23 (1972): 221–68.

Gomillion v. Lightfoot, 364 U.S. 339 (1960).

Goodin, Robert, and John Dryzek. "Rational Participation: The Politics of Relative Power." *British Journal of Political Science* 10 (1980): 273–92.

Greenawalt, Kent. "How Empty is the Idea of Equality?" *Columbia Law Review* 83 (1983): 1167–85.

Grofman, Bernard. "For Equal Member Districts Random Is Not Equal." In *Representation and Redistricting Issues*, edited by Bernard Grofman et al., 55–58. Lexington, Mass.: Lexington Books, 1982.

Gutmann, Amy. *Liberal Equality*. Cambridge: Cambridge University Press, 1980.

Guttman, Julia E. "Primary Elections and the Collective Right of Freedom of Association" [Note]. *Yale Law Journal* 94 (1984): 117–37.

Hampton, Jean. *Hobbes and the Social Contract Tradition*. Cambridge: Cambridge University Press, 1986.

Hare, Thomas. *The Election of Representatives, Parliamentary and Municipal*. 4th ed. London: Longmans, Green, Reader, and Dyer, 1873.

Heard, Alexander. *The Costs of Democracy*. Chapel Hill: University of North Carolina Press, 1960.

Herndon, James F. "Access, Record, and Competition as Influences on Interest Group Contributions to Congressional Campaigns." *Journal of Politics* 44 (1982): 996–1019.

Herodotus. *The History of Herodotus*. Translated by George Rawlinson. New York: Tudor Publishing, 1928.

Hoag, C. G., and G. H. Hallett, Jr. *Proportional Representation*. New York: Macmillan, 1926.

Hobbes, Thomas. *Leviathan* [1651]. New York: Collier Books, 1962.

Howard, Alan, and Bruce Howard. "The Dilemma of the Voting Rights

Act—Recognizing the Emerging Political Equality Norm." *Columbia Law Review* 83 (1983): 1615–63.

Jacobson, Gary C. "Money and Votes Revisited: Congressional Elections, 1972–1986." *Public Choice* 47 (1985): 7–62.

———. *Money in Congressional Elections*. New Haven: Yale University Press, 1980.

Jenness v. Fortson, 403 U.S. 431 (1968).

Jones, Peter. "Political Equality and Majority Rule." In *The Nature of Political Theory*, edited by David Miller and Larry Siedentop, 155–82. Oxford: Clarendon Press, 1983.

Kalai, E., and M. Smorodinsky. "Other Solutions to Nash's Bargaining Problem." *Econometrica* 43 (1975): 513–18.

Kant, Immanuel. "On the Common Saying: 'This May be True in Theory, but it does not Apply in Practice' " [1793]. *Kant's Political Writings*, edited by Hans Reiss and translated by H. B. Nisbet, 61–92. Cambridge: Cambridge University Press, 1970.

Karcher v. Daggett, 462 U.S. 725 (1983).

Kateb, George. "The Moral Distinctiveness of Representative Democracy." *Ethics* 91 (1981): 357–74.

Katz, Richard S. *A Theory of Parties and Electoral Systems*. Baltimore: Johns Hopkins University Press, 1980.

Keeter, Scott, and Cliff Zukin. *Uninformed Choice: The Failure of the New Presidential Nominating System*. New York: Praeger, 1983.

Kirkpatrick, Evron M. "Toward a More Responsible Party System: Political Science, Policy Science, or Pseudo-Science?" *American Political Science Review* 65 (1971): 965–90.

Lakeman, Enid. *Power to Elect: The Case for Proportional Representation*. London: Heinemann, 1982.

Lijphart, Arend. *Democracy in Plural Societies*. New Haven: Yale University Press, 1977.

Lijphart, Arend, and Bernard Grofman, eds. *Choosing an Election System*. New York: Praeger, 1984.

Lindblom, Charles E. *Politics and Markets*. New York: Basic Books, 1977.

Lindsay, A. D. *The Essentials of Democracy*. Lectures on the William J. Cooper Foundation of Swarthmore College. Philadelphia: University of Pennsylvania Press, 1929.

Lipset, Seymour Martin, and Stein Rokkan. "Cleavage Structures, Party Systems and Voter Alignments: An Introduction." In *Party Systems and Voter Alignments*, edited by S. M. Lipset and S. Rokkan, 1–64. New York: Free Press, 1967.

Little, I.M.D. "Social Choice and Individual Values." *Journal of Political Economy* 60 (1952): 422–32.

Lively, Jack. *Democracy*. Oxford: Basil Blackwell, 1975.

Low-Beer, John R. "The Constitutional Imperative of Proportional Representation" [Note]. *Yale Law Journal* 94 (1984): 163–88.

Lukes, Steven. *Power: A Radical View*. London: Macmillan, 1974.

Lynd, Staughton. "The Compromise of 1787." In *Class Conflict, Slavery, and the United States Constitution*, 185–213. Indianapolis: Bobbs-Merrill, 1967; reprint, Westport, Conn.: Greenwood Press, 1980.

McLean, Iain. *Public Choice: An Introduction*. Oxford: Basil Blackwell, 1987.

Malbin, Michael J. "Of Mountains and Molehills: PACs, Campaigns, and Public Policy." In *Parties, Interest Groups, and Campaign Finance Laws*, edited by Michael J. Malbin, 152–84. Washington, D.C.: American Enterprise Institute, 1980.

Manning, Brian. *The English People and the English Revolution*. London: Heinemann, 1975.

Mansbridge, Jane. *Beyond Adversary Democracy*. New York: Basic Books, 1980.

March, James G. "Bounded Rationality, Ambiguity, and the Engineering of Preferences." *Bell Journal of Economics* 9 (1978): 587–608.

Marshall, T. H. "Citizenship and Social Class" [1949]. In *Class, Citizenship, and Social Development*, 65–122. Garden City, N.Y.: Doubleday, 1964.

May, Kenneth O. "A Set of Independent Necessary and Sufficient Conditions for Simple Majority Decision." *Econometrica* 20 (1952): 680–84.

Meiklejohn, Alexander. *Political Freedom*. New York: Harper & Brothers, 1960.

Meyers, Diana T. "In Defense of Blind Apportionment Criteria." Comment presented to the Conference on Equal Opportunity, University of Delaware, May 1985. Photocopy.

Mill, John Stuart. *Autobiography* [1873]. In *Collected Works*, vol. 1, edited by J. M. Robson and J. Stillinger, 1–290. Toronto: University of Toronto Press, 1981.

———. *Considerations on Representative Government* [1861]. In *Collected Works*, vol. 19, edited by J. M. Robson, 371–577. Toronto: University of Toronto Press, 1977.

———. *On Liberty* [1859]. In *Collected Works*, vol. 18, edited by J. M. Robson, 213–310. Toronto: University of Toronto Press, 1977.

———. "Thoughts on Parliamentary Reform" [1859]. In *Collected Works*, vol. 19, edited by J. M. Robson, 311–39. Toronto: University of Toronto Press, 1977.

Miller, David. "The Competitive Model of Democracy." In *Democratic Theory and Practice*, edited by Graeme Duncan, 133–55. Cambridge: Cambridge University Press, 1983.

———. "Democracy and Social Justice." *British Journal of Political Science* 8 (1978): 1–19.

Miller, Nicholas R. "Pluralism and Social Choice." *American Political Science Review* 77 (1983): 734–47.

———. "Power in Game Forms." In *Power, Voting, and Voting Power*, edited by M. J. Holler, 33–51. Würzburg, Germany: Physica-Verlag, 1981.

Mobile v. Bolden, 446 U.S. 55 (1980).

Mueller, Dennis C. *Public Choice*. Cambridge: Cambridge University Press, 1979.

Musgrave, R. A., and P. B. Musgrave. *Public Finance*. 3d ed. New York: McGraw-Hill, 1980.

Nagel, Thomas. *Mortal Questions*. Cambridge: Cambridge University Press, 1979.

———. *The View from Nowhere*. New York: Oxford University Press, 1986.

Nelson, Alan. "Economic Rationality and Morality." *Philosophy & Public Affairs* 17 (1988): 149–66.

Nelson, William N. *On Justifying Democracy*. London: Routledge & Kegan Paul, 1980.

Nicholson, Marlene A. "Campaign Financing and Equal Protection." *Stanford Law Review* 26 (1974): 815–54.

Niemi, Richard G., and John Deegan, Jr. "Competition, Responsiveness and the Swing Ratio." *American Political Science Review* 72 (1978): 1304–23.

Nixon v. Condon, 286 U.S. 73 (1932).

Nixon v. Herndon, 273 U.S. 536 (1927).

Ortiz, Daniel R. "Alternative Voting Systems as Remedies for Unlawful At-Large Systems" [Note]. *Yale Law Journal* 92 (1982): 144–60.

Ostrogorski, M. *Democracy and the Organization of Political Parties*. 2 vols. Translated by F. Clarke. New York: Macmillan, 1902.

Ostwald, Martin. *Nomos and the Beginnings of the Athenian Democracy*. Oxford: Clarendon Press, 1969.

Overacker, Louise. *Money in Elections*. New York: Macmillan, 1932.

Parent, T. Wayne, Calvin C. Jillson, and Ronald E. Weber. "Voting Outcomes in the 1984 Democratic Party Primaries and Caucuses." *American Political Science Review* 81 (1987): 67–84.

Parsons, Talcott. "On the Concept of Influence" [1963]. Reprinted in *Sociological Theory and Modern Society*, 355–82. New York: Free Press, 1967.

Pateman, Carole. *Participation and Democratic Theory*. Cambridge: Cambridge University Press, 1970.

Pattanaik, P. K. *Voting and Collective Choice*. Cambridge: Cambridge University Press, 1971.

Patterson, Orlando. *Slavery and Social Death*. Cambridge: Harvard University Press, 1982.

Patterson, Samuel C. "Campaign Spending in Contests for Governor." *Western Political Quarterly* 35 (1982): 457–77.

Pennock, J. Roland. *Democratic Political Theory*. Princeton: Princeton University Press, 1979.

Plamenatz, John. *Democracy and Illusion*. London: Longman, 1973.

Pole, J. R. *The Pursuit of Equality in American History*. Berkeley: University of California Press, 1978.

Powell, G. Bingham. *Contemporary Democracies*. Cambridge: Harvard University Press, 1982.

Rae, Douglas W. "Decision-Rules and Individual Values in Constitutional Choice." *American Political Science Review* 63 (1969): 40–56.

———. *The Political Consequences of Electoral Laws*. Rev. ed. New Haven: Yale University Press, 1971.

Rae, Douglas W., with Douglas Yates, Jennifer Hochschild, Joseph Morone, and Carol Fessler. *Equalities*. Cambridge: Harvard University Press, 1981.

Railton, Peter. "Moral Realism." *Philosophical Review* 95 (1986): 163–207.

Ranney, Austin. *Curing the Mischiefs of Faction*. Berkeley: University of California Press, 1975.

Rawls, John. "The Basic Liberties and Their Priority." In *The Tanner Lectures on Human Values*, vol. 3, edited by Sterling McMurrin, 1–87. Salt Lake City: University of Utah Press; Cambridge: Cambridge University Press, 1982.

———. "Justice as Fairness: Political not Metaphysical." *Philosophy & Public Affairs* 14 (1985): 223–51.

———. "Kantian Constructivism in Moral Theory." *Journal of Philosophy* 77 (1980): 515–72.

———. *A Theory of Justice*. Cambridge: Harvard University Press, 1971.

Reiter, Howard L. "The Limitations of Reform: Changes in the Nominating Process." *British Journal of Political Science* 15 (1985): 399–417.

Reynolds v. Sims, 377 U.S. 533 (1964).

Riker, William H. *Liberalism Against Populism*. San Francisco: W. H. Freeman, 1982.

———. "The Two-party System and Duverger's Law." *American Political Science Review* 76 (1983): 753–66.

Riker, William H., and Peter C. Ordeshook. *An Introduction to Positive Political Theory*. Englewood Cliffs, N.J.: Prentice-Hall, 1973.

Ripon Society v. National Republican Party, 525 F.2nd 567 (1975) (D.C. Circuit).

Robertson, David. *A Theory of Party Competition*. London: John Wiley, 1976.

Rogers v. Lodge, 458 U.S. 613 (1982).

Rogowski, Ronald W. "Representation in Political Theory and in Law." *Ethics* 91 (1981): 395–430.

———. "Trade and the Variety of Democratic Institutions." *International Organization* 41 (1987): 203–24.

Rokkan, Stein. *Citizens, Elections, Parties*. New York: David McKay, 1970.

Roth, Alvin E. *Axiomatic Models of Bargaining*. Berlin and New York: Springer Verlag, 1979.

Rousseau, Jean-Jacques. *The Social Contract* [1762]. In *The Social Contract and Discourses*. Translated G.D.H. Cole. London: J. M. Dent, 1973.

Samuelson, Robert J. "The Campaign Reform Failure." *The New Republic*, 5 September 1983, 28–36.

Sartori, Giovanni. *The Theory of Democracy Revisited.* 2 vols. Chatham, N.J.: Chatham House, 1987.

Satterthwaite, M. A. "Strategy-proofness and Arrow's Conditions: Existence and Correspondence Theorems for Voting Procedures and Social Welfare Functions." *Journal of Economic Theory* 10 (1975): 187–217.

Scanlon, T. M. "Contractualism and Utilitarianism." In *Utilitarianism and Beyond*, edited by Amartya Sen and Bernard Williams, 103–28. Cambridge: Cambridge University Press, 1982.

————. "Freedom of Expression and Categories of Expression." *University of Pittsburgh Law Review* 40 (1979): 519–50.

————. "Liberty, Contract, and Contribution." In *Morals and Markets*, edited by Gerald Dworkin, Gordon Bermant, and Peter G. Brown, 43–67. Washington, D.C.: Hemisphere, 1977.

————. "Preference and Urgency." *Journal of Philosophy* 72 (1975): 655–69.

————. "Rights, Goals and Fairness." In *Public and Private Morality*, edited by Stuart Hampshire, 93–111. Cambridge: Cambridge University Press, 1978.

Schattschneider, E. E. *Party Government.* New York: Rinehart, 1942.

————. *The Semi-Sovereign People* [1960]. Hinsdale, Ill.: Dryden Press, 1975.

Schumpeter, Joseph. *Capitalism, Socialism, and Democracy.* 5th ed. London: Allen and Unwin, 1976.

Sen, Amartya K. *Collective Choice and Social Welfare.* San Francisco: Holden-Day, 1970.

————. "Personal Utilities and Public Judgements: Or, What's Wrong with Welfare Economics?" *Economic Journal* 89 (1979): 537–58.

Shafer, Byron E. *The Quiet Revolution.* New York: Russell Sage Foundation, 1983.

Shapiro, Howard M. "Geometry and Geography: Racial Gerrymandering and the Voting Rights Act" [Note]. *Yale Law Journal* 94 (1984): 189–208.

Shapley, L. S., and Martin Shubik. "A Method for Evaluating the Distribution of Power in a Committee System." *American Political Science Review* 48 (1954): 787–92.

Sidgwick, Henry. *The Methods of Ethics.* 7th ed. London: Macmillan, 1907.

Simon, Herbert A. "A Behavioral Model of Rational Choice." *Quarterly Journal of Economics* 69 (1955): 99–118.

————. "Rationality as Process and as Product of Thought." *American Economic Review* 68 (May 1978): 1–16.

Singer, Peter. *Democracy and Disobedience.* New York: Oxford University Press, 1973.

Smith v. Allwright, 321 U.S. 649 (1944).

Sorauf, Frank J. *Party Politics in America.* 5th ed. Boston: Little, Brown, 1984.

Sterne, Simon. *On Representative Government and Personal Representation.* Philadelphia: J. B. Lippincott, 1871.

Still, Jonathan. "Political Equality and Election Systems." *Ethics* 91 (1981): 375–94.

Stokes, Donald E. "Spatial Models of Party Competition." *American Political Science Review* 57 (1963). Reprinted in Angus Campbell, Philip E. Converse, Warren E. Miller, and Donald E. Stokes, *Elections and the Political Order*. New York: John Wiley, 1966: 161–79.

Storer v. Brown, 415 U.S. 724 (1974).

Storing, Herbert J., ed. *The Complete Anti-Federalist*. 7 vols. Chicago: University of Chicago Press, 1981.

Strasnick, Steven. "The Problem of Social Choice: Arrow to Rawls." *Philosophy & Public Affairs* 5 (1976): 241–73.

Sugden, Robert. "Free Association and the Theory of Proportional Representation." *American Political Science Review* 78 (1984): 31–43.

Taagepera, Rein. "The Effect of District Magnitude and Properties of Two-Seat Districts." In *Choosing an Electoral System*, edited by Arend Lijphart and Bernard Grofman, 91–102. New York: Praeger, 1984.

Taylor, Michael. "The Theory of Collective Choice." In *Handbook of Political Science*, vol. 3, edited by Fred I. Greenstein and Nelson W. Polsby, 413–81. Reading, Mass.: Addison-Wesley, 1975.

Taylor, Michael, and V. M. Herman. "Party Systems and Government Stability." *American Political Science Review* 65 (1971): 28–37.

Terry v. Adams, 345 U.S. 641 (1953).

Thernstrom, Abigail M. *Whose Votes Count?* Cambridge: Harvard University Press, 1987.

Thomas, Keith. "The Levellers and the Franchise." In *The Interregnum: The Quest for Settlement 1646–1660*, edited by G. E. Aylmer, 57–78. London: Archon, 1972.

Thompson, Dennis F. *The Democratic Citizen*. Cambridge: Cambridge University Press, 1970.

———. *John Stuart Mill and Representative Government*. Princeton: Princeton University Press, 1976.

Thucydides. *The Peloponnesian War*. Translated by John H. Finley, Jr. New York: Modern Library, 1951.

Tribe, Laurence H. *American Constitutional Law*. Mineola, N.Y.: Foundation Press, 1978.

Tufte, Edward. "The Relationship between Seats and Votes in Two-Party Systems." *American Political Science Review* 67 (1973): 540–54.

United Jewish Organizations v. Carey, 430 U.S. 144 (1977).

Verba, Sidney, Norman H. Nie, and Jae-on Kim. *Participation and Political Equality: A Seven-Nation Study*. New York: Cambridge University Press, 1978.

Vickery, William. "On the Prevention of Gerrymandering." *Political Science Quarterly* 76 (1961): 105–10.

Vlastos, Gregory. "Isonomia." *American Journal of Philology* 74 (1953): 337–66.

Waldron, Jeremy. "Theoretical Foundations of Liberalism." *Philosophical Quarterly* 37 (1987): 127–50.

Walzer, Michael. "The Moral Standing of States." *Philosophy & Public Affairs* 9 (1980): 209–29.

———. "Philosophy and Democracy." *Political Theory* 9 (1981): 379–99.

———. *Spheres of Justice*. New York: Basic Books, 1983.

Wasby, Stephen L. *Vote Dilution, Minority Voting Rights, and the Courts*. Washington, D.C.: Joint Center for Political Studies, 1982.

Weber, Max. *The Theory of Economic and Social Organization*. Translated by A. M. Henderson and Talcott Parsons. New York: Free Press, 1947.

Weiszacker, C. C. von. "Notes on Endogenous Change of Tastes." *Journal of Economic Theory* 3 (1971): 345–72.

Welch, W. P. "Campaign Contributions and Legislative Voting: Milk Money and Dairy Price Supports." *Western Political Quarterly* 35 (1982): 478–95.

Wells, David. "Against Affirmative Gerrymandering." In *Representation and Redistricting Issues*, edited by Bernard Grofman et al., 77–89. Lexington, Mass.: Lexington Books, 1982.

Wells v. Rockefeller, 394 U.S. 542 (1969).

Wesberry v. Sanders, 376 U.S. 1 (1964).

White v. Regester, 412 U.S. 755 (1973).

Wicksell, K. *Finanztheoretische Untersuchungen* (Jena, 1896). Selections translated and reprinted as "A New Principle of Just Taxation." In *Classics in the Theory of Public Finance*, edited by R. Musgrave and A. Peacock, 72–118. New York: St. Martin's Press, 1967.

Williams, Bernard. *Ethics and the Limits of Philosophy*. Cambridge: Harvard University Press, 1985.

Williams v. Rhodes, 393 U.S. 23 (1968).

Winter, Ralph K. *Campaign Finance and Political Freedom*. Domestic Affairs Study 19. Washington, D.C.: American Enterprise Institute, 1973.

Wollheim, Richard. "A Paradox in the Theory of Democracy." In *Philosophy, Politics, and Society*, 2d series, edited by Peter Laslett and W. G. Runciman, 71–87. Oxford: Basil Blackwell, 1962.

Woolrych, Austin. *Soldiers and Statesmen: The General Council of the Army and Its Debates, 1647–1648*. Oxford: Clarendon Press, 1987.

Wright, J. Skelly. "Money and the Pollution of Politics: Is the First Amendment an Obstacle to Political Equality?" *Columbia Law Review* 82 (1982): 609–45.

Wright v. Rockefeller, 376 U.S. 52 (1964).

Index

Abramowitz, Alan I., 198n

access to the ballot. *See* ballot access

Ackerman, Bruce, 58n, 60–64; on Neutrality principle, 61n; theory contrasted with Rousseau's, 63

Adamany, David W., 195n, 196n, 200n

agenda. *See* ballot access, political agenda

Agree, George E., 196n

Agreement of the People (1647) (Leveller manifesto), 3n

Alexander, Herbert E., 193n, 195n, 196n, 199n, 200n, 204n, 206n

Alfange, Dean, Jr., 145n

Almond, Gabriel A., 28n

American Party v. White, 166n

American Political Science Association, 182n

Anderson v. Celebreeze, 166n

anonymity, 9n; in May theorem, 59–60

Anti-Federalists, 134n

Aristotle, 16

Arrow, Kenneth J., 21n, 49, 50n, 67–74, 67n, 73n, 119, 171; conception of social choice, 70; conditions, 69n; impossibility theorem stated, 69–70; interpretation of impossibility theorem, 70–74

Bagehot, Walter, 126n, 155n

Baier, Kurt, 71n

ballot access, 11–14, 164–91; abstract conception of problem, 166; and deliberative interests, 166; and distribution of political resources, 187; of minor parties and independent candidates, 186; and party governance, 165n; and political liberty, 173; and political parties, 164; and preference aggregation, 12–13, 170–73; prima facie unfairness of restricting, 164; unfair regulation of, 108; in

U.S. constitutional law, 166n. *See also* political agenda

Barry, Brian, 5n, 8n, 9n, 11n, 26n, 27n, 46n, 52n, 55n, 63n, 82n, 153n, 182n; on majority rule, 75–77, 75n, 86n

Barton, John H., 165n, 186n

Baty, Th., 64n

Berger, Fred R., 34n, 35n

Bergson, A., 20n, 21n, 26n, 73n

Bergson-Samuelson social welfare function, 20n

best result theories, 20, 31–48; ambiguity of, 43; compared with popular will theories, 21, 49; contractualist critique of, 39–40; enlarged criteria of best results, 40–46; Mill's theory as, 32–40; and procedural fairness, 46–48; two-dimensional criteria of best results, 44

Black, Duncan, *xvn*, 51n, 63n, 68n, 69n, 130n

blind apportionment criteria, 147n

Bogdanor, Vernon, 124n, 127n, 128n, 130n

Brams, Steven J., *xvn*, 128n

Brittan, Samuel, 184n

Buchanan, James M., 25n, 26n, 66n

Buckley, James (Senator), on incumbency, 199n

Buckley v. Valeo, *xn*, 194n, 198n, 209n, 211n; on freedom of expression and campaign finance regulation, 209–13

Burkart, Michael P., 198n

campaign finance. *See* political finance

campaigns for office, communicative purposes of, 202

candidate selection procedures of political parties, 165, 186, 190

Ceaser, James W., 165n, 186n

Chamberlin, John R., 139n

Chandler, J. A., 130n

citizenship roles, 97, 98; complexity of, 117

Cohen, Joshua, *xvin*, 52n, 53n, 124n, 136, 137n, 169n, 193n

Coleman, Jules, 21n

Common Cause, 146n

communitarianism, 223

competitiveness of elections, defined, 197, 197n; and political finance, 200

complex proceduralism, 97–119; central idea, 99; contrasted with other views, 117–19; egalitarianism of, 116, 219; and ideal of citizenship, 116, 220–21; introduced, 23; indeterminacy, 225–27; justification of, 218, 220–21; negative force of, 118, 219; normative content of, 105–6; outcome-oriented features of, 112–13; and "paradigmatic" cases of unfairness, 108, 221; pluralism of, 219; relativism of, 221–25; and social contract doctrine, 104–7; stated, 100; subject-matter of, 218; virtue of fairness in, 227–29. *See also* regulative interests of citizenhip

Condorcet candidate, 51, 170–71; "paradox" of voting, 68

constituencies: fairness of territorial basis of, 148; and qualitative fairness, 146–47; "voluntary" and "compulsory" contrasted, 133

constitutional convention, Rawls on, 87

contractualism. *See* social contract

corruption, 203–5

Courant, Paul N., 139n

Cousins v. Wigoda, 188n

Crotty, William, 190n

cyclical majorities, 68–69

Dahl, Robert A., 5n, 8n, 57n, 62n, 66n

Daniels, Norman, 193n

Davis, J. C., 103n

Davis v. Bandemer, 142n, 143n, 152n

decisiveness (universal domain), in May theorem, 58

Deegan, John, Jr., 152n, 157n

deliberative responsibility, regulative interest in, 23n, 100, 113–16, 179, 219; and political agenda, 173, 175–76, 178–79, 184–87; and political finance, 202–3, 205–7; potential for

conflict, 115; and proportional representation, 136–38

democracy: definition of, 7, 17n; and deliberation, 114, 230; flourishing of, 229; generic conception of, 16, 32, 98; ideal of, contrasted with Hobbes's vision, 98; as preference aggregating device, 114, 228–29; Schumpeter's "classical" model of, 180

Democratic National Committee, 165n

Democratic Party of the United States v. LaFollette, 188n

distributive injustice: influence on politics of, 15, 192; remedies for, 193

district representation: and decision rule, 129; forms of, 128; and minorities, 138

Dixon, Robert G., 124n, 142n, 148n, 149n

Downs, Anthony, 182n

Drew, Elizabeth, 194n, 208n

Dryzek, John, 16n

Dummett, Michael, *xvn*, 50n, 52n, 54n, 70n, 126n, 171n

Dunleavy, Patrick, 172n

Duverger, Maurice, 28n, 130n, 165n

Dworkin, Gerald, 105n, 189n

Dworkin, Ronald, 4n, 18n, 108n

Eismeier, Theodore J., 204n, 205n

Eldersveld, Samuel J., 165n, 182n

elections, agenda-formation and campaign stages distinguished, 207. *See also* political finance, voting

elite competition: doctrine of, 180–82; as political oligopoly, 183; Schattschneider on, 183

Elkins, David J., 197n

Elster, Jon, 168n, 172n

Ely, John Hart, 161n

Epstein, Leon, 28n

equal satisfaction of preferences, 153

equality (anonymity), in May theorem, 58

equality, political. *See* political equality

equilibrium, in voting, 69

equitable treatment, regulative interest in, 23n, 100, 110–13, 203, 219; and fair representation, 155–58; outcome-oriented character of, 112–13; and po-